GUIDE TO
MARC 21

For Cataloging of Books and Serials

With functional definitions, examples and
working resources

Asoknath Mukhopadhyay

Chandos Publishing
Oxford • England

First Published in 2007 by Viva Books Private Limited

This edition published by

Chandos Publishing (Oxford) Limited
Chandos House
5 & 6 Steadys Lane
Stanton Harcourt
Oxford OX29 5RL UK
Tel: +44 (0) 1865 884447 Fax: +44 (0) 1865 884448
email: info@chandospublishing.com
www.chandospublishing.com

This edition is for distribution outside of the Indian subcontinent only

ISBN 10 : 1-84334-407-6
ISBN 13 : 978-1-84434-407-0

Printed and bound in India.

GUIDE TO
MARC 21

For Cataloging of Books and Serials

With functional definitions, examples and working resources

*A snowball
to little Rupsa and
her generation*

Contents

SUMMARY

January 28, 2006

PREFACE

MARC has come a long way to achieve the status of the supreme world standard for bibliographic information interchange. It had gone through a critical phase of technological advancement much ahead of the cultural change. This might be one of the reasons why even today MARC 21 needs strengthening promotion of its missions for resource sharing at a global plane.

From day one of mechanization, the Library of Congress pursues the policy of sharing benefits of their machine-readable catalogue with libraries having no machine to read, by the way of distributing printed catalogue cards in conventional format. We, at IIMC Library in Calcutta, happened to be one of the early beneficiaries. It was all before the microprocessor era. The recent technological boom has empowered libraries to exploit computer and communication facilities, and implement MARC standard for interchange of bibliographic information to their best advantage. Besides institutional will, what the libraries need most is the knowledge and skill to develop MARC compliant databases addressing local as well as global requirements. Since it is not being taught in university courses, the opportunity for developing knowledge of MARC, in most of the developing countries, is restricted to self-study. Going through the massive learning resources on MARC completely unguided is almost like crossing a desert all alone with full of uncertainties.

During the last two decades, often I experienced uncertainties in grasping the intents of MARC specifications. The definitions at times leave their implications open-ended. Lack of readily available instructive documents at affordable cost is perhaps one of the major reasons for inconsistent content designations found in different MARC 21 databases, particularly in fields associated with problem issues like multi-part or multi-script documents. A good number of official and unofficial publications are available today on web and in print; some regularly updated, others dated. These include freely accessible training ware and tutorials, mostly developed by various libraries for their internal communities.

The book, Guide to MARC 21, is intended to serve as a short handbook to MARC catalogers and as a learning resource to the student. The book represents a subset of MARC 21 fields delineating scope, content designations, interpretations and examples related to cataloging of language materials — mainly books and serials. The subset contains only those fields which are likely to be used in average libraries with or without vernacular collections.

To provide the catalogers with all-round support, I have gathered selectively MARC resources available in numerous websites, and repackaged them with elucidations and examples keeping in mind the requirements of those who know cataloging norms, but little about computer applications. The terminology and definitions used in this book are in tune with MARC documentation, CCP, OCLC, AACR2, and ISBD. For interpretations and examples I depended largely on Library Corporation's site *ITS.MARC* and other sources that include a variety of instructive materials and utilities developed by institutions and individuals. Without sharing their resources the purpose of the book would have been lost. With deep appreciation I acknowledge the unique contributions made by the organizations and individuals including MARC21 development authorities. Their names and web addresses have been mentioned in *Acknowledgements* page.

I am thankful to the National Library authorities for providing me with a rare opportunity to look over their huge collections picking examples of varied types of cataloguing problems; and also to the officials and experts, involved in the retro-conversion project, for the gainful discussions I had with them. I take this opportunity to thank Ubique Technology for providing my book with a training ware which I believe will help the users in building skill and confidence.

My special thanks go to Geeti, my wife, for her encouragement and care I needed in completing the work in time.

Asoknath Mukhopadhyay
asoknath@hotmail.com

ACKNOWLEDGEMENTS

The book concentrates on MARC 21 cataloging, and its ingredients are primarily sourced from *MARC 21 documentations,* developed and maintained by the Library of Congress, Network Development and MARC Standard Office. Among other resources, Library Corporation's ITS.MARC has been extensively used, particularly for application oriented elucidations of content designations. Many more sources of supportive information have been networked into this book to provide readers with multidimensional perspectives and necessary working tools for cataloging MARC way. The author is indebted to the individuals and organizations for using their valuable resources:

Banerjee, Kyle

- **Cataloging Calculator**
  http://home.earthlink.net/~banerjek/calculate/search.html

Graham, Peter S.

- **The Mid-decade catalog and its environment**
  http://aultnis.rutgers.edu/texts/cffc.html

Huthwaite, Ann
- **AACR2 and its place in the digital world:** near-term solutions
  and long-term direction

Ann Huthwaite, Bibliographic Services Manager, Queensland
University of Technology Library

InfoWorks Technology Company

- **INTERNET Library for Librarians: Cataloging: MARC Formats**
  http://www.itcompany.com/inforetriever/cat_marc.htm

IFLANET

- **Mailing Lists (Online Discussion Forum)**
- **Webography on Cataloguing Resources**
  www.ifla.org/index.htm

Johnson, Timothy G.

- **Book Cataloger's Cheat-Sheet**
  **Written by Timothy G. Johnson. HTML coding by Christian
  Thomason**
  www.music.indiana.edu/tech_s/manuals/training/marc/
  bookcheat.html

The Library Corporation

- **Cataloger's Reference Shelf**
  http://www.itsmarc.com/crs/crs0000.htm

Library of Congress
NETWORK DEVELOPMENT AND MARC STANDARDS OFFICE

- **A Brief Bibliography of Writings on MARC**
  www.loc.gov

- **Cataloger's Desktop**
  www.loc.gov/cds/desktop/contacts.html

- **MARC 21 Organization Codes: Request form**
  www.loc.gov/marc/organizations/orgshome.html#requests

- **MARC FORUM**
  http://sun8.loc.gov

- **MARC RECORD SERVICES**
  www.loc.gov/marc/marcrecsvrs.html

- **MARC Specialized Tools**
  www.loc.gov/marc/marctools.htm

- MARC Systems
  www.loc.gov/marc/marcsysvend.htm

- Z39.50 Implementations
  www.loc.gov/z3950/lcserver.html

- Library of Congress Online Catalog (Sample Search Hits)
  http://catalog.loc.gov/

- MARC 21 Concise Format for Bibliographic Data
  www.loc.gov/marc/bibliographic/ecbdhome.html

Library Technologies, Inc.

- Barcode Production
  www.libtech.com

National Library, Calcutta

- Transliteration of Indian Scripts
  www.nlindia.org

Queen Elizabeth II Library

- Cataloguer's Toolbox
  http://staff.library.mun.ca/staff/toolbox/
  last revised: 13 January 2005

Queen's University Library

- Descriptive Cataloguing for Monographs
  http://130.15.161.74/techserv/cat/c001c02.html
  Page maintained by Elizabeth A. Read,
  readel@post.queensu.ca.
  Updated: 05-01-2000

- Format Integration-Serials
  Sources: Format integration workshop : major changes for
  printed serials / Crystal Graham, University of California, San
  Diego. Page maintained
  by Elizabeth A. Read, readel@stauffer.queensu.ca.

- Holdings Record : 852 Field & 86X Fields
  http://130.15.161.74/techserv/cat/sect05/holdings/852.htmlPage
  maintained by Elizabeth A. Read, readel@ post.queensu.ca.
  Created: 2002-09-25 by D. Rutherford. Updated: 08-Jun-2004

- **Uniform Titles:** Cataloguing Procedures
  http://130.15.161.74/techserv/cat/Sect02a/uniformtitles.html
  Page maintained by Elizabeth A. Read, *readel@post.queensu.ca*
  Updated: 11-Jun-2004

Sabinet Online

- **Notice of AACR2 2002 Revisions**
  http://www.sabinet.co.za/sabicatwebkey_changes_to_oclc_marc.doc

University of Virginia Library

- **Formatting Holdings Information**
  http://www.lib.virginia.edu/cataloging/manual/appendices/
  appx21.html
- **Title Access:** Cataloging Procedures Manual
  http://www.lib.virginia.edu/cataloging/manual/appendices/
  appx8.html#marc
  Rev. 10/22/03

Vianne Tang Sha

- **Ending Punctuation for Bibliographic Data**
  www.itcompany.com/inforetriever/punctuation.htm
  No longer maintained as of December 13, 2000

York University Libraries Cataloguing Resources Technical Services

- **Roman Alphabet Abbreviations**
  http://www.info.library.yorku.ca/techserv/catres.htmRoman

PART

1

Introducing MARC

CONTENTS

PART I

MARC CATALOGING ELEMENTS

FREQUENTLY ASKED QUESTIONS   39

MEANING & DESCRIPTION

Meaning of MARC

MARC stands for 'MAchine Readable Cataloging'. The word meaning as such does not distinguish MARC. In fact, any bibliographic exchange format, MARC or non-MARC, or even a non-standard computerized cataloging format, all are, by description, machine-readable.

MARC is a generic term. When loosely used, it blankets all standard machine-readable formats developed by international agencies for bibliographic information interchange. In this broad sense LCMARC, USMARC, MARC 21, UNIMARC, CCF and all other national MARCs are often referred to as MARC. In its strict sense, however, MARC refers to the typical record architecture developed at the Library of Congress as LCMARC, upgraded as USMARC, and eventually manifested as MARC 21 — an international version ready to cope with the twenty-first-century requirements.

The term MARC 21, refers to the definitions and specifications prescribed in this particular version. In this book, the term, MARC, is used to indicate the logical framework of allocation of bibliographic elements and the definitive principles underlying LCMARC–USMARC–MARC 21 hierarchy.

Bibliographic Elements

MARC comprises a detailed scheme, or a pattern, for allocation of all bibliographic and allied elements, as for example, title, author, language, target readership, etc., in an electronic file. This scheme of allocation of elements with their logical relationship is unique to MARC, and differs from other parallel schemes in scope of its applications and in nature and definitions of the bibliographic elements.

Physical Structure

However, for enabling the machine to identify and process the data elements, whenever needed, MARC follows a physical structure and a set of control mechanism. This physical data structuring scheme, originally developed as a carrier of MARC data, is now being used as a standard, in the USA (ANSI Z39.2) and internationally (ISO 2709), by other communication formats for bibliographic information interchange, like UNIMARC, CCF, national MARCs, etc. They all are implementations of ANSI Z39.2/ISO 2709 standard.

The merit of this standard lies on its ability to communicate and archive bibliographic data reliably, and negotiate with library management programs without requiring much of technological sophistry.

Dual Role

Though MARC came out of the program for mechanization of the LC catalog, its primary objective happens to be the communications of bibliographic information.

MARC serves as a system of bibliographic information interchange, that is, for importing one or many records from another MARC compliant online catalog located anywhere in the world, or exporting records to other on demand. Once a record enters another computer database through this system, or protocol, it should be readily visible and controllable there.

The best way to achieve this great benefit is to ensure that the patterns of data allocation in the importing and exporting databases resemble each other. MARC format specifications serve that purpose unfailingly. Here lies the key to the growing popularity of MARC in today's resource-sharing environment.

Importance & Advantages

It is important for the implementing agencies to note the plus points of MARC, particularly MARC 21, and its advantages over other bibliographic exchange formats, like UNIMARC, CCF and National MARCs:

- MARC is a collaborative effort. The MARC scheme, with its massive structure and exceedingly ambitious planning for upgrading its capabilities, depends on active participation of expert agencies. Primarily, the Library of Congress is responsible for creation and upkeeping of the scheme. The National Agricultural Library, National Library of Medicine, United States Government Printing Office and National Library of Canada, together with the Library of Congress, serve as sources of authoritative cataloging and provide most of the codes and standards used for MARC cataloging.

- MARC is one of the very few international schemes that sustain the tempo of development and continuously update its resources. It stands current and serves as a reliable processing instrument for machine-readable cataloging. The Library of Congress made no revisions in MARC specifications unilaterally. Two Committees were set up to review and update MARC 21 format documentation. One is the MARC Advisory Committee and the other, Machine-Readable Bibliographic Information (MARBI) Committee of the American Library Association (ALA). The MARC Advisory Committee is composed of the representatives from libraries and scholarly associations, as well as from the bibliographic utilities and vendor groups. The MARC authorities welcome proposals from all professional institutions and experts for incorporating changes in specifications in the interest of the user community at large.

- MARC 21 embraces all media of documents in its scheme. In 1970, the Library issued specifications for magnetic tapes containing *monographic* records in *MARC II format,* as they named it. The first document published with USMARC in title appeared in 1990. After a decade a revised edition of USMARC format for bibliographic data, has been produced in collaboration with the British Library and National Library of Canada as MARC 21. As its variant name suggests the revised format aims to meet the challenge of the 21st century.

- There is hardly anything in MARC that falls outside the scope of standardization. Being a bibliographic information interchange format, MARC in principle does not dictate use of any particular standard, but allows its users to follow any one of the available standards or authorities, especially for data rendering, choice of access points, codes, classifications and choice of subject headings, name authorities, etc. MARC Program for Cooperative Cataloging (PCC), as an international cooperative effort emphasizes on greater flexibility in tailoring local cataloging practice to local needs and priorities maintaining relative standards.

- MARC databases are multiplying. The Library of Congress, the official depository of United States publications, is a principal source of cataloging records for US and international publications. The OCLC's shared database, another enormous source of MARC records, available online for downloading against fees. These apart, many a public library and institutional library in USA, Canada, Britain, Australia and some other countries offer MARC records, often at no cost. The population of MARC databases is growing fast. In India, under Government patronage, MARC 21 implementations are in progress in a number of libraries, including the National Library of India. The increase in accessibility of MARC records tends to boost up MARC implementations in turn.

Origin & Development

In early 1960s the Library of Congress had developed a schematic design to help transfering its card catalog records into newly installed computer. The design provided a way to pass on coded instructions to the computer, made of numbers, alphabets and special characters, along with bibliographic data. The computer requires all those for identifying cataloging data elements, and reproducing LC Catalog Cards, and Tapes for distribution among the member institutions. This was how MARC began. The communication format of the MARC records, in the beginning, was suitable for encoding the bibliographic elements of books in roman script. During the span of four decades, the Library of

Congress, with collaborators, enriched MARC in terms of document-types and contents. They enhanced its structural design to accommodate requirements of all kinds of recorded knowledge—from prehistoric artifacts to web-publications.

For efficient management of bibliographic data in networking environment five separate formats are defined to handle five types of data: bibliographic, holdings, authority, classification, and community information.

Bibliographic format

MARC 21 Format for Bibliographic Data is central to MARC system. It is an integrated format defined for the identification and description of different forms of bibliographic material, no more restricted to monographs as it was, but extends specifications in detail for encoding elements of documents of any description, shape and material type—such as books, serials, computer files, maps, music, visual materials, websites, databases and mixed materials too.

Holding format

Format for Holdings Data serves as a subset of Bibliographic format. It contains that portion of format specifications which a library may require for encoding data elements pertinent to the holdings and physical location of the items the library holds.

Authority format

This is a format of the Authority Record. Libraries maintain the files of records as cataloging tools. Authority Records help inputting consistently and uniformly personal & corporate names, subject headings, which serve as preferred access points in records. Format specifications for encoding these bibliographic elements standardize the textual representations of these bibliographic elements and ensure data consistency—a precondition for effective search.

Classification format

MARC 21 Format for Classification Data contains format specifica-tions for encoding classification numbers and their descriptive terms. It serves as an in-house tool for maintaining consistency in library classification, and helps catalog search by class numbers and browsing books on shelves.

Community information format

Format for Community Information provides format specifications for records containing house-keeping information, events, programs, services, etc. required for running circulation system and other library management programs.

Multilingual/ Multi-script Support

MARC 21 extends support for multilingual documents using romanized script or in a non-Latin script designated for a language. Its effective and efficient implementation has been possible in recent time after the introduction of Unicode system.

Versions & Updates

The LC MARC found its way to US MARC, as an acknowledged national format for bibliographic communications, and after that evolved into MARC 21. Although, one finds there little change content-wise, MARC 21 differs significantly in its vision. It tends to take issues beyond national preferences, and to negotiate with the up-coming events as well. Being its focus shifted from geographic to temporal zone, MARC 21 appears as a MARC version for the century.

It all started in early 1960s with the mechanization of Library of Congress Card Catalog. MARC II format was published in 1968. LCMARC became USMARC in the next decade and continuously updated its formats till 1997. MARC 21 is not a new format, but a harmonized edition of USMARC and CAN/MARC updates of 1997-1998 brought out as a consolidated scheme.

The first edition of the document *MARC 21 Specifications for Record Structure, Character Sets, and Exchange Media* came out in 1999. New editions followed every year, the latest being the 2005 edition. The document provides technical information on the structure of MARC records, the character sets used in MARC records, and the format for distribution media for MARC 21 records. The Library of Congress issued the document for helping libraries and bibliographic agencies engaged in designing and maintaining systems for the exchange and processing of MARC records.

Resource Sharing Initiative

In manual environment, libraries had no other options but invest huge staff time in creating catalog entries of their own for every document they acquire. When MARC files became available, individual libraries, with no computer facility, started buying computer-printed cards from the Library of Congress. In due course, more and more libraries installed computers. Those who designed their databases MARC compliant, preferred to download MARC from the Library of Congress or from other bibliographic utilities, like OCLC, WLN, RLIN and A-G Canada. The agencies extended their online services based on their high-power mainframe system, against fee-plus-communication-cost. Output was a magnetic tape containing bibliographic information tagged in modified MARC I format. The academic institutions, having sufficient fund and sophisticated library software, joined bibliographic utilities. They enjoyed benefit of sharing their collective resources by downloading and contributing MARC records. With the advancement of information technology, computer systems are getting more powerful, affordable and friendlier day-by-day. Libraries have found automated systems are cost-effective as well as efficient, and resource sharing is the key to solve the problem of unleashed proliferations of information and ever-increasing information price. This happens to be the backdrop of coming of MARC into prominence.

The scenario is not exactly the same in less-advanced countries. Although computer power is within easy reach of the libraries, the benefits of sharing MARC records is still untasted in the developing countries. This is largely due to want of practical knowledge about the benefits MARC offers, and absence of opportunity to gain sufficient exposure to MARC cataloging. Recently, a number of large libraries are in the process of converting their card catalogs into MARC 21 format. With the increasing population of MARC databases, these pioneering projects, hopefully, will bring about a congenial atmosphere for bibliographic information sharing. Further, it is expected to lead way to setting up local service agencies to supply MARC records in the fashion of the foreign utilities.

Implementing MARC

The people working with MARC standards, directly or indirectly, stand responsible for success and failure of MARC in playing its primary role, which is to develop sharable bibliographic resources.

The software developers building MARC utility programs, the database vendors distributing MARC records and the professionals cataloging MARC records must know MARC adequately to do their part responsibly. The individual professionals are expected to format the records with utmost care adhering strictly to the norms and standards. If one misinterprets a specification, or makes unauthorized use of any exchangeable MARC field for local data, or commits some minor errors, then such imperfections may ruin functioning of a shared database in effect.

In implementing MARC-compliant library automation system, it is important that the people at the top acquire clear-cut understanding about MARC to support their decision-making and help them see that their:

- Library Management Package includes efficient MARC utility programs
- MARC data files, whenever downloaded from external sources, hold no substandard records
- MARC catalogers work proficiently adhering to MARC specifications.

INSIDE MARC:
TECHNICAL OVERVIEW

Internal Structure

Physical formats of MARC File and of MARC Record are essentially communication formats. The communication formats are machine-generated and interpreted by the machine. However, by understanding the way machine handles the cataloging data, a MARC Cataloger should be in a better position to follow MARC 21 specifications that have been discussed later.

Physical file format

MARC files were distributed earlier on electronic tape. The tape carries MARC records in a sequential file following a unique structural design. This design of physical carrier of bibliographic data has been registered as National and International Standards for Bibliographical Information Interchange, under ANSI Z39.2, and ISO 2709, respectively.

MARC File stores a continuous stream of innumerable records consecutively placed in a single row.

record 1▲record 2▲record 3▲record 4▲record5▲...▲record n↔

Figure 1 Marc File

Computer singles out the records one by one by tracing the predetermined record-separator, which is a special character rarely used in text, often a non-printable sign. Figure 1 shows the use of an *up-pointed solid triangle* sign as record separator. Besides the record separator, the standardized physical format uses other control characters to dissect the contents of a record into sections and sub-sections. Further discussion on this point will be more fitting after giving an exposure to the physical format of a MARC record.

Physical Record Format

A MARC record, in communication format, comprises three sections of data:

- Leader or Record Label
- Directory
- Data Content

Leader

The Leader includes mostly coded information all about the organization and features of the record itself in a string of 24 characters, 00 to 23.

Position: 01←————————————→24
String: 01218cam _ _ 22003134a _ 4500

Figure 2 Leader

The code may be a letter, number, or a Blank Space. As illustrated here in Figure 2, an underscore '_' represents a blank space.

The meaning of any one-lettered code depends on its relative position in the string. For example, letter 'a' in position 06 indicates that the Record is for a language material, whereas in position 18 it means that the Record conforms to AACR2 in rendering values in certain fields. The positions are programmatically filled in either by extracting values from the record itself, e.g. Record Length (position 00-05), or by setting default values applicable to all records following Library policy, e.g. Character Coding Scheme coded in position 09.

Only a few coded data are needed to be determined by the Catalogers, e.g. Type of Record (06), Bibliographic level (07). Record Type is always Language Material for cataloging books and serials. For Bibliographic Level (Position 07), however, Catalogers are required to provide the computer program with appropriate coded data. It is either 'm' for Monograph, or 's' for Serial. Detailed specifications for Leader are given in Part III.

Record Directory

The Directory serves as road map of the Data Contents area. Directory information is dynamically gathered and stored in a place between the Leader and the Data Contents sections. The Directory is generated programmatically by computer for locating data fields with the help of their address, which is a string of 12 numeric characters. The size of Directory area varies depending on the number of times the address repeats in Directory. The address mechanism consists of three components, placed successively without any partition in between:

- Field Tag: A three-character ID of a bibliographic information type given in the field. It consists of digits, no alphabet. Example: '001' Tag for Record ID Field. (First three digits in Figure 3)

- Field Length: Computer calculates field length taking the size of the bibliographic data string and one character for the Field Terminator. It takes at the most four character positions. Example: '0009'. (From the fourth to seventh positions in Figure 3)

- Starting Position: It is the relative position in reference to the base address, i.e. taking the first position in the Data Content section as 0. It consists of five character positions. Example: '00000' indicates that the Tagged Field '001' starts from the very beginning of the Data Content section. (From the eighth to twelfth positions in Figure 3)

001000900000005001700009008004100026906004500067925004200112955021300154010001700367020002700384020002200411040001800433042001400451050002400465082001600489100001900505245003700524260004200561300003800603490002500641500002100666650400590068750500710074665000330081765000012008508080000420086207100746650003300817650000120085080800004200862

Figure 3 Directory

Data Contents

The Data Content section holds related cataloging data as data fields. The data fields are separated by the Field Terminator which is a predetermined special character, such as, a hash sign '#', an 'at' sign '@', etc. or a non-printable character as generally used in MARC files. The terminator helps to recognize the fields as distinctive physical units of data content arranged in a row as a character string in the Data Content Section.

```
13020293▲20030923103827.0▲021204s2003      nyua   b b    001 0 eng ▲  ▼a7▼bcbc▼co
rignew▼di▼eecip▼f20▼gy-gencatlg▲0 ▼aacquire▼b1 shelf copy▼xpolicy default▲  ▼ajb
12 2002-12-04▼cjb12 2002-12-04▼djb04 2002-12-06▼ejb02 2002-12-06 to Children's▼a
1b00 2002-12-10▼dlb04 2002-12-12▼aaa07 2002-12-16▼aps07 2003-08-25 1 copy rec'd.
, to CIP ver.▼fpv06 2003-08-28 CIP ver to BCCD▲ ▼a  2002154957▲ ▼a0516242946 (
lib. bdg.)▲  ▼a0516278819 (pbk.)▲  ▼aDLC▼cDLC▼dDLC▲  ▼apcc▼alcac▲00▼aQL737.C23▼b
E34 2003▲00▼a599.756▼221▲1 ▼aEckart, Edana.▲10▼aBengal tiger /▼cby Edana Eckart.
▲  ▼aNew York :▼bChildren's Press,▼cc2003.▲  ▼a24 p. :▼bcol. ill. ;▼c16 x 19 cm.
▲1 ▼aAnimals of the world▲  ▼a"Welcome books."▲  ▼aIncludes bibliographical refe
rences (p. 23) and index.▲0  ▼aBengal tigers -- Cubs -- Roaring -- New Words -- T
o find out more.▲ 0▼aTigers▼vJuvenile literature.▲ 1▼aTigers.▲1 ▼aEckart, Edana.
▼tAnimals of the world.▲↩
```

Figure 4 Data Content

The Data Content resides in the final section of a Record, and ends with the Record Terminator. In Figure 4, the Record Terminator is a Double-headed Arrow—a non-printable character. The example is presented here in graphic form to display all special characters.

A Bibliographic Communication Record is constituted integrating Leader, Directory, and Data Content all together as illustrated below.

```
01218cam  22003134a 4500001000900000005001700000900800410002690600450006792500420
01129550213001540100017003670200027003840200022004110400018004330420014004510500
02400465082001600489100001900505245003700524260004200561300003800603490002500641
50000210066650400590068750500710074665000330081765000120085080000420086241302029
3▲20030923103827.0▲021204s2003      nyua   b b    001 0 eng ▲  ▼a7▼bcbc▼corignew▼
di▼eecip▼f20▼gy-gencatlg▲0 ▼aacquire▼b1 shelf copy▼xpolicy default▲  ▼ajb12 2002
-12-04▼cjb12 2002-12-04▼djb04 2002-12-06▼ejb02 2002-12-06 to Children's▼alb00 20
02-12-10▼dlb04 2002-12-12▼aaa07 2002-12-16▼aps07 2003-08-25 1 copy rec'd., to CI
P ver.▼fpv06 2003-08-28 CIP ver to BCCD▲ ▼a  2002154957▲ ▼a0516242946 (lib. bd
g.)▲  ▼a0516278819 (pbk.)▲  ▼aDLC▼cDLC▼dDLC▲  ▼apcc▼alcac▲00▼aQL737.C23▼bE34 200
3▲00▼a599.756▼221▲1 ▼aEckart, Edana.▲10▼aBengal tiger /▼cby Edana Eckart.▲  ▼aNe
w York :▼bChildren's Press,▼cc2003.▲  ▼a24 p. :▼bcol. ill. ;▼c16 x 19 cm.▲1 ▼aAn
imals of the world▲  ▼a"Welcome books."▲  ▼aIncludes bibliographical references
(p. 23) and index.▲0  ▼aBengal tigers -- Cubs -- Roaring -- New Words -- To find
out more.▲ 0▼aTigers▼vJuvenile literature.▲ 1▼aTigers.▲1 ▼aEckart, Edana.▼tAnima
ls of the world.▲↩
```

Figure 5 MARC 21 Record in communication format

PRELUDE TO
MARC CATALOGING

Logical Record Structure

MARC cataloging basically involves the logical record structure, the content designation and the data content.

Before taking up the logical construct of a MARC record, it should be worthwhile to find out what the components of a logical record are, and how those are organized into a machine-readable record serving as functional library catalog. For understanding the rationale of record structure, the content designation needs to be discussed first due to the reason that the content designators provide clues for logical analysis and interpretations of bibliographic records in communication format.

Content Designation

The data units are clustered in Data Content Section, as illustrated in Figure 4. While reading the continuous character string, computer picks up units of data with the help of predetermined control characters that separate the physical units as fields and subfields. Hence, Fields and Subfields are in fact logical names of physical units and sub-units of data.

By the same logic, the actual text, or value, of a data unit is defined as Field Content. The meaning of a data unit, or field content, is established only by putting it in context of Field Tag. The Field Tags, however, are kept in the Directory section, away from their respective data fields, but programmatically linkable. The three digit Field Tag, as indicated earlier, represents the type of bibliographic data contained in the field, e.g. Tag '245' signifies that the field contains *title statement* of the record item. This clarifies that the Field Tag serves a logical purpose of recognizing the relationship of the field content with the record item, or the document.

Like Field Tag, there are other tools to analyse and extract the field values discretely, reveal their identities explicitly, and manipulate field contents programmatically. Such tools are known as Content Designators. There are two devices for physical control that help Content Designators to function.

Physical Control of Data Content

The two control devices, Subfield Delimiter and Field Terminator, work like traffic signals. The Subfield Delimiters (e.g. '$') embedded in field contents alert computer programs to take the immediate next character (e.g. 'a') as a data identifier code and not as a part of text. This way, the computer continues to read the text string as a subfield till it encounters another Subfield Delimiter or a Field Delimiter.

The control characters used for Subfield Delimiter and Field Delimiter are special characters, rarely used, and most often nonprintable. The nonprintable ones are preferred because their use eliminates chances of occurrence of a control character as a part of text. For example, a Hash sign '#', often employed as Field Terminator, used sometimes in text for a number symbol. In MARC 21 records, an upright solid triangle and an upside-down solid triangle serve as the Field Separator and Subfield Delimiter respectively. Figure 4 and Figure 5 display these nonprintable characters in graphic form; otherwise, the printer would have ignored those and replaced all unseen characters with null in outputs. To overcome print hazards, when a MARC record is printed in Tagged Format the nonprintable characters get transformed into some legible signs by proxy. As shown in Figure 6, the two nonprintable symbols used for Field Terminator and

Subfield Delimiter in the example of MARC Communication Format (Figure 5) are replaced in Tagged Format.

```
LDR 01218cam 22003134a 450
001 13020293
005 20030923103827.0
008 021204s2003 nyua b b 001 0 eng
906 __ $a 7 $b cbc $c orignew $d 1 $e ecip $f 20 $g y-gencatlg
925 0_ $a acquire $b 1 shelf copy $x policy default
955 __ $a jb12 2002-12-04 $c jb12 2002-12-04 $d jb04 2002-12-06
$e jb02 2002-12-06 to Children's $a lb00 2002-12-10 $d lb04 2002-
12-12 $a aa07 2002-12-16 $a ps07 2003-08-25 1 copy rec'd., to CIP
ver. $f pv06 2003-08-28 CIP ver to CCD
010 __ $a 2002154957
020 __ $a 0516242946 (lib. bdg.)
020 __ $a 0516278819 (pbk.)
040 __ $a DLC $c DLC $d DLC
042 __ $a pcc $a lcac
050 00 $a QL737.C23 $b E34 2003
082 00 $a 599.756 $2 21
100 1_ $a Eckart, Edana.
245 10 $a Bengal tiger / $c by Edana Eckart.
260 __ $a New York : $b Children's Press, $c c2003.
300 __ $a 24 p. : $b col. ill. ; $c 16 x 19 cm.
490 1_ $a Animals of the world
500 __ $a "Welcome books."
504 __ $a Includes bibliographical references (p. 23) and index.
505 0_ $a Bengal tigers − Cubs − Roaring − New Words − To find
out more.
650 _0 $a Tigers $v Juvenile literature.
650 _1 $a Tigers.
800 1_ $a Eckart, Edana. $t Animals of the world.
```

Figure 6 Tagged MARC Record for visual representation

Functions of Content Designators

As Content Designators, the Field Tag, Indicator 1 and Indicator 2, and Subfield Code, all contribute to computer performance in reading the content of a bibliographic record meaningfully. The main objectives of the content designation are to support computer programming in:

- Searching and retrieving all identifiable bibliographic data elements
- Formatting of retrieved data for visual presentation on screen and in print.

Field Tag

In MARC format, there is no reserved space for any particular type of data as one finds often in a relational database record, where pre-labelled data spaces are allocated for every identifiable data unit, such as title, author, physical description, etc. Instead of pre-labelled fixed plots, MARC reserves a number of Field Tags, or three digit codes, each meant for a particular type of data. The three digit codes are, in fact, abbreviated form of the field names used for describing bibliographic units, or group of units. Field Tag is an efficient identifier. It is short, standard and easy to handle for the computer. Field Tag, on top of that, provides bibliographic format with flexibility. This is an indispensable feature for recording bibliographic elements since many data fields, e.g. Title, Author, etc. vary in length. Field Tag, being potentially a repeatable device, supports multiple occurrences of any field specified as 'Repeatable' in MARC 21 documentation. When a field, e.g. Tag 700, repeats twice, it will produce two Alternate Authors fields. The nature of the data content of a field type determines repeatability/non-repeatability of fields. For example, a bibliographic record supports only one non-repeatable main entry field 100 for Personal Author.

The primary function of a Field Tag is to provide a data field with

100 1_ $a Spilsbury, Richard, $d 1963-	NR
020 __ $a 0516242946 (lib. bdg.)	R
020 __ $a 0516278819 (pbk.)	
650 _1 $a Tigers.	R
650 _1 $a Endangered species.	

Figure 7 Examples of Repeatable Field Tags

its context. For example, Tag 100 stands for main author, and interprets the data within the field as all about the main author of the document. Without the context of Field Tag the content of field is meaningless junk of data.

Indicators

Indicators are two: Indicator 1 and Indicator 2. Both the Indicators work together as Content Designators. Indicator 1 holds the first position at the beginning of a variable data field; the Indicator 2 holds the next position. Each of these provides some supplementary information about the field content, mostly related to visual presentation of the field. Use of Indicators varies depending on the types of data field represented by their corresponding Tags.

Each Indicator holds single-character code. The code may be a numeric or a lowercase alphabetic character or a blank space. Use of a blank (#) Indicator is inconsistent. A blank space may mean:

- Indicator undefined
- No value provided, or
- A specific meaning assigned.

Here are few examples:

- Value 3 in first indicator of field 246 indicates that field content is a parallel title; while value 3 in second indicator indicates that there will be no notes but an added entry under the parallel title.

- A '0' value of 1st indicator in field 245 indicates that the title is the main entry; in field 246 it indicates that the field content is a portion of title.

- A '0' value of second indicator in field 650 indicates that for subject heading LCSH is followed; in field 245 the second indicator value 3 indicates that the title begins with an article with three non-filing characters ('An' and a space). Indicator value 9 is reserved for local implementation.

TAG	INDICATORS		FIELD-CONTENT
	1st	2nd	
246	3		Parallel Title
246	3		No Notes. Added Entry
245	0		Main Entry under Title
245		3	Skip 3 characters in sorting/filing
650		0	LCSH used for Subject Heading

Figure 8 Changing values of Indicators in variant fields

Subfield Code

Subfield Codes identify data elements within a field for enabling the computer to manipulate each one separately. A Subfield Code is composed of a Subfield Delimiter and a Data Element Identifier. In reference to the earlier discussion on physical control, it is quite apparent that Subfield Delimiter remains unchanged in all records in a database. It is a necessary component of Subfield Code, but not a code by itself. A delimiter's function ends with passing a signal to computer predicting the presence of a Data Element Identifier. On the other hand, Data Element Identifier is a code, and has a crucial role to play in analysing bibliographic data content in a MARC format.

Data Element Identifier consists of either a lowercase alphabetic character or numeric character. In most cases, numeric identifiers are defined for processing parameters. Alphabetic identifiers, and rarely some numeric ones, are defined for typifying every identifiable element that constitutes the field content. The character '9' is kept reserved for local use as data element identifier.

Subfield codes are defined not for the purposes of arranging the subfields in order within a field. The order of subfields is specified by the bibliographic standards followed by the cataloging agency, e.g., cataloging rules, ISBD, giving priority to MARC 21 specifications wherever available.

245	Title statement	NR
$a	Title proper/short title	NR
$b	Remainder of title	NR
$f	Designation of vol./issue and/or date	NR
$g	Miscellaneous information	NR
$h	Medium	NR
$i	Display text	NR
$n	Number of part/section of a work	R
$p	Name of part/section of a work	R
$5	Institution to which field applies	NR
$6	Linkage	NR
$8	Field link and sequence number	R

Figure 9 Examples of Subfield Codes with Dollar sign as Subfield Delimiter

Subfield Code does not repeat unless it is specified as repeatable for a particular field in MARC 21 documentation. Besides repeatability (R) and non-repeatability (NR), Figure 9 illustrates use of numeric character in Subfield Code as processing parameters $6 and $8.

A Note to MARC Catalogers

Whatever said so far in this section reveals sufficiently the intricacies of MARC 21 mechanism for analysing bibliographical record contents. While the physical identification of fields and subfields is achieved by simple algorithms, the applications of analytical tools, namely the content designators, prove to be highly complicated. This is largely because of the unpredictable behaviour of bibliographic data, amount of denotable data types and uncertainty in their relationship. Any isolated attempt to invent a solution locally by deviating from the standard practice should invariably frustrate the consolidated efforts to solve bibliographic information problems globally. Therefore, it is all important for MARC catalogers to strictly abide by the MARC 21 specifications.

MARC Cataloging Elements

Logical Data

The logical structure of bibliographic data content is primary concern of catalogers, be it in manual card format or MARC 21. The rules formulated for management of bibliographic data aim to provide ready access and precise descriptions of the recorded items. In developing normative principles for identifying discrete data elements and their syntactic relationship, the experts have taken comparable approaches under traditional as well as electronic environment; even though the definition of a catalog has been revolutionized during the transition period. Those with exposure to cataloging practices should not feel alien to the basic features of MARC 21 data structuring.

Structural Framework

The building blocks in logical structure of data content are data fields. Data field is a logical representation of a character string identified as a unit of information (e.g. R. K. Narayan), and qualified by its corresponding field name (e.g. Author). The field tag transforms the field content into a meaningful unit of information.

The MARC field tag consists of a three digit character (e.g. 100). It acts like a sticker label; attach a machine-readable descriptive name to the field (e.g. tag 100). Tag 100 stands for 'Personal Author - Main Entry'. It is interesting to note that MARC 21 defines a field not only by the nature of its association with the record item (or the target work), but also by taking into account the processing requirements of the field. This explains why there are so many field tags for name of personal author, e.g. 100, 700, 800 instead of one. There are many instances of multiple functionality of a field serving as descriptive representation of bibliographic unit and as an access point too. Fields may be divided further into subfields containing specific data elements, e.g. 245 Title Statement field has subfield $c Statement of Responsibility.

The data content section holds essentially two types of fields: Data fields and Control fields. Since data fields are of variable length, they are called variable data fields, unless the data are in coded form. The coded data fields, e.g. 007, 008, are fixed length fields. The control fields are referred to at times as fixed fields, though some of those are in fact variable in length. There are as many as 999 potential MARC tags. A complete list of field tags is provided in Part 3 for a bird's eye view of MARC data map. As the List reveals, few of those remain unassigned; and few assigned previously, now deleted leaving out nearly 200 active fields. Amongst those, about 42 fields are designated for local use, and some other reserved for libraries in US/Canada. Only a handful of fields are being used over and over again in current catalogs, the rest intermittently or barely ever, depending upon the nature of available resources.

It would be rewarding for a cataloger to study the distribution pattern of MARC tags and keep in mind its regulatory principles.

Field Tag Distribution

Tag number indicates the field type. The tagging system follows a hierarchical scheme. The three numeric characters in field tags behave like a DDC in assigning field types in decimal order. The first character in a tag indicates functional characteristics of data, and on those criteria, it makes the primary grouping of related data fields in blocks. The second and third characters generally determine the data type. Figure 10 explains the underlying pattern of field distributions.

The book follows the convention of using an upper case letter, 'X', as a dummy notation that may substitute any numeric character in the given tag position.

X10 gets fields	010	110	210	310	etc.
1X0 gets fields	110	120	130	140	etc.
11X gets fields	110	111	112	114	etc.

Figure 10 Hierarchical Pattern of Field Tagging

There is a set of content designators that may be assigned with common values in fields, whenever applicable, across the blocks.

#	Undefined (element not defined)
n	Not applicable (element is not applicable to the item)
u	Unknown (record creator was unable to determine value)
z	Other (value other than those defined for the element)
$	Fill character (record creator has chosen not to provide information)

Figure 11 Parallel use of hash signs #, and subfield element identifiers in MARC

Control fields

The first block of fields is made under tag 00X that contains variable control fields, e.g. 001, and fixed-length position-specific data fields, e.g. 008; none of those contain indicators or subfield codes. For cataloguing of books and serials, the only relevant 00X field is Field 008, which has separate formats for monographic materials, continuous resources, which includes serials, and other document types. It may be noted that 008 is an optional field, and required only if the Library's application software makes use of the coded data profitably, otherwise not. It is also possible for a computer to generate the field programmatically. Therefore, it is inadvisable to opt for a 008 field without checking with the systems adminis-trator.

It may be mentioned here that the record's Leader is not a field, and does not have a tag of its own. However, following conventions, sometimes a triple zero '000', or alpha code 'LDR' is used as a virtual tag for Leader in a tagged display of MARC records.

Variable data fields

All fields except 00X are variable data fields. These fields consist of indicators, one or more Subfield codes, variable data, and a field terminator. The blocks of data fields are organized by the nature of relations of data with the record item (or the target work), taking processing requirements into account.

0XX = Control information, numbers, codes
1XX = Main entry
2XX = Titles, edition, imprint
3XX = Physical description, etc.
4XX = Series statements
5XX = Notes
6XX = Subject access fields
7XX = Name, etc. added entries or series; linking
8XX = Series added entries; holdings and locations
9XX = Reserved for local implementation

Figure 12 Primary Grouping of Variable Fields

A subset of the primary blocks contains fields of accessible data. For maintaining these data in consistent form the cataloging agencies must employ appropriate authority control tools. It may also require them to build authoritative tools to control culture-specific vocabulary and their renderings.

1XX = Main entry
4XX = Series statements
6XX = Subject access fields
7XX = Name, etc. added entries or series; linking
8XX = Series added entries; holdings and locations

Figure 13 Access Field blocks

2nd level fields

Second level organization of blocks involves the final two numeric characters of field tags. At this level, some content designators are set for select fields across the blocks, which function as access points.

X00	Personal names
X10	Corporate names
X11	Meeting names
X30	Uniform titles
X40	Bibliographic titles
X50	Topical terms
X51	Geographic names

Figure 14 Selective Second-level Fields serving as Access Points

3rd level fields

The hierarchical pattern of field structuring may be found in some places at the third level of field allocations. Particularly in title, notes and subject blocks the trend is visible.

500	General Note
501	With Note
502	Dissertation Note
503	Bibliographic History Note [obsolete]
504	Bibliography, etc. Note
505	Formatted Content Note
506	Restrictions on Access Note
507	Scale Note for Graphic Material
508	Creation/Production Credit Note
509	Unassigned [may be used for local note]

Figure 15 Hierarchic distribution of third level fields

Parallel fields

The principle of parallel tagging is followed only in selective fields where a common set of second level tagging may be used with same meaning across primary blocks. There are, however, exceptions to this principle of parallel meaning of field designation where historical legacy dominates over the new directions.

Personal Name	
	Title: India, development and participation.
100 Auth. Main	Drèze, Jean
700 Auth. Alt.	Sen, Amartya Kumar
	Tile: The Calcutta municipal gazette: Tagore memorial special supplement.
600 Subject	Tagore, Rabindranath
Corporate Name	
	Title: Founding Conference of the Club of Life.
110 Auth. Main	Club of Life
610 Subject	Club of Life
	Title: Centenary review of the Asiatic Society, 1784-1884.
110 Auth. Main	Asiatic Society (Calcutta, India)
610 Subject	Asiatic Society (Calcutta, India)
Conference Name	
	Title: Basic national education: report of the Zakir Husain Committee and the detailed syllabus
111 Auth. Main	All India National Education Conference, Wardha, 1937
711 Auth. Alt.	Wardha Conference
611 Subject	Wardha Conference

Figure 16 Examples: Parallel meaning in context of Author Types

Implementation Decisions

MARC 21 specifications provide its implementers with opportunities for adopting alternative means and measures in dealing with some specific types of data elements to suit their national and institutional requirements. MARC 21, being promoted to an international format, aims to embrace the diverse segments of the universe of knowledge, irrespective of the differences in their ethnicity, ethos and communicability. Instead of the classical principle of unification, MARC 21 approaches toward harmonization and tends to keep individual bibliographic resources and formats within the folds of its schematic organization. It is an enormous and highly involved task for MARC 21, particularly because of the fact that it is a process of reengineering of the old framework originally oriented as a local and then a national device.

Today, the MARC 21 bibliographic format offers a number of flexible modular mechanisms to cataloging agencies to make choices that suit their national as well as institutional requirements, from within a range of options as to the data fields, content designations, authority files, bibliographic standards, uncontrolled data, local data, language and scripts. Sometimes the alternatives are declared and authoritative sources, including different cataloging rules, classification schemes or subject heading authorities, are enumerated with specifications. There is also a kind of bucket fields/subfields designated for 'Others' that appear at the bottom in a list. The provision of 'others' does not include 'any other' elements, but only those enlisted separately with approved codes.

Customary Field Sets

While it is unwarrantable to exclude outright any of the field provisions for local use, no library may need all as evidenced from the online databases. The criteria of selection are basically twofold:

- Nature of library's collections
- Nature of library's readership that determines the development trend of the library's collections, in other words, the nature of future collections

Taking these two aspects in view a policy may be framed to concentrate on a set of relevant fields, indicators, subfields. That should not, however, stop an able cataloger to use fields outside the selection whenever justified. A library may start working with the commonly used fields clubbed with other fields related to their special requirements, and then go on adding up while gathering experience. This is true not only for bibliographic fields but filter through the indicators and subfields. The bare minimum starting pack for book cataloging may look something like the following:

020	ISBN
040	Cataloging Source
09X	Local Call Number
100	Personal Name – Main Entry
110	Corporate Name – Main Entry
130	Uniform Title – Main Entry
240	Uniform Title
245	Title of the Work
246	Varying Form of Title
250	Edition Statement
260	Imprint: Publication, Distribution
300	Physical Description
440	Series Statement/ Series Title Added Entry
500	General Note
504	Bibliographic Note
505	Formatted Contents Note
520	Summary Note (abstracts, etc)
59X	Local Notes
600	Subject Added Entry - Personal
630	Subject Added Entry – Uniform Title
650	Subject Added Entry - Topical
651	Subject Added Entry - Geographic
69X	Local Subject Access Fields
700	Personal Names - Additional Access Point
710	Corporate Name - Additional Access Point
730	Uniform Title - Additional Access Point
700	Personal - Additional Access Point
9XX	Local Data Elements

Figure 17 Example of a Basic Set of Bibliographic Fields

The first important question about the basic field-set may relate to legitimacy of fields it includes. Inclusion of each field should be validated by frequent use. If a library does not access series editors, the field 440 stands valid, otherwise there should be another pair of fields - field 490 to describe series title and field 800 to provide access to series editor. When the basic fields are identified the indicators and subfield codes are required to be evaluated in the same fashion. The set of fields may grow with the changing pattern of the collections. The MARC 21 fields are dynamic. A new field may be introduced, existing field dropped, reallocated or redefined. The customized field-set must remain tuned with such revisions.

Serials-related fields

Supposedly a library decides to catalog serials for the first time. The basic field-set, as Figure 17 displays, would be quite insufficient to support serials data elements unless some special fields are added.

020	ISSN
222	Key Title
247	Former Title
362	Dates/Sequential Designation
310	Current Frequency
710	Supplement/Special Issue

Figure18 Essential fields for Serials

Like that, very many changes may take place in library's resource profile over time compelling the authorities to append more fields. Here are certain instances of collection types that call for expansion of the set shown in Figure 17.

Conference related fields

As generally understood, conferences or meetings are *temporary* corporate bodies. MARC 21 has assigned fields X11 for independent conference, meeting, workshop, etc. identifiable by its own name.

111	Meeting Name – Main Entry
611	Meeting Name – Subject Added Entry
711	Meeting Name – Added Entry
811	Meeting Name – Series Added Entry

Figure19 Essential fields for meetings, etc. as independent bodies

MARC 21 treats meetings, conferences, etc. differently and specifies fields X10 instead of X11, in such cases:

- where those are entered under a corporate name, or
- where the words 'conference', 'congress', etc. are included in the name of the corporate body, like Standing Conference on Library Materials on Africa; or United Nations Conference on Trade and Development.

Language-related fields

Libraries serving a multilingual nation, like India, involve critical issues relating to language and script in bibliographic data communications. For developing a multilingual/multiscript record, it is imperative to declare specific information about language and script used in appropriate coded fields. Any bibliographic data element may be represented in different script in a record. Language of cataloging may also differ from the bibliographic item recorded. The fields dealing with identification, description, and linking are to be used selectively to avoid undue complications in format—both for man and machine performances.

041	Language Code
546	Language Note
880	Alternate Graphic Representation

Figure 20 Fields related to Language and Script data

Field 041 is used in conjunction with 008/35-37 (Language). The languages may also be recorded in textual form in field 546. Field 880 contains the fully content-designated representation, in a different script, of another field in the same record. It is used when data needs to be duplicated to express it in both the original vernacular script and those transliterated into one or more scripts. MARC 21 prescribes two different models for building multiscript records.

Model A: Vernacular and transliteration.
The regular fields may contain data in different scripts and also in the vernacular or in transliterated form. Bibliographic data in the regular fields is linked to the data in 880 fields by a subfield $6.

Model B: Simple multiscript records.
A record contains bibliographic data in regular fields only. Script varies in one or more fields as required. No bibliographic element is duplicated for presentation in different script or transliterated form in a link field.

The Cooperative Cataloging Program (CCP) identified a set of fields required additionally for *core record* containing Non-Latin scripts.

1XX	Main Entry
245	Transcription of title, other title, SOR
246	Varying form of title
250	Edition Statement
260	Imprint (pub. place, pub. name and pub. date)
4XX	Series statement
5XX	Note Fields
500	Source of title if not from t.p.
502	Dissertation note
505	Contents note for multipart items + separate titles
533	Reproduction note
6XX	Subject Headings
7XX	Added Entries

Figure 21 Additional requirements for core records containing non-Latin scripts

For CCP *core record* visit www.loc.gov/catdir/pcc/pcc.html. Fields 066, 041 provide script and language information, and may be included in the subset.

As regards to the character sets, MARC 21 has provided specifications for character sets and repertoires for scripts. The resources available under UCS/Unicode environment may be found more relevant today both technologically and culturally. Many Asiatic and Indic scripts are now ready for web-enabled database applications. MARC 21 authorities have taken special initiative for implementing UCS/Unicode character set.

There are some basic requirements to be fulfilled by the local agencies for successful Unicode implementation. Those are:

- In MARC 21 records, Leader character position 9 contains value 'a'.
- UCS/Unicode characters not to be used partially.
- The record length contained in Leader positions 0-4 is a count of the number of octets in the record, not characters.

See discussion on Unicode under FAQ for further details.

Holding data fields

MARC record provides the copy-specific information in local fields and partly in holding data fields. The importance of copy availability information in a resource sharing and networking environment can not be overestimated. MARC 21 has introduced Holding Data Format to handle holding data elements in two ways. First, holding data in a separate record linked with bibliographic record:

Fields of Bibliographic Record or Holding Record	
840	Holding Institution
852	Location
853	Caption and Pattern - Basic bibliographic unit [Structured]
863	Enumeration and Chronology [Structured]
866	Textual Holdings –Basic bibliographic unit [Unstructured]

Figure 22 Holding Information in Bibliographic and Holding fields

Optionally, holding data may take place in the bibliographic record itself. The fields that provide minimum level holding information are:

Fields of Bibliographic Record	
049	Local Holdings
856	Electronic Location and Access

Figure 23 Holding Information in Bibliographic Fields

Field 850 contains merely the name of the host institution, whereas field 852 provides extensive location data, including full form of institution name, address, etc. As regards the holding details, field 866 accommodates the volume/copy and chronological data in textual format, whereas field 853 and field 863 together provide those details in a structured formats suitable for captioned display and print.

Local data fields

Cataloging rules describe bibliographic elements based on available copy. MARC 21 record provides the copy-specific information in local note fields considered not a logical part of the exchangeable record.

A large number of fields have been provided in MARC 21 formats for local use without detail specification. It is up to the local implementation to design and define the fields in context of their possible contents. The following are the fields denoted for local use, which are defined normally as non-exchangeable data fields providing bibliographic or housekeeping information, such as Barcode, Accession Numbers, Acquisition references, 'etc.

009	Variable Control Field - free for local use
049	Local Holdings - used by OCLC
09X	Local Call Number Fields
59X	Local Note Fields
69X	Local Subject Access Fields
9XX	Additional Fields - free for local use

Figure 24 Free Fields for Local Use

The freedom of using locally defined fields given to the implementing agencies may prove disastrous if not the provisions are used judiciously, abiding by the normative principles of MARC 21 bibliographic record structuring.

Display Formatting Issues

One of the major administrative decisions an implementing agency needs to take is about the form of catalog. Should the card catalog facility continue for a while? Should the records displayed on Online Catalog look like a card entry? If the answer is Yes for any of the two, in the Record Leader/18 the control data for Descriptive Cataloging Form will be set with code 'a', otherwise code 'i' to pass on to the system for processing data accordingly.

#	Non-ISBD
a	AACR 2
i	ISBD
u	Unknown

Figure 25 Code for Descriptive Cataloging Form

The code 'a' specifies that the choice and form of entry of the access points are formulated according to AACR2, which abides by the ISBD specifications.

The code 'i' indicates that only the punctuation practices in some designated fields are followed in accordance with ISBD specifications.

Libraries in the process of computerization sometimes believe that the manual catalog should go on parallel until the users get used to OPAC — the Online Public Access Catalog. Those who share this belief wish to see the records on screen or in print displayed in card catalog-like fashion meticulously following AACR2 rules and library conventions. MARC 21 specifications support application programs in displaying records in alternative formats. At the time of data transcription, the catalogers are required to embed data elements with appropriate punctuation. This makes process of catalog generation slower, and production cost and the risk of human errors higher.

Title and Statement of Responsibility
Edition
Material or type of publication specification
Publication, Distribution (etc.)
Physical Description
Series
Notes
Standard Numbers

Figure 26 Application areas for ISBD Punctuation

Taking the above points into account, an implementing agency may like to agree with the increasing population of automated libraries to adopt Labelled Display format that has been gaining popularity among the user communities worldwide. Even in labelled display, the end-punctuation specified by ISBD needs to appear. ISBD specified punctuation is applicable in the following field areas:

Fields	
1xx	5xx
245	6xx
260	700-730
362	8xx

Figure 27 Fields end with punctuation

Many instructive documents prepared by libraries to help their own community are available for viewing in their websites. These offer opportunities to find different perspectives of using MARC fields and take practical lessons.

FREQUENTLY ASKED QUESTIONS

Here are some general questions on and about MARC, and some pertinent to MARC 21, that may not have been answered clearly enough in introductory discussions.

Do all computerized catalogs follow MARC?

No. Many machine-readable catalogs follow no bibliographic standard at all, and few follow different ones, like UNIMARC. A non-standard computerized catalog system can serve the current and local needs satisfyingly. However, the good and committed libraries are expected to move toward standardization sooner or later.

Why MARC is needed when a machine-readable catalog can do without?

MARC is a format for bibliographic data communications, which is a necessary functionality of shared cataloging. Libraries using MARC compliant database are capable of reading MARC records originated somewhere else. Based on Z39.50 protocol, MARC records can be accessed online from remote computers. Union catalogs comprising MARC records can be generated and maintained efficiently by using MARC 21 holding format. MARC 21 bibliographic format offers full coverage of bibliographic elements related to every possible type of documents. Its integrated design allows records of varied types and sizes to be kept together, and searched together.

Being a flexible and modular in structure, MARC formats allow a library to add, revise, delete fields through utility programs. The feature also enables a library to customize imported MARC records for copy cataloging.

Why MARC records look so bizarre?

To a viewer, a MARC record in its communication format is an unreadable junk of characters; to a computer it is a meaningful item of communication. Computer processes the bibliographic data following MARC specifications and transform those into different display formats for public viewing. The display formats commonly referred to as:

- Tagged display
- Labelled display
- Card format display

The tagged display format is generally used by the professional familiar with MARC content designators. Relatively, a tagged record provides fuller details.

The labelled display format is the most popular among the online users, as revealed in survey literature. This is because the labels qualify the fields, or group of fields, the representations are straightforward and discrete.

The card format, however, is often the best choice for the users nostalgic about good old cataloging system. For more see discussion on this issue under section 'Prelude to MARC Cataloging'.

What is a MARC-compliant database? Is it same as MARC database?

No, MARC database and MARC compliant database are not same. A MARC database contains a sequential file of hierarchically arranged records following ANSIZ39.2/ISO2709 specifications and MARC defined content designation for every field in every record; whereas a MARC compliant database may be a relational, or a different model, holding records comprising elements equivalent to MARC fields by definition. A database in compliance with MARC can transform its records into MARC communication format and exchange records with any MARC database or with another MARC compliant database; otherwise it cannot.

Copy Cataloging sounds new terminology. What does it mean?

Yes. The term stands for a new concept of cataloging work that includes finding sources of MARC records of target documents, downloading records, eliminating unwanted fields, and adding fields of local relevance. Since copy cataloging procedures are carried out programmatically, it takes less time, involves less cost and less intellectual effort.

Can someone do Copy Cataloging without knowledge of MARC ?

No. Only a professional conversant with MARC specifications can read MARC data fields correctly and accomplish editing for customization.

Does Copy Cataloging make in-house cataloging outmoded?

No. Copy Cataloging is not a substitute of Original Cataloging—a new term used for complete cataloging of a document from scratch. The obvious reason is the unavailability of downloadable records of all documents that a library needs to process. Hence a library is required to undertake both the cataloging procedures for gaining full advantage of computerization.

Where from are MARC records obtained for copy cataloguing?

There are websites offering free catalog search and download options for records retrieved. LC database is one of them. This gesture helps researchers. The free service allows them downloading records one at a time. For library cataloging the facility proves unaccommodating. The sources of MARC records are either database vendors, and/or utility networks.

The utility networks operate at regional and international levels and extend variety of bibliographic support services. Distribution of cataloging data in MARC format against subscriptions is one common agenda. Top organizations like Library of Congress and

OCLC are among them. Libraries in India and neighbouring countries may make use of some reputed utilities as cost-effective solution for getting quality records in short time, provided they have

- Suitable MARC editing software, and

- Adequate trained professionals.

Competing local enterprises are expected to come up sooner or later to grab the potential market opportunities. Names and whereabouts of MARC service providers are available at www.loc.gov/marc/marcrecsvrs.html

Few of them are mentioned under the heading 'MARC Resource', in Appendix.

MARC fields seem too many. Do Libraries really need them all?

MARC can describe in depth documents of every conceivable type and shape. The enormous size of field population makes MARC format highly accommodating. No libraries need them all; some require fields that others may not need. This is why no valid MARC field can be permanently discarded without risking loss of useful information. Depending on their types of collections, libraries select fields for their regular use. For general guidance, MARC 21 documentations suggest a *minimal level* of records containing essential cataloging information. Borrowing words from MARC 21 documentations one can say that there is 'no list of "mandatory" data elements that must appear in a MARC 21 record. Theoretically, a record could simply consist of a leader and a 245 (title) field.' MARC authorities define the minimal level record in terms of US libraries, and expect other nations to define the same for their own use. There is another model developed by the Cooperative Catalog Program (CCP), known as *core level* which is less than *full level*, and more than the *minimal*. Until decisions at national level are taken, libraries may base their minimum level format on one of these models with necessary modifications. The agencies may not hesitate to go beyond the defined set and use any valid MARC 21 fields whenever a cataloging target calls for.

More on this point has been discussed under section: 'Prelude to MARC Cataloging.'

A list enumerating minimal and national level requirements from US point of view can be seen at www.loc.gov/marc/bibliographic/nlr/.

MARC cataloging might be easier with software help. Is there any?

Large resources are available providing help in all spheres of MARC cataloging. Quite a few simple and user-friendly applications are there, as well as highly sophisticated ones supporting specific jobs. The activities demand too many types of skills, starting with web hunting for records. While many of them are priced, some are free. There are in fact some excellent products, like Cataloging Calculator, which are free of cost. Cataloging Calculator functions as a smart ready reckoner that fetches for a cataloger correct codes, content designators, standard abbreviations, etc. In general, cataloging tools offer the following types of supports:

- Simultaneous searching, downloading, uploading, filtering
- Spell checking and cleaning up bibliographic databases
- Editing, script-making and translating delimited texts into MARC format
- Finding variable and fixed MARC field tags, language codes, geographic area codes, publication country codes, abbreviations, etc.
- Converting MARC records to and from other formats
- Validating MARC records
- Finding URL links in MARC 21 records

A list of bibliographic tools that support the MARC 21 formats is maintained by the MARC 21 authority at www.loc.gov/marc/marctools.html. See a select list of specialized tools extracted from MARC 21 Documentations page in Appendix.

What matters in developing quality records?

Libraries need to identify the format correctly, and transcribe accurately bibliographic elements, both in text and coded forms, following adopted standards and norms. Selection of standards—name and subject authorities, classification systems, or authorized code lists—are critical for developing quality records. Before deciding to adopt any of them, a cataloging agency must think twice about its relevance to national and local requirements.

What bibliographic tools help developing correct MARC records?

Library of Congress is currently offering access to cataloging tools as a support service package *Catalogers' Desktop* at www.loc.gov/cds/dektop.html. This fee-based service provides electronic access to most commonly used bibliographic standards and authority documents. Some of them may be found indispensable for a cataloging agency. The subscription package includes:

- Anglo-American Cataloguing Rules (AACR2)

- Library of Congress Rule Interpretations

- Subject Cataloging Manuals

- MARC 21 Formats

- Latest editions of all MARC code lists

- There are many more (see full list at www.loc.gov/cds/dektop resourcelist.html)

Do libraries require all the tools, or select few?

MARC 21 formats and Library of Congress Rule Interpretations are surely instances of fundamental requirements. As for descriptive cataloging, MARC 21 offers alternatives in Leader/18. MARC has however a close affinity with AACR2. Moreover, AACR2 continues as a de-facto standard and being updated regularly comes closer to MARC, though basically the two are different and are expected to remain so.

The selection of subject authorities, however, is not simple. For various reasons, use of Library of Congress Subject Headings (LCSH) is much less than use of Sears' Subject List. None of them are found unquestionably acceptable due to such reasons as:

- Ideas, concepts and events culturally important to societies with long traditions are poorly represented in available authorized subject headings.
- Secondly, the forms of the subject headings, including spelling, play a vital role in search and retrieval. Readership in countries like India are not comfortable with American spelling and expressions.

The situation should improve with active participation of the user societies over time. It is a professional obligation to propose revisions and additions to LCSH authorities through prescribed form (*see* Appendix).

As a temporary measure, libraries may choose fields 690-699 for subject headings of local significance, and start building local thesaurus and authority files that may eventually contribute to making integrated authority systems for national level use.

Catalogers' Tools page precludes Classification. Why?

Recently Library of Congress comes up with another fee-based service package *Classification Web* at www.loc.gov/cds/classweb/ #NewServer . The service offers opportunities to access correlations between tools of content analysis:

LC Subject headings	<->	LC Classification Numbers
LC Subject headings	<->	Dewey Classification Numbers
LC Classification Numbers	<->	Dewey Classification Numbers

Selection of classification may not be a problem. The majority follows DDC, some UDC; and a few use LC Classification. All have their designated fields. If a library uses a different scheme and wants to stick to that, the library may use the field reserved for all other classification systems, duly posting its code, if available. Otherwise the scheme must get registered with MARC 21 authorities.

Is it possible to create MARC records in vernacular languages?

Yes, MARC 21 supports multilanguage transcriptions. The cataloging language itself may be English or non-English, e.g. German, Arabic, Hindi; certain fields may contains text in a different language, say Bengali. It is possible then to create bibliographic record in English with Title field in Bengali, or vice versa, or entirely in vernacular. MARC 21 bibliographic format provides special linking fields with specifications necessary for accommodating multi-lingual and multi-script fields.

Until recently, the only way to transcribe languages, which fall back on non-roman alphabets, was transliteration using diacritics. Today with the development of Unicode technology it has been possible to use native scripts for representing texts of any vernacular language of the world with no hassle.

What is Unicode? How it can be used in MARC 21 records?

Unicode is an international standard for character encoding—an industry subset of Universal Coded Character Set (UCS) that supports over 90,000 characters of which the first 256 are ASCII. MARC 21 adopted Unicode as an alternative character set in 1994. It enables MARC 21 to support far more characters than are in the MARC-8 sets and share with other communities a single character set, universal in scope.

MARC authorities maintain a large repertoire of Basic and Extended Latin characters defined for use in MARC-8 environment. At present the use of UCS/Unicode and UTF-8, which represents the encoding rules, is restricted within that repertoire, so that systems not having the full range of UCS/Unicode character sets may continue interchanging bibliographic data. It is believed, Unicode is going to be the only character coding standard in near future. Until then MARC 21 formats are expected to remain broad based and accommodate MARC-8, UCS, or UTF-8 encoding rules, or UCS/Unicode UTF-8 as referred to in MARC 21 documentation.

For details access http://www.loc.gov/marc/specifications/speccharintro.html

Questions Unanswered

Many questions have not been raised; some may not have been answered well enough here or anywhere in the book. Those unasked questions are not yet lost. All roads conveying MARC-related questions lead to MARC Homepage in Library of Congress website. The Homepage is practically the centre of all that happens around MARC. It has a section on FAQ too. A small set of probable questions is reproduced from there indicating the locations where from the best answers can be had.

Who maintains the MARC 21formats?
http://www.loc.gov/marc/overview.html

Are there any discussion groups or forums for the MARC 21 formats?
http://www.loc.gov/marc/marcforum.html

What documentation is available and how do I obtain it?
http://www.loc.gov/marc/
Are SGML or XML versions of the MARC 21 formats available?
http://www.loc.gov/marc/marcxml.html
How do I report errors in MARC 21 documentation?
mailto: ndmso@loc.gov & ndmso@loc.gov
How do I propose making a change to the MARC 21 formats?
mailto: marc@nlc-bnc.ca
MARC 21 Formats Proposed Change Form may be had from:
http://www.loc.gov/marc/chgform.html

PART

2

MARC 21 Fields

Contents

PART 2

Main Entry Variable Data Fields

Title Variable Fields

Edition, Imprint, etc.

Physical Descriptions, etc.

Series Statements

Notes

LEADER (NR)

The Leader is the first field of a bibliographic record. It is fixed in length at 24 character positions (00-23). The Leader consists of data elements containing coded values that provide the system with required information for processing the record. The Leader has no indicators or subfield codes. The data elements are positionally defined.

Data elements:		
00-04	Logical record length	NR
05	Record status	NR
06	Type of record	NR
07	Bibliographic level	NR
08	Type of control	NR
09	Character coding scheme	NR
10	Indicator count	NR
11	Subfield code count	NR
12-16	Base address of data	NR
17	Encoding level	NR
18	Descriptive cataloging form	NR
19	Linked record requirement	NR
20-23	Entry map	NR

The following Leader elements are system generated:

00-04	Logical record length
09	Character coding scheme
10	Indicator count
11	Subfield code count
12-16	Base address of data
20-23	Entry map

Other Leader elements may also be system generated depending upon the capabilities of an individual system.

05	Record status
06	Type of record
07	Bibliographic level
08	Type of control
17	Encoding level
18	Descriptive cataloging form
19	Linked record requirement

Normally, the positions 05, 06, 07 and 18 need human interference.

Leader/05 Record status

The character position contains a one-character alphabetic code that indicates the relationship of the record to a file for file maintenance purposes. Leader/05 and its codes in the table below are valid for all material types.

a	Increase in encoding level
c	Corrected or revised
d	**Deleted** - The record has been *logically deleted.*
n	**New** - The record is *a newly input* record.
p	Increase in encoding level from prepublication

Leader/06 Type of record

The *Type of record* character position contains a one-character alphabetic code that indicates the characteristics of and defines the components of the record, usually describing in general the type of material, for example, printed music, musical sound recording, kit, etc. The code is also used to determine the appropriateness and validity of certain data elements in the record.

Microforms , whether original or reproductions, are not identified by a distinctive *Type of record* code. The type of material characteristics described by the codes take precedence over the microform characteristics of the item.

The table below includes only the codes related to Books, Serials, Manuscripts and Mixed materials.

a	**Language material**	
	Leader/07 = a, c, d, or m:	**Books**
	Leader/07 = b or s:	**Serials**
p	Mixed materials	Mixed materials
t	Manuscript language material	Books

Leader/07 Bibliographic level

The *Bibliographic level* character position contains a one-character alphabetic code that indicates the bibliographic level of the record. Leader/07 and its codes in the table below are valid for all types.

a	Monographic component part
b	Serial component part
c	Collection
d	Subunit
m	Monograph/Item
s	Serial

Leader/18 Descriptive Cataloging Form

The codes in the table are valid for all types.

#	Non-ISBD
a	AACRZ
i	ISBD
u	Unknown

Leader/19-23

The character positions 19-23 comprise Linking and Entry map coding are generated programmatically. *See* discussions on Leader under *'Prelude to MARC Cataloging'* in Part 1.

008 Control Field: Books (NR)

Fixed-Field Data Elements

The field contains character positions 00-39 that provide coded information

- *about the record as a whole* and
- *about special bibliographic aspects* of the item.

The data elements are potentially useful for retrieval and data management purposes.

All defined character positions must contain a defined code. Fill character (|) may be used except in positions 00-05, 07-10, 15-17, 23 or 29.

Position-Specific Values 00-39

00-05 - Date entered on file

The computer-generated, six-character numeric string that indicates the date the MARC record was created. The date is recorded in the pattern *yymmdd*.

06 - Type of date/Publication status

A one-character code that categorizes the type of dates given in 008/07-10 (Date 1) and 008/11-14 (Date 2).

The choice of code for 008/06 is made concurrently with a determination of the appropriate dates for 008/07-14. For most records data is derived from information in field 260 (Publication, Distribution, etc. (Imprint)), field 362 (Dates of Publication and/ or Sequential Designation), or from note fields.

b -	No dates given; B.C. date involved [fields 008/07-10 and 008/11-14 are blank (#)]
c -	Continuing resource: currently published [Date 2 (008/11-14) contain 9999]
d -	Continuing resource: ceased publication [Date 1 and Date 2 both provided]
e -	Detailed date [Date 1 contains *YYYY*, and Date 2 *mmdd*]
i -	Inclusive dates of collection
k -	Range of years of bulk of collection [Contain the range of years covered by most of the material in the collection. if the bulk dates are represented by only a single year *the same date* in both the places is given.]
m -	Multiple dates [usually contain the beginning date and the ending date. If both dates for a multipart item are represented by a single year, then code s (Single date) is used.]
n -	Dates unknown [e.g., when no dates are given in field 260]
p -	Date of distribution/release/issue and production/recording when different
r -	Reprint/reissue date and original date [Date 1 contains date of reproduction/reissue; Date 2 the date of the original (code u ("uuuu"), if unknown)]
s -	Single known date/probable date [Date 2 contains blanks (####)]
t -	Publication date and copyright date
u -	Continuing resource status unknown [Date 2 contains code u ("uuuu")]
| -	No attempt to code

Note:

- A span of dates associated with a single item of uncertain date is coded as questionable (code q).
- Multiple dates associated with a single item are coded as multiple dates (code m).
- Single or multiple dates associated with a collection are coded as either bulk dates (code k) or inclusive dates (code i).
- A collection, whether or not it consists of individually published items, is not considered to exist in published form.
- Multipart items are not treated as a collection, see code m
- (Multiple dates).

07-10 - Date 1

The determination of dates for 008/07-10 is made concurrently with the choice of code for 008/06 (Type of date/publication status). When fill is used in 008/07-10, all four positions must contain the fill character

1-9	Date digit
#	Date element is not applicable
u	Date element is totally or partially unknown
I	No attempt to code

11-14 - Date 2

1-9	Date digit
#	Date element is not applicable
u	Date element is totally or partially unknown
I	No attempt to code

15-17 - Place of publication, production or execution

Choice of a MARC code is generally related to information in field 260 used in conjunction with field 044. The use of fill characters (| | |) in 008/15-17 is discouraged. When more than one place of publication, production or execution is involved, the first-named country is coded in 008/15-17. Additional codes are recorded in field 044.

18-21 - Illustrations

Up to four one-character codes (recorded in alphabetical order). The codes are derived from terms entered in field 300 (Physical Description).

- No illustrations
a - Illustrations
b - Maps
c - Portraits
d - Charts
e - Plans
f - Plates
g - Music
h - Facsimiles
i - Coats of arms
j - Genealogical tables
k - Forms
l - Samples
m- Phonodisc, phonowire, etc.
o - Photographs
p - Illuminations
	- No attempt to code

[The presence of the term *table* or *tables* alone mandates the use of code *a*. This, however, *differs from AACR2*]

22 - Target audience

A one-character code indicates the target audience of the item, in other words, for whom the item is intended.

#	Unknown or not specified
a	Preschool
b	Primary
c	Pre adolescent
d	Adolescent
e	Adult
f	Specialized [the item is narrowly aimed at a particular audience and of little interest to other audiences.]
g	General [the item is of general interest and not aimed at a particular target audience.]
j	Juvenile [item is intended for use by children/ young people through the age of 15.]
l	No attempt to code

23 - Form of item

A one-character code that indicates the form of material for the item.

#	None of the following
a	Microfilm
b	Microfiche
c	Microopaque
d	Large print
f	Braille
r	Regular print reproduction [Eye readable]
s	Electronic
l	No attempt to code

24-27 - Nature of contents

Codes, recorded in alphabetical order, indicate whether a significant part of the item *is* or *contains* certain types of material. Each unused position contains a blank (#).

- No specified nature of contents

a - Abstracts/summaries [It is or it contains abstracts/summaries of other publications.]

b - Bibliographies [all or part of an item is a bibliography or bibliographies. This code is used   only if the bibliography is substantial enough to be mentioned in the bibliographic record.]

c - Catalogs

d – Dictionaries [also used for a glossary or a gazetteer]

e - Encyclopedias

f - Handbooks

g - Legal articles

i – Indexes [The item is or contains an index to bibliographical material *other* than itself]

j - Patent document

k - Discographies

l – Legislation [Contains full or partial texts of enactments or texts of rules and regulations]

m – Theses [or dissertation or work created for an academic certification or degree]

n - Surveys of literature in a subject area [authored surveys]

o – Reviews [It is or it contains critical reviews of published or performed works]

p - Programmed texts

q - Filmographies

r - Directories

s - Statistics

t - Technical reports

u - Standards/specifications

v - Legal cases and case notes

w - Law reports and digests

z - Treaties [a treaty or accord negotiated between two or more parties]

| - No attempt to code

28 - Government publication

A one-character code that indicates whether the item is published or produced by or for a government agency, and, if so, the jurisdictional level of the agency.

#	Not a government publication
a	Autonomous or semiautonomous component
c	Multi-local
f	Federal/national
i	International intergovernmental
l	Local
m	Multi-state
o	Government publication level undetermined
s	State, provincial, territorial, dependent, etc.
u	Unknown if item is government publication
z	Other
|	No attempt to code

29 - Conference publication

0	Not a conference publication
1	Conference publication
|	No attempt to code

30 - Festschrift

A complimentary or memorial publication usually in the form of a collection of essays, and often embodies the results of research, issued in honor of a person, an institution, or a society, as a rule, on the occasion of an anniversary celebration. The title of the work may or may not use the word *festschrift*. Other indicative words are: *papers in honor of*, *in memory of*, *commemorating*, and their equivalents in foreign languages.

0	Not a festschrift
1	Festschrift
I	No attempt to code

31 - Index

Indicates whether the item includes an index to its own contents.

0	No index
1	Index present
I	No attempt to code

32 - Undefined

Contains a blank (#) or fill character (I)

33 - Literary form

Numeric codes 0 and 1 provide a generic identification of whether or not the item is a work of fiction. Alphabetic codes may be used to identify specific literary forms.

0	Not fiction (not further specified)
1	Fiction (not further specified)
c	Comic strips
d	Dramas
e	Essays
f	Novels
h	Humor, satires, etc. [or of a similar literary form]
i	Letters [a single letter or collection of correspondence]
j	Short stories [a short story or collection of short stories]
m	Mixed forms [a variety of literary forms e.g., poetry and short stories]
p	Poetry
s	Speeches
u	Unknown
I	No attempt to code

34 - Biography

#	No biographical material
a	Autobiography
b	Individual biography
c	Collective biography
d	Contains biographical information
		No attempt to code

35-37 - Language

Choice of a MARC code is based on the predominant language of the item.

38 - Modified record

A one-character code that indicates whether any data in a bibliographic record is a modification of *information that appeared on the item being cataloged* or that *was intended to be included in the MARC record*. Codes are assigned as in the order of the following priority list.

#	Not modified
d	Dashed on information omitted [use discouraged in MARC records]
o	Completely romanized/printed cards romanized [MARC record and printed cards both completely romanized]
r	Completely romanized/printed cards in script [MARC record completely romanized but the printed cards are in vernacular script]
s	Shortened [Some of the data omitted. Rarely used in current MARC records]
x	Missing characters [Not machine-readable. Use of **x** in current records unlikely]
		No attempt to code

39 - Cataloging source

A one-character code that indicates the creator of the original cataloging record. If the cataloging source is known, it is identified in subfield $a of field 040 (Cataloging Source).

#	National bibliographic agency [e.g., U.S. Library of Congress or National Library of Canada]
c	Cooperative cataloging program [other than a national bibliographic agency]
d	Other
u	Unknown
|	No attempt to code

EXAMPLES

008/06 Type of date

Code i - Inclusive dates of (made-up) collection

008/06 i
008/07-10 1943
008/11-14 1947
260 ##$c1943-47.

Code k - Range of years of the bulk, or most of the materials in (made-up) collection

008/06 k
008/07-10 1854
008/11-14 1854
260 ##$c1854. (There might be few outside the range.)

Code m - Multiple dates

008/06 m
008/07-10 1941
008/11-14 9999
260 ##$aCalcutta : $bRoyal Asiatic Society of Bengal,$c 1941-
[Multipart item for which the earliest volume is held.]

008/06 m
008/07-10 1943
008/11-14 1945
260 ##$aLondon : $bGollancz,$c1943-1945.

[A Single part item for which the publication date spans more than one year]

Code n - Dates unknown

008/06 n
008/07-10 uuuu
008/11-14 uuuu
260 ##$a[Spain]

Code q - Questionable date

008/06 q
008/07-10 1901
008/11-14 1965
260 ##$c [19 -]
505 1#$av.1 1884-1896; v.2 1896-1897; v.3 1898-1903

Code r - Reprint/reissue and Original date

008/06 r
008/07-10 2002
008/11-14 1941
260 ##$aKolkata :$bKolkata Municipal Corporation and New Age Publishers, $c2002.
500 ##$aPreviously published in 1941.

008/06 r
008/07-10 1966
008/11-14 uuuu
500 ##$aReprinted from Green Howard's Gazette.
       [Original date of publication is unknown.]

Code s Single known date/probable date

008/06 s
008/07-10 1977
008/11-14 ####
260 ##$aWashington : $bDept. of State,$c1977.

008/06 s
008/07-10 2001
008/11-14 2001
260 ##$aNew York : $bRoutledge,$c2001

Code t - Publication date and copyright date

008/06 t
008/07-10 1970
008/11-14 1958
260 ##$ San Diego, Calif. : $bGreenhaven Press, $c1970, c2001.

008/15-17 Place of publication, production, or execution

008/15-17 gw
260 ##$aBerlin ;$aNew York : $bSpringer-Verlag, $c c1992.

008/15-17 xx#
260 ##$aS.1. : $bs.n.,$c1983. [Place completely unknown]

008/18-21 Books : Illustration

008/18-21 a###
300 ##$a271 p. : $bill. ; $c21 cm.

008/18-21 ae##
300 ##$bill., plans (in pocket)

008/18-21 acfh
300 ##$bill., facsims, plates, ports.

008/18-21 ####
300 ##$a367 p. ; $c23 cm.
[no illustrations in the item]

008/22 Books : Target audience

008/22 g
245 10$aWonderland : $ba fiction. [General]

008/22 f
245 10$aPersonal documentation. [Special]

008/22 j
650 #0$aAlibaba and forty thieves$xJuvenile literature. [Juvenile]

008/23 Books : Form of item

008/23 d
250 ##$aLarge print ed.

008/23 r
500 ##$aPhoto-reproduction of 1941 edition.

008/23 b
300 ##$a8 microfiches.
400 #0$aSouth Asia ephemera collection. $v I-CLR-783

008/24-27 (BK) Nature of contents

008/24-27 b###
504 ##$aBibliography: p. 202-222.
008/24-27 bu#
504 ##$aBibliography : p. 230-264.
504 ##$aStandards : p. 265-272

008/24-27 d###
245 10$aDictionary of Indic languages.

008/24-27 ####
245 10$aMaking of man
[No special nature of contents given]

008/24-27 i###
245 ##$aNineteenth Century Studies
504 ##$aComplete index to Bengal Magazine : p. 130-155.

008/30 (BK) Festschrift

008/30 1
245 00$aFacets of Indology : $b Mahamahopadhyaya Pandit
     Damodhar Mahapatra Shastri commemoration volume.
520 ##$aFestschrift in honor of Damodhar Mahapatra Shastri,
     1890-1975...

008/31 Index Indicator

008/31 1
500 ##$aIncludes index. [includes an index to its own contents]

008/34 Biography

Code a: Autobiography

008/34 a
100 1#$aRay, Annadashankar
245 0#$aBinur bai.
500 ##$aAutobiography.

Code b: Individual biography

008/34 b
100 1#$aBagchi, Nirmalya.
245 10$aRammohun : $b a study.
600 00$aRammohun Roy, $c Raja, $d 1772?-1833.

Code c: Collective biography

008/34 c
100 1#$aSlide, Anthony.
245 12$aA biographical and autobiographical study of 100 silent film actors and actresses.

Code d: Contains biographical information

008/34 d
245 12$aA history of the renaissance in Bengal : Ramtanu Lahiri, Brahman & reformer. ...

008/35-37 Language
008/35-37 eng
041 0#$aengspa
546 ##$aText in English and Spanish. [no predominant language]

008/35-37 eng
041 0#$aeng$aper
546 ##$aIncludes passages in Persian.

008/35-37 eng
041 1#$aeng$hspafre
500 ##$aTranslated into English from the Spanish translation of the French original.

008/39 Cataloging Source
008/39 #
040 ##$aliCaNL$cliCaNL [Record created and transcribed by the National Library,Calcutta]

008/39 d
040 ##$aWyU$cWyU [Record created and transcribed by the Univ.of Wyoming.]

008/39 u
040 ##$cWMUW [Univ.of Wisconsin-Milwaukee is responsible for the content designation and transcription of cataloging from an unknown source.]

008 Control Field: Continuing Resources (NR)

Fixed-Field Data Elements related to *Serials* and *Integrating Resources*

Scope

The field contains character positions 00-39 that provide coded information

- *about the record as a whole* and
- *about special bibliographic aspects* of the item.

The coded values are positionally defined, and are potentially useful for retrieval and data management. Every character position requires to contain a defined code. For some positions, this may be the fill character (|) - *excepting for Dates and for the Form of item, that is,* positions 00-14, 22-23.

Position-Specific Values 00-39

00-05 Date entered on file [As in 008 Control Field: Monographs]

06   **Type of date/Publication status** [As in 008 Control Field: Monographs]

07-10 Date 1   [As in 008 Control Field: Monographs]

11-14 Date 2   [As in 008 Control Field: Monographs]

15-17 Place of publication, production, or execution [As in 008 Control Field: Monographs]

18 Frequency

This element is used in conjunction with 008/19 (Regularity) and is based on the information found in field 310 (Current Publication Frequency)

#	No determinable frequency *intentionally irregular*
a	Annual
b	Bimonthly *6, 7, or 8 numbers a year*
c	Semiweekly
d	Daily
e	Biweekly
f	Semiannual *two numbers a year*
g	Biennial
h	Triennial
i	Three times a week
j	Three times a month
m	Monthly *9, 10, 11, or 12 numbers a year*
q	Quarterly *four numbers a year*
s	Semimonthly
t	Three times a year
u	Unknown
w	Weekly
z	Other

19 Regularity

A one-character alphabetic code that indicates the intended regularity of a serial. This element is used in conjunction with 008/18 (Frequency) and is based on the information found in field 310 (Current Publication Frequency). The coding depends on the stated intention of the publisher. When a serial is declared as a Monthly but scheduled to publish only 10 monthly issues, instead of 12, the Regularity Code should be 'n' . Similarly Code 'x' should be used when the publisher states that the serialized publication maintains no definite periodicity.

Code:	Description:
n	Normalized irregular
r	Regular
x	Completely irregular
u	Unknown

20 ISSN centre

A one-character code that indicates the ISSN Network centre. In cases where the country of publication has changed, the code in 008/20 represents the centre currently responsible for maintaining the data assigned. A Cataloging agency may prefer to use '#' or '|'.

Code:	Description:
#	No ISSN centre code assigned
0	**International Centre** *International Centre of the ISSN Network (Paris, France)*
1	**United States** *United States National Serials Data Program (NSDP)*
4	**Canada** *ISSN Network/Canada*
z	**Other** *ISSN Network centre other than the one for which codes are defined.*

21 Type of serial

Code:	Description:
#	None of the following
m	Monographic series
n	Newspaper
p	Periodical

Code **m** is a **monographic series** and is used for any title that is a series, regardless of its treatment. A monographic series is a group of analyzable items related to one another by a collective title. The individual items may or may not be numbered.

22 Form of original item

A one-character alphabetic code stands for the **form of material** in which the serial was **originally published**. When it is difficult to determine the originally published form, the first item appeared in the database may be treated as the original physical form

Code:	Description:
#	None of the following
a	Microfilm
b	Microfiche
c	Microopaque
d	Large print
e	Newspaper format
f	Braille
s	Electronic
|	No attempt to code

Microfilm Code 'a' is also used for the long strips of photographic film on reels, in cartridges and in cassettes. They are all roll formats in linear rather than grid array.

Electronic Code 's' is *not* used for items that do not require the use of a computer.

23 Form of item

The alphabetic code specifies the form of material for the item being recorded.

The Form of Material Code: Same as under position 22 above

24 Nature of entire work

A one-character alphabetic code indicates the nature of a serial as a whole. It specifies by nature what type of serial *it is* as opposed to what *it contains*. If the item is of varied types, i.e. more than one, those are coded in 008/25-27 (Nature of contents), and the 008/24 position is coded # (blank).

#	**Not specified** *Nature of the entire serial is not specified.*
a	**Abstracts/summaries** *Entire serial consists of abstracts or summaries of other publications.*
b	**Bibliographies**
c	**Catalogs** *Entire serial is a catalog (i.e., a list of items in a collection, such as a collection of books, a collection of art objects, etc.).*
d	**Dictionaries**
e	**Encyclopedias** *Entire serial is an encyclopedia or an encyclopedic treatment of a specific topic.*
f	**Handbooks**
g	**Legal articles** *Entire serial contains substantive articles on legal topics, such as those published in law school reviews.*
h	**Biography**
i	**Indexes** *Entire serial is an index to bibliographical material other than itself (e.g., an indexing journal).*
k	**Discographies** *Entire serial is a discography or discographies, or other bibliography of recorded sound.*
l	**Legislation**
m	**Theses** *Entire serial contains theses, dissertations, or works identified as having been created to satisfy the requirements for an academic certification or degree.*
n	**Surveys of literature** in a subject area
o	**Reviews** *Entire serial is devoted to critical reviews of published or performed works (e.g., books, films, sound recordings, theater, etc.).*
p	**Programmed texts**
q	**Filmographies**
r	**Directories**
s	**Statistics** *Entire serial is a collection of statistical data on a subject. The code is not used for works about statistical methodology.*
t	**Technical reports**

v	Legal cases and case notes
w	Law reports and digests
z	Treaties

25-27 Nature of contents

One-character alphabetic codes indicate that the serial *contains* more than one type of materials by nature. Generally, a specific code is **used only if the code holds good for a significant part of the item.**

If fewer than three codes are assigned, the codes are left justified and each unused position contains a # (blank). If no codes are applicable, all positions contain blanks.

The Nature of Contents Code: *Same as under position 24 above*

28 Government publication [As in 008 Control Field: Books]

29 Conference publication [As in 008 Control Field: Books]

30-32 Undefined

33 Original alphabet or script of title

The code indicates the original script of the language of the title on the source item, upon which the key title (field 222) is based. If there is no key title present, the code value may relate to the title proper (field 245).

Code:	Description:
#	No alphabet or script given/No key title
a	Basic roman
b	Extended roman
c	Cyrillic
d	Japanese
e	Chinese
f	Arabic
g	Greek

h	Hebrew
i	**Thai** *Original script of the title is the Thai syllabary.*
j	Devanagari
k	Korean
l	Tamil
u	**Unknown**
z	Other

For bibliographic records that do not contain field 222 (Key Title), code # (blank) is often used instead of coding for the original alphabet or script of the title proper in field 245 (Title Statement).

Basic roman:

Code **a** indicates that the original alphabet of the title is roman and it **does not include any diacritics or special characters.** Languages that are usually associated with code **a** include: Basque, English, Latin, Welsh, and many languages of Central and Southern Africa.

Extended roman:

Code **b** indicates that the original alphabet of the title is a roman alphabet language that includes diacritics and special characters. Most western European languages use alphabet that fall into this group. As for Indic scripts, only two have their own script code, Devanagari and Tamil. The scripts belonging to the Devanagari, like Bengali, Gujarati, Gurumukhi, Oriya may share code for Devanagari. Similarly, Telegu, Kanada, Malayalam which belong to Tamil group of scripts may use the code assigned to Tamil.

Note*:* Code b is used **if the language itself has diacritics** even if the title *in hand* does not contain any characters from the extended alphabet.

Devanagari:

Code **j** indicates that the original script of the title is the Devanagari syllabary.

Note: Bengali, Gujarati, Gurumukhi, Oriya may share Code **j** being considered as members of the same family.

Code l indicates that the original script of the title is the Tamil syllabary.

Note: Telegu, Kanada, Malayalam may share Code l since they belong to the same family.

Other:

Code z indicates an original script of the title of a serial for which none of the other defined codes are appropriate.

Note: Code z also used when the title is transcribed in more than one alphabet or script.

34 Successive/latest entry

A one-character numeric code that indicates whether the serial was cataloged according to successive entry or latest entry

Code:	Description:
0	Successive entry
1	Latest entry

Code **0** indicates that the record follows the *successive entry convention* in which a new bibliographic record is created each time that:

- a title changes; or,
- a corporate body used as a main entry or uniform title qualifier changes.

Code **1** indicates that the record follows the *latest entry* convention in which a record is cataloged under its most recent (latest) title or issuing body. All former titles and/or issuing bodies are given in notes. The practice has been abandoned with the introduction of AACR cataloging rules.

35-37 Language [As in 008 Control Field : Books]

38 Modified record [As in 008 Control Field : Books]

39 Cataloging source [As in 008 Control Field : Books]

EXAMPLES

008/06 Type of date
Code n - Dates unknown

008/06 n
008/07-10 uuuu
008/11-14 uuuu
245 00 $a Alameda magazine.
310 ## $a Unknown

Code q - Questionable date

008/06 q
008/07-10 1901
008/11-14 1965
260 ##$c [19 -]
505 1#$av.1 1884-1896; v.2 1896-1897; v.3 1898-1903

Code r - Reprint/reissue and Original date

008/06 r
008/07-10 2002
008/11-14 1941
260 ##$aKolkata : $bKolkata Municipal Corporation and New Age
    Publishers, $c2002.
500 ##$aPreviously published in 1941.

008/18 Frequency

008/18 #	008/19 x	310 ##$aIrregular
008/18 a	008/19 r	310 ##$aAnnual
008/18 b	008/19 r	310 ##$aBimonthly
008/18 c	008/19 r	310 ##$aSemiweekly
008/18 d	008/19 r	310 ##$aDaily

008/19 Regularity

008/19 n	008/18 m	310 ##$aMonthly (except July and Aug.)
008/19 n	008/18 b	310 ##$aMonthly (Nov.-Dec. issue combined)
008/19 r	008/18 m	310 ##$aMonthly
008/19 r	008/18 q	310 ##$aQuinquennial
008/19 x	008/18 z	310 ##$aFive no. a year

008/21 Type of Serial

008/21 p   245   00$aMonthly review of investment projects.
008/21 n   245   04$aThe Statesman.

008/24 Nature of Serial

008/24 b   245   00$aJournal of Asian bibliography.
008/24 l   245   00$aQuarterly index to Africana periodical literature.
008/24 e   245   04$aThe Software encyclopedia.
008/24 c   245   00$aNew products catalog.
008/24 q   245   00$aWorld filmography.
008/24 m   245   00$aTheses in progress in Commonwealth studies.
008/24 s   245   00$aPocket book of labour statistics/India. Labour Bureau.

008/25-27 Nature of Contents

008/25-27 b##   008/24 #   245   00$aEmerald intelligence+ full-text.
                                             520   ## Articles from 1989 to 1993 are provided with abstracts and keywords only.

008/25-27 p##   008/24 #   245   00$aClinical exercises in internal medicine.
                                             650   #2$aInternal medicine$xProgrammed texts.

008/25-27 a##   008/24 #   245   00$aReview of applied entomology.$nSeries B.
                                             650   #2$a Veterinaryentomology $x Abstracts $x Periodicals

008/33 Original Script/Alphabet of Title

008/33 a   222   #0$aNewsweek.
008/33 b   222   #0$aRevista de biología del Uruguay
008/33 b   222   #0$aNew Brunswick police journal
                 245   00$aJournal de la police de Nouveau Brunswick.

008/33 j   245 00$aÂtmaúakti
008/33 l   245 00$aKirutayukam.
008/33 z   245 00$aSak'art'velos muzeumis moambe
                     =$bBulletin du Muséum de Géorgie. *[Title in the Georgian and Extended Roman alphabet.]*

008/34 Successive/latest entry

008/34 1   247 10$aBritish Columbia financial times$f1914-June 1951

008/34 1   111 2#$aSymposium on Underwater Physiology.
                     245 10 $aUnderwater physiology; $b proceedings.
                     550 ##$aVol. for 1955 issued by the symposium under its earlier name: Underwater Physiology Symposium

020 International Standard Book Number (R)

Field 020 contains the International Standard Book Number (ISBN), the terms of availability, and any cancelled or invalid ISBN. Each field 020 contains all the information relevant to one ISBN, or if no ISBN exists, relevant to one item.

Indicator		
1st	Undefined	
2nd	Undefined	
Subfield code:		
$a	International Standard Book Number	NR
$c	Terms of availability	NR
$z	Cancelled/Invalid ISBN	R
$6	Linkage	NR
$8	Field link and sequence number	R

SCOPE & EXAMPLES

Subfields

Subfield $a

Contains a valid ISBN for the item. Parenthetical qualifying information, such as the publisher/distributor, binding/format, and volume numbers.

020 ##$a0761418911

020 ##$a0714652288(cloth)

[Three ISBNs associated with one catalog record.]

020 ##$a1565109880 (v.2 : pbk. alk. : paper)

020 ##$a1565109910 (v.2 : lib. bdg. : alk. paper) : c4.95

020##$a1565109902 (v.2 : pbk. : alk. paper)

Subfield $c

Subfield **$c** contains the price or a brief statement of availability and any parenthetical qualifying information concerning the item. If only price information is present in field 020, data relevant to a single item is given in one subfield **$c** in one field 020 and data relevant to another item is given in another subfield **$c** in a subsequent 020 field.

020 ##$a1555874835(pbk.) : c35.00

020 ##$cRs. 18.00

020 ##$cRental material

020 ##$cFor sale ($450.00) or rent ($45.00)

Two prices for two items on one catalog record. Second one does not show price:

020 ##$a1557860033 : c11.75

020 ##$a069101071 (pbk)

022 International Standard Serial Number (R)

Field 022 contains the International Standard Serial Number (ISSN), a unique identification number assigned to a serial title, and/or any incorrect or cancelled ISSN. The ISSN is assigned to a serial publication by a national centre under the auspices of the ISSN Network.

The initialism **ISSN** and the phrases **ISSN (incorrect)** and **ISSN (cancelled)** are not carried in the MARC record. The hyphen separating the two groups of digits is carried in the MARC record. (The ISSN is an agency-assigned data element.)

Indicator:		
1st	Level of international interest	
#	No level specified	
0	Serial of international interest	
1	Serial not of international interest	
2nd	Undefined; contains a blank	
Subfield code:		
$a	International Standard Serial Number	NR
$y	Incorrect ISSN	R
$6	Linkage	NR
$8	Field link and sequence number	R

Value # (blank) indicates that the level of international interest is unknown or not specified.

SCOPE & EXAMPLES

Subfields

Subfield **$a** contains a valid ISSN for the serial.

022 ##$a0942-5225

Subfield **$y** contains incorrect ISSN for the serial .

022 0#$a0018-5817$y0018-5811

Display constants [to be generated by system]:

- **ISSN** [associated with the content of subfield $a]
- **ISSN (incorrect)** [associated with the content of subfield $y]
  ISSN 0018-5817 ISSN (incorrect) 0018-5811

040 CATALOGING SOURCE (NR)

Field 040 contains the MARC code or the name of the organization(s) that created the original record,

- assigned MARC content designation and
- transcribed the record into machine-readable form, or
- modified (except for the addition of holdings symbols) an existing MARC record.

The MARC codes in field 040 and the code in 008/39 (Cataloging source) specify the category of the organization responsible for the content, content designation, and transcription of a bibliographic record. For organizations outside of Canada, the source of these codes is *MARC Code List for Organizations* maintained by the Library of Congress.

Indicator:		
1st	Undefined	
2nd	Undefined	
Subfield code:		
$a	Original cataloging agency	NR
$b	Language of cataloging	NR
$c	Transcribing agency	NR

$d	Modifying agency	R
$e	Description conventions	NR
$6	Linkage	NR
$8	Field link and sequence number	R

EXAMPLES

Subfields

008/39 # *national bibliographic agency*

040 ##$aDLC$cDLC$dDLC

[Cataloging produced, input, and modified by the Library of Congress.]

008/39 d *other sources*

040 ##$aDLC$cDLC$dFBR

[Cataloging produced and input by the Library of Congress, and modified by Manatee County Public Library.]

008/39 d *other sources*

040 ##$aCaOTY$cCaOTY

[Cataloging produced and input by York University.]

041 LANGUAGE CODE (NR)

The field contains three-character *MARC alphabetic codes* for languages associated with an item.

Field 041 is used when one or more of the following conditions exist:

- The item contains more than one language
- The item is or includes a translation
- The language of the summaries, abstracts, or accompanying material differs from the language of the main item
- The language of a table of contents differs from the language of the main item.

Note: The subfields have been recently defined as *repeatable*.

Indicator:	
1st	Translation indication
0	Item not a translation or does not include a translation
1	Item is or includes a translation
2nd	Source of code
#	MARC language code
7	Source specified in $2

Subfield code		
$a	Code of text/sound track or separate title	R
$b	Code of summary or abstract/subtitle	R
$d	Code of sung or spoken text	R
$e	Code of librettos	R
$f	Code of table of contents	R
$g	Code of accompanying material	R
$h	Code of original or intermediate translations of text	R
$2	Source of code	
$6	Linkage	NR
$8	Field link and sequence number	R

SCOPE & EXAMPLES

Subfields

Subfield $a

Contains codes for languages associated with the item being cataloged. The first code in subfield $a is also recorded in 008/35-37.

For works in multiple languages, the codes for the languages of the text are recorded in the order of their predominance in the text. If no language is predominant, the codes are recorded in English alphabetical order. For practical purposes, if there are more than six languages, the code for the title (or the first title, if there are more than one) and the code **mul** (multiple languages) are recorded.

Subfield $h

Subfield **$h** contains the code(s) for language(s) of the original work and/or intermediate translations of a work. Codes for intermediate translations are recorded *before codes for languages of the original*.

EXAMPLES

008/35-37 eng
041 0# $aeng$afre$ager [Text is in English, French, and German]

008/35-37 rus
041 0#$arus$aeng [Item is in Russian (the predominant language) and English]

008/35-37 cze
041 0#$aeng$hspa$hfre [Translated into English from the Spanish translation of a French original]

008/35-37 eng
041 1#$aeng$agrc$hgrc [Text in original Greek and in English translation]

008/35-37 eng
041 1#$aeng$hund [Text is an English translation; the original language undetermined]

008/35-37 fre
041 1#$afre$hger$hrus [Text in French; contains three works, the first translated from German and two from Russian]

008/35-37 eng
041 1#$aeng$hmul [Item is an anthology of Indic poems translated into English from eight Indic languages]

044 Country of Publishing/ Producing Code (NR)

Contains a two- or three-character MARC Country Code, when field 008/15-17 is insufficient to convey full information for an item published or produced in more than one country. The code in 008/15-17 is recorded in the first occurrence of subfield $a of field 044.

For indicator and subfield code definitions and examples, and designator repeatability, see table below:

Indicators		
First	Undefined	
Second	Undefined	
Subfield code:		
$a	Country of publishing/producing entity code	R
$b	Local subentity code	R
$c	ISO subentity code	R
$2	Source of local subentity code	R
$6	Linkage	NR
$8	Field link and sequence number	R

Scope & Examples

Subfield $a

Contains the three digit MARC code for the country of the publishing or producing entity. The code for each country is given in a separate subfield $a. The code appearing in 008/15-17 is given as the first subfield $a.

008/15-17 it#

044 ##aitafr$asp [Co-publishing countries: Italy, France, and Spain]

008/15-17 xxk

245 00$aLife on earth.$pThe swarming hordes$h [videorecording]/$cproduced by British Broadcasting Corporation in association with Warner Brothers.

044 ##$axxk$axxu [Producing countries: United Kingdom and United States]

Subfield $b

008/15-17 at#

044 ##$bxna$2<source of local code> [Place of publication: New South Wales]

Subfield $c

Subfield $c contains subentity code taken from the International Organization for Standardization's *Codes for the representation of names of countries and their sub-divisions: Part 2, Country subdivision codes*, ISO3166-2.

008/15-17 sz#

044 ##$cCH-ZH [Place of publication: *Zürich* (ISO 3166-2 code)]

049 LOCAL HOLDINGS (NR)

Field 049 is *not* a part of the standard MARC formats, but a MARC21 defined field, that may be used by libraries for local holdings information. Typically, Field 049 is used to designate locations (holding libraries), copies, and/or volumes of a bibliographic item owned by a local institution. The regular MARC fields for holdings information, however, belong to *MARC Holding Format* that fully support information requirement of a shared database or a union catalog, or of a library desiring to maintain holding data in a systematic programmable format.

Since MARC21 does not provide any fixed structural design for field 049, it is up to the cataloging agency to define the content designators to suit their purpose best. The indicators and subfield codes presented here are based upon the specifications followed by OCLC participating institutions, which may serve as a prototype.

Indicator	
1st	Controls printing
#	Undefined
0	Print dataFrom subfield $a only
1	Locally deLocally defined

2	Locally deLocally defined	
2nd	Completeness of holdings data	
#	Undefined	
0	Holdings information complete	
1	Locally defined	
Subfields		
$a	Holding library	R
$c	Copy statement	R
$d	Definition of bibliographic subdivisions	R
$l	Local processing data	R
$m	Missing elements	R
$n	Notes about holdings	NR
$o	Local processing data	R
$p	Secondary bibliographic subdivision	R
$q	Third bibliographic subdivision	R
$r	Fourth bibliographic subdivision	R
$s	Fifth bibliographic subdivision	R
$t	Sixth bibliographic subdivision	R
$u	Seventh bibliographic subdivision	R
$v	Primary bibliographic subdivision	R
$y	Inclusive dates of publication or coverage	NR

SCOPE & EXAMPLES

Indicators

First Indicator - Display/Print control

Values # and 0 as defined above may be found useful for local applications.

Values 1 may be defined for displaying/printing all elements.

Second Indicator - Extent of data representation

Values # and 0 as defined above may be found useful for local applications.

Values 1 may be defined as partial holdings data.

Subfields

Subfield $a

The library code needs to be case-insensitive to include upper and lower case or their combinations, as found in MARC organization codes, e.g. **IiCaNL** (National Library of India).Example of possible codes for a University's central library and two other departmental libraries:

$aIiCalCUc $aIiCalCUs $aIiCUa

Subfield $c

Subfield $c is repeatable. Each subfield $c may represent one or more copies. Each subfield $c is subordinate to or related to the last preceding subfield $a. A single 049 field may have multiple subfield $a's each with one or more related subfield $c's.

049     $aIiCalSP $c1 $c2 $aLIB-a $c3

Note: Accession numbers may be entered in subfield $c in brackets.

049 $aIiCalSP $c1 [476532], 3 [479569] $aLIB-g $c2 [477343]

Subfiled $d

The subfield includes words or abbreviations that customarily identify a bibliographic unit, particularly the numbering of an item's volumes or parts. Each word or abbreviation relates the subfield code to the level of bibliographic subdivision. The content may be entered in brackets.

049 $d[$v vol. $ppt.]

049 $c1 $d[$vser. $pvol. $qno.]

$d Missing elements

Subfield $d is used to record status of a bibliographic unit as 'Missing', 'Not found', or as defined. Fields $v through $u are recorded in brackets within subfield $m to identify the lacking units.

Subfield $m is subordinate to the immediately preceding subfield $c. All the information in subfield $m relates to every copy in subfield $c. If no subfield $c is present, subfield $m is subordinate to the immediately preceding subfield $a.

049    $aLIB-A $c1 $v1-7 $p1-4 $m[$v2 $p3 $v5 $p1,4]

049    $aLIB-B $c2 $v1-3 $p1-6 $v4 $p1-2 $m[$v 1 $p1-2,6 $v2 $p2-5 $v3 $p1, 3 $v4$p1]

049    $aLIB-C $c2 $v1 $p3-5 $v2 $p1,6 $v3 $p2,6 $v4 $p2

Subfield $y may be used in subfield $m to identify the dates of publication or coverage of the missing units.

049    $aLIB-D $v1-34 $y1906/07-1939/40 $m[$v 28-29 $y1934/35-1935/36]

Sufield n

Notes in $n amplify or clarify holdings data. It includes data which cannot be recorded in other subfields. Subfield $n is subordinate to subfield $a or to subfield $c,

Sufield $p

Each subfield $p is subordinate to the immediately preceding subfield $v. All the information in subfield $p pertains to every unit in the last preceding subfield $v.

049    $aLIB-E $v1-10 $p1-

049    $aLIB-F[Reading Room] $c1 $v1-2 $p1-6 $aLIB-G $c2 $v2 $p1-6

Sufield $q

Each subfield $q is subordinate to the immediately preceding subfield $p. All the information in subfield $q pertains to every unit in the last preceding subfield $p.

049    $aLIB-H $d [$v vol. $p pt. $q no.] $v 1-10 $p A $q 1-6 $p B $q 1-12

Sufield $r to $u

The level of subdivisions is recognized by the subfield codes assigned. The governing principle for organizing the subfields within field 049 is: Each subfield is subordinate to the immediately preceding subfield. All the information in a subfield pertains to every unit in the last preceding subfield.

Sufield $v

It includes the identity of the first division of a publication, which may be described as a 'volume', 'tome', 'band' or other synonym; or a 'series' one level up in hierarchy.

049 $aLIB-F $d [$v Tome] $v 5-26

If holding library LIB-B holds volumes 1-13 and volume 8 is incomplete, enter:

049 $aLIB-B $v 1-7 $v 8 [inc.] $v 9-13

Sufield $y

The subfield contains the inclusive dates of holdings. Ordinarily, particularly for monographs, dates supplement other numbering (subfields $v through $u). In absence of a systematic volume designation, dates may serve as a primary level identity.

049 $aLIB-A $c3 $y1919

049 $aLIB-R $c1 $v1-10 $p1-6 $y1901-1909

049 $aLIB-M $c1-2 $v1-16 $y1963-1978 $c3 $v4-8 $y1960-1970

049 $aLIB-B $v1-8 $y1967/68-1974/75

049 $aLIB-M $c1-4 $v1 $p1 $yMar./Apr. 1979

Further Examples of   Subfield applications

049 $aLIB-r $aLIB-e $aLIB-4

049 $c1 $c2 $c3

049 $d[$vvol. $ppt.]

049 $d[$vser. $pvol. $qno.]

049 $v1[inc.] $v2-5

049 $v1, 5 [inc.], 7-16, 17 [inc.], 18-20

049 $v1-15 [most vols.inc.]

080 UNIVERSAL DECIMAL CLASSIFICATION NUMBER (R)

Field 080 contains the class number (and item number) following Universal Decimal Classification (UDC) scheme.

Indicator:		
1st	Undefined	
2nd	Undefined	
Subfield code:		
$a	Universal Decimal Classification number	NR
$b	Item number	NR
$x	Common auxiliary subdivision	R
$2	Edition identifier	NR
$6	Linkage	NR
$8	Field link and sequence number	R

SCOPE & EXAMPLES

Subfields

Subfield $a contains the principal part of the UDC notation stands for the subject contents of the item.

Subfield $b contains the item number according to the practice followed for author mark, date, term, etc.

Subfield **$x** contains a common auxiliary subdivision of UDC that qualifies the concept represented by the main UDC number.

080 ##338.9bSAN(1934)$x(540)

080 ##$a94$x(474)$x"19"$x(075)$2[edition information]

Subfield **$2** contains the edition number, date, or other textual designation of the edition of UDC used to compose the classification number.

080 ##$a63:338.9$21993

082 Dewey Decimal Classification Number (R)

Field 082 contains classification number assigned to the item following Dewey Decimal Classification schedules. The second indicator values distinguish between content actually assigned by the Library of Congress and content assigned by an organization other than LC.

Indicator		
1st	Type of edition	
0	Full edition	
1	Abridged edition	
2nd	Source of call number	
#	No information provided	
0	Assigned by LC	
4	Assigned by agency other than LC	
Subfield code		
$a	Classification number	R
$b	Item number	NR
$2	Edition number	NR
$6	Linkage	NR
$8	Field link	R

Note: The Second Indicator Value **4** should always be used *unless* a cataloging agency prefers to use DDC number assigned by LC.

SCOPE & EXAMPLES

Subfield

Subfield $a

Subfield **$a** contains the classification number portion of the call number.

Subfield $b

082 00$a355.02/17**$2**19

Subfield **$b** contains the item number portion of the call number. [No more in use]

084 OTHER CLASSIFICATION NUMBER (R)

Field 084 contains classification number assigned by a cataloging agency using a scheme other than the schemes provided with designated fields, e.g. *Library of Congress Classification*, Dewey Decimal Classification schemes, etc. The field also supports inclusion of alternative classification number with or without item number.

Note: If a classification system does not have a designated field of its own, but does have a MARC code *only then* field 084 is used for recording classification numbers in subfield $a and the Classification system code in subfield $2.

Indicator:		
1st	Undefined	
2nd	Undefined	
Subfield code:		
$a	Classification number	R
$b	Item number	NR
$2	Source of number	NR
$6	Linkage	NR
$8	Field link and sequence number	R

Scope & Examples

Subfields

Subfield $a

- Subfield $a contains the classification number portion of the call number, $b for item number.
- Subfield $a is repeated to record an alternative class number following the last subfield of any primary call number.
- Subfield $a when used for an alternate class number it includes item number along with, instead of using subfield $b for that purpose.

  084 ##$a014$2frbnpnav

  084 ##$a016$a014$a018$a122$2frbnpnav

Subfield $b

084 ##$a84.7$bSShA$2rubbk

084 ##$aKB112.554$bU62 1980$2laclaw

Subfield $2

Subfield $2 contains a *MARC code* for the source of the classification system or scheme from which the number was assigned. The source of the code is *MARC Code List for Relators, Sources, Description Conventions* maintained by the Library of Congress.

084 ##$a8501(043)$2rueskl

100 Main Entry - Personal Name (NR)

Main entry is assigned according to various cataloging rules (such as AACR 2), usually to the person chiefly responsible for creation of the intellectual or artistic content of a work.

The content designators identify the sub-elements occurring in personal name fields constructed according to the generally accepted cataloging and thesaurus-building rules, e.g. AACR 2, LCSH.

Personal names used in phrase subject headings (e.g. *John, the Baptist, saint, in the Koran*) are contained in field 650 (Subject Added Entry - Topical Term).

Indicator:		
1st	Type of personal name	
0	Forename	
1	Surname	
3	Family name	
2nd	Undefined; contains a blank	
Subfield code:		
$a	Personal name	NR
$b	Numeration	NR

$c	Titles and other words	R
$d	Dates associated with a name	NR
$e	Relator term	R
$f	Date of a work	NR
$g	Miscellaneous information	NR
$n	Number of part/section of a work	R
$p	Name of part/section of a work	R
$q	Fuller form of name	NR
$t	Title of a work	NR
$u	Affiliation	NR
$4	Relator code	R
$6	Linkage	NR
$8	Field link and sequence number	R

SCOPE & EXAMPLES

Subfields

Subfield $a contains a personal name. The name may be a surname and/or forename; letters, initials, abbreviations, phrases, or numbers used in place of a name; or a family name.

Subfield $a

100   0#$aDr. X.

100   0#$aRajendra Prasad,$d1884-1963.

100   0#$aClaude,$cd'Abbeville, pere,$dd.1632.

100   0#$aAuthor of The diary of a physician,$d1807-1877.

100   1#$aBlackbeard, Author of,$d1777-1852.

100   1#$aVérez-Peraza, Elena,$d1919-

100   1#$aLe Conte, John Eatton,$d1784-1860.

100   1#$aWatson,$cRev.

100   1#$aSarkar, Badal, $d1925-

Subfield $b

Subfield $b contains a roman numeral or a roman numeral and a subsequent part of a forename. *It is used only in a forename heading (first indicator, value 0).*

100   0#$aJohn Paul$bII, $cPope,$d1920

100   0#$aEdward$bVIII, $cKing of Great Britain, $d1894-1972.

Subfield $c

The subfield contains titles and other qualifying information such as:

- titles designating rank, office, or nobility, e.g., *Sir*
- terms of address, e.g., *Mrs.*
- initials of an academic degree or denoting membership in an organization, e.g., *Ph.D.*, *F.L.A*
- a roman numeral used with a surname, e.g., *II*
- other words or phrases associated with the name, e.g., *clockmaker, Saint*

100   1#$aVivekananda, $cSwami.

100   1#$aChurchill, Winston,$cSir, $d1874-1965.

100   1#$aWard, Humphrey, $cMrs., $d1851-1920.

100   0#$aThomas, $cAquinas, Saint, $d1225?-1274.

100   0#$aBlack Foot, $cChief, $dd. 1877 $c(Spirit)

100   1#$aBeeton, $cMrs.$q(Isabella Mary), $d1836-1865.

Note: If the heading is a surname followed directly by a prefix without intervening forenames or forename initials, the prefix is contained in subfield $c to prevent its being processed as a forename in searching and sorting.

100   1#$aWalle-Lissnijder, $cvan de.

Subfield $d

Subfield $d contains dates of birth, death, or flourishing, or any other date associated with a name. A qualifier used with the date (e.g., *b.*, *d.*, *ca.*, *fl.*, *?*, *cent.*) is also contained in subfield $d.

100   0#$aClaude, $cd'Abbeville, pere, $dd. 1632.

100   0#$aH. D.$q(Hilda Doolittle), $d1886-1961.

100 1#$aEl-Abiad, Ahmed H., $d1926-

100 1#$aJoannes Aegidius, Zamorensis, $d1240 or 41-ca. 1316.

Subfield $e

100 1#$aThapar, Karan, $d1938-$einterviewer.

100 1#$aMorgan, John Pierpont, $d1837-1913, $ecollector.

Subfield $j

100 1#$aAmir Khan,$cUstad,$d1912-1974,$jPupil of

100 0#$aE.S.,$cMeister,$d15th cent.,$jFollower of

Subfield $q

100 1#$aBuck, Pearl S.$q(Pearl Sydenstricker), $d1892-1973.

100 1#$aBanaphul$q(Balaichand Mukhopadhyay), $d1899-1979.

Subfield $u

100 1#$aChan, Lois Main.$uCollege of Lib. & Info. Sc., Kentucky University.

110 MAIN ENTRY - CORPORATE NAME (NR)

Field 110 contains a corporate name used as a main entry. By definition, main entry under corporate name is assigned to works that represent the collective thought of a corporate body.

The defined content designators identify the sub-elements occurring in corporate name fields constructed according to the generally accepted cataloging and thesaurus-building rules, e.g. AACR2, LCSH.

Indicator		
1st	**Type of Entry element**	
1	Jurisdiction	
2	Corporate Name in Direct Order	
2nd	**Undefined**	
Subfield code		
$a	Corporate/Jurisdiction name	NR
$b	Subordinate unit	R
$c	Location of meeting	NR
$d	Date of meeting or treaty signing	R
$e	Relator term	R
$f	Date of a work	NR

$g	Miscellaneous information	NR
$k	Form subheading	R
$l	Language of a work	NR
$n	Number of part/section/meeting	R
$p	Name of part/section of a work	R
$t	Title of a work	NR
$u	Affiliation	NR
$4	Relator code	R
$6	Linkage	NR
$8	Field link and sequence number	R

Scope & Examples

Indicators

Value 1: Jurisdiction - indicates that the entry element is a name of a jurisdiction (but *not an integral part of the name*).

110   1#$aCyprus (Archdiocese)

110   1#$aWest Bengal.$bBoard of Secondary Education.

110   1#$aIndia.$bPresident (2002- : Abdul Kalam)

Value 2: Name in direct order - indicates that the name is in direct order. The heading may contain a parenthetical qualifier or may be an acronym or initialism.

110   2#$aVidyasagar University.

110   2#$aNational Gardening Association (U.S.)

110   2#$aTISCO (Firm)

Jurisdiction as an integral part of the name or qualified by a jurisdiction name :

110   2#$aUniversity of Calcutta.$bCentral Library.

110   2#$aBombay Natural History Society.

Subfields

Subfield $a

Contains a name of a corporate body or the first entity *when subordinate units are present*; a jurisdiction name under which a corporate body, city section, or a title of a work is entered; or a jurisdiction name that is also an ecclesiastical entity. A parenthetical qualifying term, jurisdiction name, or date (other than the date of a meeting) is *not separately subfield coded.*

110   1#$aIndia.$bDept of Culture.

110   2#$aMartin & Burn.

110   2#$aScientific Society of San Antonio (1892-1894).

110   2#$aSt. James Church (Calcutta).

Subfield $b

Contains a name of a subordinate corporate unit, a name of a city section, or a name of a meeting entered under a corporate or a jurisdiction name.

110   2#$aIndian Library Association.$bMeeting.

110   2#$aNational Association of Library and Information Science Educators. $bConference $n(10th : $d1999 : $cUniversity of Ibadan)

110   2#$aBrahmasamaj.$bBhowanipur (Calcutta).

Subfield $c

Contains a place name or a name of an institution where a meeting was held. Multiple adjacent locations are contained in a single subfield $c.

110   2#$aSoutheastern VHF Society. $bConference $d(2003 : $cHuntsville, Ala.*)*

110   2#$aIndian Association of Special Libraries and Information Centre.$bConference$c(Kuruskhetra)

Note: Place name added parenthetically as a qualifier is not separately subfield coded.

110   2#$aRamakrishna Mission (Penang).

Subfield $d

Contains the date a meeting was held.

110   2#$aInternational Labour Organisation.$bEuropean Regional Conference$n(2nd:$d1968:$cGeneva, Switzerland)

Note: In a name/title X10 field, subfield **$d** also contains the date a treaty was signed.

710   1#$aAlgeria.$tTreaties, etc.$gEngland and Wales,$d1682 Apr. 20.

Subfield $e

Contains a designation of function describing relationship between a name and a work.

110   2#$aK.P. Bagchi & Co.,$epublisher.

Subfield $g

Contains a data element that is not more appropriately contained in another defined subfield. *In a heading for a meeting, entered under a corporate body*, subfield $g also contains sub-element that is less appropriate for subfields $c, $d, or $n .

110   1#$aMinnesota.$bConstitutional Convention$d(1857 :$gRepublican)

Note: *In a name/title X10 field*, subfield $g contains the name of the *other party* to treaties, intergovernmental agreements, etc.

610   10$aGreat Britain.$tTreaties,etc.$gIreland,$d1985Nov.15.

Subfield $4

Contains a MARC code for relators. More than one relator code may be used if the corporate name has more than one function. The code is given *after* the name portion in name/title fields.

110   1#$aIndia.$bUniversity Grant Commission.$4fnd

110   2#$aIndian Institute of Design.$4clb

Note: Relator terms, which also specify the relationship of a corporate body to a work, are contained in subfield $e.

Subfield $k

Contains a form subheading. A form subheading may occur in either the name or the title portion of an **X10** field. Form subheadings used with corporate names include: *Manuscript, Protocols, etc.*, and *Selections.*

710 22$aCatholic Church.$bPope (1958-1963 : John XXIII). $tMater et magistra. $lFrench. $kSelections.$f1963.

610 20$aBritish Library.$kManuscript.$nArundel 384.

610 10$aUruguay.$tTreaties, etc.,$d1974 Aug.20.$kProtocols, etc.$d1982 Dec. 20.

111 Main Entry - Meeting Name (NR)

The field contains a meeting or conference name used as a main entry. According to cataloging norms, main entry under a meeting name is assigned to work that contains proceedings, reports, etc. The defined content designators identify the sub-elements occurring in corporate name fields constructed according to the generally accepted cataloging and thesaurus-building rules, e.g. AACR2, LCSH.

Meeting under Corporate Name

1. A named meeting *under a corporate name* is contained in the X10 fields

2. Corporate names that include such words as *conference* or *congress* are also contained in the X10 fields. For example; *the Congress of Neurological Surgeons,* a professional group, is a corporate name.

Meeting under Meeting Name

A meeting entered directly under its own name is contained in the X11 fields.

Indicators		
1st	Type of meeting name entry element	
0	Inverted name	
1	Jurisdiction name	
2	Name in direct order	
2nd	Undefined; contains a blank	
Subfield code		
$a	Meeting name or jurisdiction name	R
$c	Location of meeting	NR
$d	Date of meeting	NR
$e	Subordinate unit	R
$f	Date of a work	NR
$g	Miscellaneous information	NR
$k	Form subheading	R
$l	Language of a work	NR
$n	Number of part/section/meeting	R
$p	Name of part/section of a work	R
$q	Name of meeting following jurisdiction name	NR
$t	Title of a work	NR
$u	Affiliation	NR
$4	Relator code	R
$6	Linkage	NR
$8	Field link and sequence number	R

SCOPE & EXAMPLES

Indicators

First indicator: Value 1 - Jurisdiction name

This indicator value is unlikely to be used in AACR 2 records.

First indicator: Value 2 - Name in direct order

Value **2** indicates that the name is in direct order. The heading may contain a parenthetical qualifier or may be an acronym or initialism.

111   2#$aClub of Life Founding Conference $d (1982 : $c Rome, Italy)

111   2#$aGovernor's Conference on Aging (N.Y.)$d(1982: $cAlbany, N.Y.)

711   2#$aThe Films of the Year (Festival)

Meeting names with a jurisdiction name as its integral part or qualified by a place name.

111   2#$aIASTED International Symposium$d(1982 : $cDavos, Switzerland)

111   2#$aBrussels Hemoglobin Symposium$n(1st : $d1983)

Subfields

The subfield codes specified in MARC21 documentation are defined for possible applications in X11 fields; many of those may not be relevant to the requirements of a particular instance of X11 fields.

Examples include only for those subfields which are relevant and commonly found in international databases.

Subfields $a

Contains name of a meeting, or the first entity when subordinate units are present; or a jurisdiction name under which a meeting name is entered.

111   2#$aInternational Palaeontological Congress $n(1st : $d2002 :$cSyndey, N.S.W.)

111   2#$a Autotestcon $n (38th : $d2002 : $cHuntsville, Ala.)

111   2#$a All India Library Conference $n(49th : '$d2003 : $c Bundelkhand University)

111   2#$aBritish and Intercolonial Exhibition $d(1924: $cHokitika, N.Z.)

111   2#$aSeminar on Judicial and other Remedies against the Abuse of Administrative Authority $d(1959 : $cKandy, Sri Lanka)

Note: Parenthetical qualifying information is not separately subfield coded. Meeting names are not entered *under jurisdiction names in AACR 2 formulated X11 fields.*

111 2#$a Military History Symposium (U.S.)**$n**(9th :**$d**1980 :**$c**United States Air Force Academy)

Subfield $c

Contains a place name or a name of an institution where a meeting was held.

111 20$a**AACOBS Seminar on Library Acquisitions Rationalization **$d(1987 : **$c**Queensland Museum)

111 2#$a Workshop-cum-Expert Consultation on National Accounts Compilation of Bangladesh **$d**(1994 : **$c**Dhaka, Bangladesh)

711 2#$a Conference on Philosophy and Its History **$d**(1983 : **$c**University of Lancaster)

Note: Multiple adjacent locations are contained in single subfield **$c**.

111 2#$a World Peace Conference **$n**(1st : **$d**1949 : **$c**Paris, France and Prague, Czechoslovakia)

Note: A place name added parenthetically to a meeting name to distinguish between identical names is not separately subfield coded.

111 2#$a Governor's Conference on Aging (N.Y.)

Subfiled $d

Indecates the date of a meeting

111 2#$a Colloquio franco-italiano di Aosta**$d**(1982)

111 2#$a African Seminar on International Human Rights Standards and the Administration of Justice **$d**(1991 : **$c**Cairo, Egypt)

111 2#$a International Workshop on Physics and Technology of Thin Films **$d**(2003 : **$c** Tehran, Iran)

Subfield $e

The name of a subordinate unit entered under a meeting name.

111 2#$a International Congress of Gerontology **$e**Satellite Conference **$d**(1978 : **$c**Sydney, N.S.W.)

Subfield $n

A number of a meeting or a number designation for a part or section of a work.

111 2#$aAsian Games $n(9th : $d1982 : $cDelhi, India)

Note: Subfield $n also contains a number designation for a part or section of a work. Numbering is defined as an indication of sequencing.

Subfield $p

A name designation of a part or section of a work used with a title in a name/title field.

Subfield $p contains a *name* designation of a part or section of a work in a name/title field.

111 2#$aInternational Conference on Gnosticism $d(1978 : $cNew Haven, Conn.). $tRediscovery of Gnosticism. $pModern writers.

Subfiled $q

Note: This construction is not used in AACR 2 formulated X11 fields.

Subfield $t

Contains a uniform title, a title-page title, or series title used in a name/title field.

111 2#$aInternational Conference on Gnosticism $d(1978 : $cNew Haven, Conn.).$tRediscovery of Gnosticism. $pModern writers.

Subfield $4

Contains a MARC code that specifies the relationship between a name and a work. More than one relator code may be used if the meeting has more than one function. The code is given *after* the name portion in name/title fields.

111 2#$aSymposium on the Underground Disposal of Radioactive Wastes $d(1979 : $cOtaniemi, Finland) $4fnd

130 Main Entry - Uniform Title (NR)

Field 130 contains a uniform titl e used *as a main entry*. It is used when a work is entered directly under title and the work has appeared under varying titles, necessitating that a particular title be chosen to represent the work. The title that appears on the work being cataloged is contained in field 245. There will be no 100, 110, or 111 field but field 130.

The content designators identify the sub-elements occurring in uniform or conventional title, title page title, or series title headings that are not entered under a name in a name/title heading and that are constructed according to the generally accepted cataloging and thesaurus-building rules, e.g., AACR2, LCSH.

A uniform title entered **under a name** is contained in field 240 {or in an appropriate field for the author's name (X00 Personal Names, X10 Corporate Names , X11 Meeting Names) under subfield $t (Title of a work)}.

Uniform titles used in phrase subject headings (e.g., *Bible and atheism*) are contained in field 650 (Subject Added Entry - Topical Term).

Indicator:		
1st	Nonfiling characters	
0	No nonfiling characters present	
1-9	Number of nonfiling characters present	
2nd	Undefined	
Subfield code:		
$a	Uniform title	NR
$d	Date of treaty signing	R
$f	Date of a work	NR
$g	Miscellaneous information	NR
$h	Medium	NR
$k	Form subheading	R
$l	Language of a work	NR
$m	Medium of performance for music	R
$n	Number of part/section of a work	R
$o	Arranged statement for music	NR
$p	Name of part/section of a work	R
$r	Key for music	NR
$s	Version	NR
$t	Title of a work	NR
$6	Linkage	NR
$8	Field link and sequence number	R

SCOPE & EXAMPLES

Subfields

Subfield $a

Note: This subfield $a definition applies to the X30 fields, field 240, and field 243. Parenthetical information added to make a title distinctive is not separately subfield coded *except in the case of the date of a treaty (see description of subfield $d).*

130 0#$aSinbad, the sailor (Fairy tale)
245 14$aThe 7 voyages of Sinbad the sailor...

130 0#$aRamayana.
245 10$aRamayani katha

130 0# $a Dialogue (Westminster (London, England))
245 00 $a Dialogue.

Subfield $f

Subfield $f contains a date of publication used in a uniform title field.

130 0#$aTosefta. $lEnglish. $f1977.

A date added parenthetically to distinguish between identical uniform titles is not separately subfield coded:

130 0#$aKing Kong (1933)

130 0#$aKing Kong (1976)

Subfield $g

Subfield $g contains a data element used in a uniform title field *that is not more appropriately contained in another defined subfield.*

Subfield $h

Subfield $h contains a media qualifier used in a uniform title field.

130 0#$aGone with the wind (Motion picture). $hSound recording.

Subfield $k

Subfield $k contains a form subheading used in a uniform title field. Form subheadings used with uniform titles include *Manuscript, Protocols, etc.,* and *Selections.*

130 0#$aBible. $pO.T. $pFive Scrolls. $lHebrew. $sBiblioteca apostolica vaticana. $kManuscript. $nUrbiniti Hebraicus1.

130 0#$aVedas. $pAtharva Vedas. $kCommentaries.

130 0#$aConvention for the Protection of Human Rights and

Fundamental Freedoms $d(1950). $kProtocols, etc., $d1963 Sept. 16.

Subfield $l

Subfield $l contains the name of a language(s) (or a term representing the language, e.g., *Polyglot*) used in a uniform title field.

130   0#$aUpanisads. $lMarathi.
245   00$aUpanisadono abhyas. $lMarathı.

130   0#$aLord's prayer. $lPolyglot.

Subfiled $n

Subfield $n contains a *number* designation for a part or section of a work used in a uniform title field. *Numbering* is defined as an indication of sequencing in any form (e.g., *Part 1, Supplement A, Book two*). In music titles, the serial, opus, or thematic index number is contained in subfield $n.

Multiple numberings for parts or sections separated by a **comma** (which are usually alternative numberings) are contained in a **single** subfield $n (see 2nd example).

130   0#$aMahabharata. $nPart III, $pVanaparva.

130   0#$aAnnale Universiteit van Stellenbosch. $nSerie A2, $pSöologie.

Subfield $p

Indicates name of part/section.

130   0#$a Tipitaka. $pSuttapitaka. $pKhuddakanikaya. $p Jataka. $pUmmaggajataka. $lSinhalese.

130   0#$aMahabharata.$nPart VI,$pVanaparva.

130   0#$aAnnale Universiteit van Stellenbosch.$nSerie A2, $pSöologie.

[Part/section is both numbered and named.]

Subfield $t

Contains a title page title of a work. *Subfield $t is unlikely to be used in an X30 field.*

222 KEY TITLE (R)

The unique name assigned to a serial by the International Serials Data System (ISDS) or by national centres under the auspices of the ISSN Network. Field 222 contains the unique name, the Key title, assigned to a serial in conjunction with an International Standard Serial Number (ISSN) recorded in field 022 (ISSN). It is formed from title information transcribed from a piece of the serial and is constructed with qualifiers to make it unique when necessary. The key title is an agency-assigned data element.

Indicator:		
1st	Undefined; contains a blank	
2nd	Nonfiling characters	
0	No nonfiling characters present	
1-9	Number of nonfiling characters present	
Subfield code:		
$a	Key title	NR
$b	Qualifying information	NR
$6	Linkage	NR
$8	Field link and sequence number	R

EXAMPLES

222	#0$aVitals $b(New *York*, N.Y.)
245	10$aVitals.
246	13$aVitals *magazine*

222	#0$aEconomic education bulletin$b(Great Barrington)
245	00$aEconomic education bulletin.

222	#0$a101 gardening and outdoor ideas
245	00$aWoman's day 101 gardening and outdoor ideas.

222	#4$aThe Worldwide art catalogue bulletin. American library edition
245	04$aThe Worldwide art catalogue bulletin.
250	##$aAmerican library edition

240 Uniform Title (NR)

Field 240 contains the uniform title for a work when the bibliographic record also has a Main entry field 100, field 110, or field 111. Field 240 is not used when field 130 (Main Entry - Uniform Title) is present. The field allows entry of uncontrolled data, that is, without checking the authority file. For instance, the field may contain the title portion of a related work that would normally be entered under a name/title heading in cataloge entry form.

- Field 240 is currently being used for collective uniform title, avoiding use of field 243.
- Uniform title added entries for related works and for analytical titles are recorded in field 730 (Added Entry – Uniform Title).

A uniform title is used when a work has appeared under varying titles, necessitating that a particular title be chosen to represent the work.

The title that appears on the work being cataloged is contained in field 245 (Title Statement).

Indicator		
1st	Uniform title printed or displayed	
0	Not printed or displayed	
1	Printed or displayed	
2nd	Nonfiling characters	
0	No nonfiling characters present	
1-9	Number of nonfiling characters present	
Subfield code:		
$a	Uniform title	NR
$d	Date of treaty signing	R
$f	Date of a work	NR
$g	Miscellaneous information	NR
$h	Medium	NR
$k	Form subheading	R
$l	Language of a work	NR
$m	Medium of performance for music	R
$n	Number of part/section of a work	R
$o	Arranged statement for music	NR
$p	Name of part/section of a work	R
$r	Key for music	NR
$s	Version	NR
$6	Linkage	NR
$8	Field link and sequence number	R

EXAMPLES

Subfield

```
100   0#$aKālidāsa.
240   10$aMeghadūta
```

```
100   1#$aTagore, Rabindranath,$d1861-1941.
240   10$aWorks.$lEnglish$f1994
```

[Following current practice Field 240 is used instead of 243]

240 10$aGulliver's travel

245 10$Voyage and adventure of Gulliver in the land of liliputs.

110 1#$aBritish Virgin Islands.

240 10$aLaws, etc. (1969-1970)

245 10$aOrdinances & statutory rules & orders of the Virgin Islands.

100 1#$aBullett, Gerald William,$d1894-1958.

240 10$aPoems.$kSelections

245 10$aPoems /$cby Gerald Bullett.

110 2#$aInter-American Commission on Human Rights.

240 10$aInforme sobre la situación de los derechos humanos en Paraguay.$lEnglish

245 10$aReport on the situation of human rights in Paraguay.

240 10$aDuoi fratelli rivali $lEnglish & Italian

245 14$aGli duoi frattelli rivali =$bThe two rival brothers $cGiambattista della Porta ; edited and translated by Louise George Clubb.

110 2#$aAustralian National Parks and Wildlife Service.

240 10$aAnnual report (1977)

245 10$aAnnual report /$cAustralian National Parks and Wildlife Service.

243 COLLECTIVE UNIFORM TITLE (NR)

Field 243 contains a generic uniform title used for bringing together works by a prolific author, and laws, treaties, etc. — the over-all conventional title for an item made up of several works.

Note: Following the current trend, a cataloguing agency may prefer to use Field 240 instead.

Indicator:		
1st	Uniform title printed or displayed	
0	Not printed or displayed	
1	Printed or displayed	
2nd	Nonfiling characters	
0	No nonfiling characters present	
1-9	Number of nonfiling characters present	
Subfield code:		
$a	Uniform title	NR
$d	Date of treaty signing	R
$f	Date of a work	NR
$g	Miscellaneous information	NR

$h	Medium	NR
$k	Form subheading	R
$l	Language of a work	NR
$m	Medium of performance for music	R
$n	Number of part/section of a work	R
$o	Arranged statement for music	NR
$p	Name of part/section of a work	R
$r	Key for music	NR
$s	Version	NR
$6	Linkage	NR
$8	Field link and sequence number	R

EXAMPLES

```
100    1#$aChattopadhyay, Bankimchandra,$d1838-1894.
243    10$a[Works].
260    ##$aCalcutta,$bBangiya Sahitya Parishat,$c1938-1946

100    1#$aTouré, Ahmed Sékou,$d1922-
243    10$aSpeeches
245    10$aDiscours du président Sékou

110    1#$aArgentina.
243    00$aLaws, etc.
245    10$aRecopilación de leyes, decretos y resoluciones ...
```

245 TITLE STATEMENT (NR)

Mandatory

The field consists of the title proper and may also contain the GMD (medium, entered in subfield $h), remainder of title, other title information, the remainder of the title page transcription/ statement(s) of responsibility.

The title proper *includes* the short title and alternative title, the numerical designation of a part/section (subfield $n) and the name of a part/section ($p).

The field may contain inclusive dates ($f) and bulk dates ($g) pertaining to a collection. For collections with no formal bibliographic title, subfield $k (Form) is used. Subfield $k may also be used to indicate "form" even if a formal title is given.

Note: Data in this field is customarily entered as specified by various rules of cataloging. Field 245 serves as primary access point in absence of field 1XX.

Indicators:	
1st	Title added entry
0	No title added entry
1	Title added entry

2nd	Nonfiling characters	
0	No Nonfiling characters present	
1-9	Number of Nonfiling characters present	
Subfield code:		
$a	Title	NR
$b	Remainder of title	NR
$c	Statement of responsibility	NR
$f	Inclusive dates	NR
$g	Bulk dates	NR
$h	Medium	NR
$k	Form	R
$n	Number of part/section of a work	R
$p	Name of part/section of a work	R
$s	Version	NR
$6	Linkage	NR
$8	Field link and sequence number	R

SCOPE & EXAMPLES

Subfield $a

1. The title proper, excluding the designation of the number or name of a part

2. Subfield **$a** also contains the first title of separate works (by the same or different authors/composers) in a collection lacking a collective title.

3. In records formulated according to ISBD principles, subfield **$a** includes all the information *up to and including the first mark of ISBD punctuation*: an equal sign, a colon, a semicolon, or a slash, or the medium designator, e.g., *[microform]*.

245   00$aProceedings /$c ...

245   00$aJLegends or lies?

245   10$aNineteenth-century bird prints.

245   10$aUnder the hill, or, The story of Venus and Tannhauser.

245　　10$a[Seventeen poems].

245　　00$aHamlet ; $bRomeo and Juliette ; Othello ...

Subfield $b

1. Subfield $b contains the remainder of the title information. The data includes titles subsequent to the first (in items lacking a collective title).

2. In records formulated according to ISBD principles, subfield $b contains all the data following the first mark of ISBD punctuation and up to and including the mark of ISBD punctuation that introduces the first author statement [i.e., the first slash (/)].

245　　14$aThe capacity to govern : $b a report to the Club of Rome.

245　　10$aContributions to the geography and history of Bengal: $bMuhammedan period.

245　　10$aWestern civilization : $boriginal and secondary source readings.

245　　10$aTrade Union Fellowship Program : $b[announcement].

Note: When each title consists of a common title and a part designation and/or title, subfield $n (Number of part/section of a work) and subfield $p (Number of part/section of a work) are input only after subfield $a (Title).

Note: *Title elements and SOR following parallel titles are not subfield coded.*

245　　10$aInternational review of applied psychology : $bthe journal of the International Association of Applied Psychology = Revue internationale de psychologie appliquée.

Subfield $c

Subfield $c contains the first statement of responsibility and/or remaining data in the field which has not been subfielded by any other subfield codes.

In records formulated according to ISBD, subfield $c contains all data following the first slash (/). *Once a subfield $c has been recorded, no further subfield coding of field 245 is possible.*

245 10$aProject directōry / $cTDC = Répertoire des projets / CDT.

245 14$aThe printer's manual$h[microform] / $cby Caleb Stower ; with a new introduction by John Bidwell. The printer's companion / by Edward Grattan ; with a new introduction by Clinton Sisson.

245 14$aThe analysis of the law / $cSir Matthew Hale. The students companion / Giles Jacob.

245 00$aManagement report.$nPart I / $cU.S. Navy's Military Sealift Command.

Subfield $h

Subfield $h contains a medium designator used in the title statement. In records formulated according to ISBD principles, the medium designator appears in lowercase enclosed within brackets, following the title proper (subfields $a , $n , $p). It *precedes* the remainder of the title ($b), subsequent titles (in items lacking a collective title), and/or SOR.

245 10$aBengal famine of 1943. $h[microform].

245 14$aThe royal gazette. $h[microform]/$cNew Brunswick.

245 00$aDaily report. $pPeople's Republic of China $h[microform]/$cFBIS.

Subfield $k

Subfield $k contains the form of the material. Specific kinds of materials are distinguished by an examination of their physical character, subject of their intellectual content, or the order of information within them (e.g., *daybooks, diaries, directories, journals, memoranda,* etc.).

245 10$aFour years at Yale : $kdiaries, $f1903 Sept.16 - 1907 Oct. 5.

245 00$aPL 17 Hearing Files : $kCase Files, $f1974 $pDistrict 6$h[microfilm (jacketted in fiche)]

Subfield $n

Numbering is identified as an indication of sequencing in any form, e.g., *Part 1, Supplement A, Book two.* In records formulated according to ISBD principles, $n data follows a period (.). Multiple alternative numberings for a part/section are contained in a single subfield $n.

245   10$aFaust.$nPart one.

245   14$aThe Bookman.$nPart B.

Subfield $p

Subfield $p contains a **name** of a part/section of a work in a title. In records formulated according to ISBD principles, subfield $p data follows a period (.) when it is preceded by subfield $a or another subfield $p and *comma (,) when it follows subfield $n*

245   10$aAdvanced calculus. $pStudent handbook.

245   00$aDissertation abstracts.$nA, $pThe humanities and social sciences.

Note: Subfields $n and $p are *repeated only if* those follow a subfield $a , $n, or $p.

If a title recorded in subfield $b or $c includes the name and/or number of a part/section, those elements are not separately subfield coded.

245   00$aZentralblatt für Bakteriologie, Parasitenkunde, Infektionkrankheiten und Hygiene. $n1. Abt. Originale. $nReihe B, $pHygiene. Krankenhaushygiene. Betrieb-shygiene, präventive Medizin.

245   00$aAnnual report of the Minister of Supply and Service Canada under the Corporations and Labour Unions Returns Act.$nPart II,$pLabour unions =$bRapport annuel du ministre des Approvisionnements et services Canada présenté sous l'empire et des syndicates ouvriers. Partie II. Syndicats ouvriers.

246 Varying Form of Title (R)

Field 246 contains varying forms of the title, whether *they are* or *are not* on the item. These are recorded in field 246 only *if they differ substantially* from the title statement in field 245 and *if they contribute to the further identification of the item*.

For *items including several works but lacking a collective title*:

- Field 246 is used only for titles related to the title selected as the title proper, *usually the first work named* in the chief source of information.

- Titles related to *other works are recorded in field 740* or *one of the other 7XX (Added Entry) fields*.

Indicator:	
First	Note controller/title added entry
0	Note, no title added entry
1	Note, title added entry
2	No note, no title added entry
3	No note, title added entry
Second	Type of title
#	No information provided

0	Portion of title	
1	Parallel title	
2	Distinctive title	
3	Other title	
4	Cover title	
5	Added title page title	
6	Caption title	
7	Running title	
8	Spine title	
Subfield code		
$a	Title proper/short title	NR
$b	Remainder of title	NR
$f	Designation of vol./issue and/or date	NR
$g	Miscellaneous information	NR
$h	Medium	NR
$i	Display text	NR
$n	Number of part/section of a work	R
$p	Name of part/section of a work	R
$5	Institution to which field applies	NR
$6	Linkage	NR
$8	Field link and sequence number	R

SCOPE & EXAMPLES

Since Field 246 is a common container for several forms of varying title, each identified by the 2nd indicator's value, annotations and examples are grouped not under subfield codes but under the second indicator values.

Indicators

Second Indicator

Value # (Blank) - No information provided

A special display may be needed by placing subfield $i (Display text) before subfield $a to provide the context of the variant.

245 10 $a Business intelligence advisory service executive report $h [electronic resource].
246 3# $a Executive report

245 00$a City of Summerside, city map : $b "the only thing we overlook is the water!".
246 1#$i *Alternate title:* $a Summerside, Prince Edward Island, Canada

245 10$aComputerized engineering index.
246 1#$iAlso known as : $aCOMPENDEX

245 10$a Map & guide, ALA/CLA Annual Conference, June 19-25, 2003 : $b [Toronto] / $c the Map Network, tradeshow map.
246 3# $a Map and guide, ALA/CLA Annual Conference, June 19-25, 2003

245 14 $a The plague ; $b The fall ; Exile and the kingdom ; and selected essays / $c Albert Camus ; with an introduction by David Bellos.
246 3#$a Plague ; The fall ; Exile and the kingdom ; and, selected essays

245 10 $a Growing up together / $c Margaret Becker ; photography by Kathleen Francour.
246 1# $i *Other title* information from cover: $a Sisters & brothers we'll always be

Value 0 - Portion of title

Indicates that the **field 246$a** is a *portion of a title* for which access is needed, but no note.

It covers part/section title in **field 245$p**, alternative title in **field 245$a**, and portion of the title proper or short title.

245 10$a 2000-2001 *annual supplement* to The piano book : $b buying & owning a new or used piano / $c Larry Fine.
246 30$a Piano book

245 10$a Father Eugene Lafont of St. Xavier's College, Kolkata and the contemporary science movement / $c Arun Kumar Biswas.
246 30$a Contemporary science movement

| 245 | 04$aThe Berkley book of modern writing. |
| 246 | 30$aModern writing |

Note: When **245 $b** consists of initialism; or, full form of title rejected as title proper:

| 245 | 10$aProceedings, International Conference on Coordinated & Multiple Views in Exploratory Visualization : $bCMV 2003, 15 July 2003, London, England / $cedited by Jonathan Roberts. |
| 246 | 30 $a CMV 2003 |

| 245 | 00$aLibrary resources market place : $bLRMP. |
| 246 | 30$aLRMP |

Value 1 - Parallel title

Value 1 indicates that the title given in field 246 is a title in another language for which access or an added entry is desired. When one or more parallel titles have been recorded in field 245, each parallel title *is also recorded in a separate field 246.*

| 245 | 00$aMyth to modernity = $bEfsanelerden günümüze. |
| 246 | 31$aEfsanelerden günümüze |

| 245 | 04$aLes anges dans nos campagnes = $bAngels o'er the fields /$cedited and arranged by J.A. Loux and J.R. Phelps. |
| 246 | 31 $aAngels o'er the fields |

| 245 | 10$aHuman dimensions of weather and climate : $bprogram and abstracts : 38th CMOS Congress, 31 May-03 June, 2004, Edmonton, Alberta = La dimension humaine de la météo et du climat : programme et résumés/ $ceditorial team, Geoff Strong... |
| 246 | 31$aDimension humaine de la métò et du climat |

Note: Following the current practice, the 2nd indicator value remains blank (#) for Parallel titles not recorded in field 245:

| 245 | 00 $6 880-01 $aJissu no shugoron to keisanron. |
| 246 | 1#$i*Parallel title* on contents p. : $aSet theory and computability theory of the reals. |

| 245 | 00$6880-01 $aKeisanki kagaku kiso riron no shintenkai. |
| 246 | 1#$i*Parallel title* on contents p. : $aEvolutionary advancement in fundamental theories of computer science |

Note: Subfields $n and $p are used even when *parallel title in field 245 not subfielded.*

Value 2 - Distinctive title

Distinctive titles are special titles appearing *in addition to the regular title* on individual issues of an item. They are most commonly found on such items as *annual reports, yearbooks,* or *conference proceedings* <u>when an issue is dedicated to a particular topic or theme</u>.

Notes: Distinctive titles should not be confused with individual titles within a series.

Subfield $f *is always* used with a distinctive title. The display constant **Distinctive title:** is associated with this indicator value.

245   00$aCommodity year book.
246   12$aCommodity statistics $f1942

245   00$aActa Polonica Monashiensis.
246   12$aActa Lemiana Monashiensis $fDec. 2002

Value 3 - Other title

Value 3 indicates that

- the title given in field 246 is another title associated with the item but which is not appropriate for one of the other second indicator values, and

- subfield $i is not being used to give specific text.

Notes: Other titles include: *masthead title, half-titles, binder's titles, colophon titles, cover titles found in an inverted format at the back of the publication, spelled out titles, etc.*

245   00$a Dialogue.
246   13$a Dialogue *magazine*

245   00$aAssembly file analysis.$h[microform].
246   13$aCalifornia State Assembly file analysis
246   13$aCalifornia Legislature State Assembly analysis

250 EDITION STATEMENT (NR)

Field 250 contains information relating to the edition of a work.

The data in this field are customarily entered as specified by various cataloging rules. AACR 2 formulated bibliographic records follow ISBD principles for description and punctuation.

Note: This field is **not used for sequential edition statements** of serialized publications, for which the field 362 (Dates of Publication and/or Volume Designation) may be used.

Indicator:		
1st	Undefined; contains a blank	
2nd	Undefined; contains a blank	
Subfield code:		
$a	Edition statement	NR
$b	Remainder of edition statement *for Serials*	NR
$6	Linkage	NR
$8	Field link and sequence number	R

SCOPE & EXAMPLES

Subfields

Subfield $a

The subfield **$a** contains the edition statement. Usually it consists of numeric and alphabetic characters and accompanying words in full or abbreviated forms.

If an edition statement appears in more than one language, only the first one is recorded in subfield **$a**.

250   ##$a3rd ed., rev. and enlarged

250   ##$aCentenary ed.

250   ##$aUpated ed.

250   ##$aSpecial education ed.

250   ##$aRev. as of Jan. 1, 1958.

250   ##$aWorld's classics ed., New ed., rev., reset, and illustrated

Subfield $b

Note: Once subfield **$b** has been recorded, no further subfield coding of **field 250** is possible.

250   ##$a4th ed. /$brevised by J.G. Le Mesurier and E. McIntosh, Repr. with corrections.

250   ##$aRev. ed. /$bwith revisions, an introduction, and a chapter on writing by E.B. White, 2nd ed. / with the assistance of Eleanor Gould Packard.

250   ##$aCanadian ed. = $bEd. canadienne.

260 PUBLICATION, DISTRIBUTION, ETC. (NR)

Field 260 contains information relating to the publication, printing, distribution, issue, release, or production of a work.

All data elements are separately subfield coded except:

- Qualifiers and subscription addresses added to place names
- Statements of the function of the publisher, printer, distributor, etc.
- Adjacent dates of publication, distribution, etc. (including dates preceded by the word *distributed*)

The data in this field are customarily entered as specified by various cataloging rules.

Indicator		
First	Undefined	
Second	Undefined	
Subfield code:		
$a	Place of publication, distribution, etc.	R
$b	Name of publisher, distributor, etc.	R
$c	Date of publication, distribution, etc.	R
$e	Place of manufacture [for serials]	NR

$f	Manufacturer [for serials]	NR
$g	Date of manufacture	NR
$6	Linkage	NR
$8	Field link and sequence number	R

SCOPE & EXAMPLES

Subfield $a

Subfield $a contains the place of publication *and any additions to the name of a place*, including an address, or bracketed clarification of a fictitious place. The subfield includes all data *up to and including the next mark of ISBD punctuation*:

- **Comma** (,) When subfield $a is followed by subfield $c
- **Colon** (:) When subfield $a is followed by subfield $b
- **Semicolon**(;) When subfield $a is followed by another subfield $a

Note: The abbreviations [S.l.] and [s.n.] may appear in $a for unknown place and in $b for unknown publisher, respectively. For uncertain dates, a note of interrogation sign '?' may be used in $c following cataloguing norms, e.g. [15–?].

260 ##$a[S.l.] :

260 ##$aKolkata :

260 ##$aHannacroix, NY (2 Hawley Lane, Hannacroix 12087):

260 ##$aBelfast [i.e. Dublin] :

260 ##$aPiscataway, NJ :

Multiple places are recorded contiguously in separate $a subfields.

260 ##$aLondon ; $aPortland, OR :

260 ##$aBerlin ; $aNew York :

Multiple units of publishers and places are recorded consecutively as separate pairs of subfield $a and subfield $b.

260　　## $a [Chicago] : $bALA ; $a[Ottawa] : $bCLA, $cc2003.

260　　## $aNew Delhi : $bLibrary of Congress Office ; $a Washington, D.C. : $bLibrary of Congress Photoduplication Service, $c1999.

Subfield $b

Subfield $b contains the name of the publisher or distributor and any qualifying terms, such as an indication of function (e.g., *[distributor]*).

Note: Subfield $b is always preceded by a *colon* (:) and includes all data up to and including the mark of ISBD punctuation that introduces the next data element.

260　　##$b[s.n.]

260　　##$b Kolkata Municipal Corporation and New Age Publishers Pvt., Ltd.

260　　##$b Parliamentary Communications Ltd.

260　　##$b Loux Music

260　　##$b [Distributed by W. Heffner]

260　　##$bNational Technical Information Service [distributor]

260　　##$b Kolkata Municipal Corporation and New Age Publishers Pvt., Ltd.

Multiple publishers are recorded in separate $b subfields.

260　　##$b Sanskrit College : $b West Bengal Government College Teachers' *Association*

260　　##$bU.S. Dept. of Agriculture, Forest Service : $bFor sale by the Supt. of Docs. U.S. G.P.O.

Subfield $c

$c contains the date of publication.

- If the date of manufacture is *substituted for* the date of publication, recorded in $c.

- Multiple adjacent publication dates, e.g., a date of publication and copyright date are recorded in a single subfield $c.

In records formulated according to ISBD principles:

- $c is always preceded by a *comma* (,) unless it is the first subfield in field 260.
- $c ends with a (.), (-) for open-ended dates, a ((]) or *closing parenthesis* ()) as the case may be.
- $c followed by some other subfield, the period is omitted.

Note: If both publication date and date of manufacture, the latter date is recorded in $g .

260   ##$c1973.

260   ##$cApril 15, 1977.

260   ##$c1968 [i.e. 1971]

260   ##$c1971$g(1973 printing)

260   ##$c1947-1979.

260   ##$c<1981- >

Subfield $e

Contains the place of manufacture and any additions to the place name. When subfield $e is recorded, subfield $f is also generally recorded. In records formulated according to ISBD principles, subfield $e is recorded after any subfield $a, $b, or $c. Subfield $e data along with any subfield $f and $g data are enclosed in parentheses. Subfield $e includes all data up to and including the next mark of ISBD punctuation i.e., a colon (:).

260   ##$aNew York : $bE.P. Dutton,$c1980$e(Moscow : $fRussky Yazyk)

260   ##$a[Pennsylvania : $bs.n.],$c1878-[1927?]$e(Gettysburg : $fJ.E. Wible, Printer)

Subfield $f

Subfield $f contains the name of the manufacturer and any qualifying terms. The abbreviation *[s.n.]* may appear when the name is unknown. In records formulated according to ISBD principles, subfield $f contains all data including the mark of ISBD punctuation that introduces the next data element:

- **Comma (,)** When subfield $f is followed by subfield $g

- **Closing Parenthesis** '( )' When subfield $f is the last subfield in field 260

260 ##$aNew York : $bPublished by W. Schaus, $cc1860 $e(Boston : $fPrinted at J.H. Bufford's)

260 ##$aLondon : $bArts Council of Great Britain, $c1976 $e(Twickenham : $fCTD Printers, $g1974)

260 ##$aBethesda, Md. : $bToxicology Information Program, National Library of Medicine [producer]; $aSpringfield, Va. : $bNational Technical Information Service [distributor], $c1974-$e(Oak Ridge, Tenn. : $fOak Ridge National Laboratory [generator])

300 PHYSICAL DESCRIPTION (R)

Field 300 contains the physical description of the item. It includes the extent, dimensions and other physical details of the item, and of the accompanying material, if any.

The data in this field are customarily formulated as specified by various cataloging rules. The prescribed ISBD principles are followed for punctuation.

Indicator		
1st	Undefined	
2nd	Undefined	
Subfield Code		
$a	Extent	R
$b	Other physical details	NR
$c	Dimensions	R
$e	Accompanying material	NR
$f	Type of unit	R
$g	Size of unit	R
$3	Materials specified	NR
$6	Linkage	NR
$8	Field link/sequence number	R

Subfields

Subfield $a

The subfield contains the number of physical pages, volumes, etc. of each type of unit. When consecutively numbered, pagination for individual volumes may also be included in parentheses, if desired.

Note: In records formulated according to ISBD principles, the subfield $a contains all data up to and including the next mark of ISBD punctuation e.g., a colon a semicolon a plus sign.

300   ##$a iv, 170 p.

300   ##$a xv, 269 p.

300   ##$av.2 (320p.)

300   ##$a11 v.

300   ##$a1 map

When the statement of pagination and illustrative matter are combined, both may be recorded in a single subfield $a.

300   ##$a74 p. of ill., 15 p.

300   ##$a27 leaves of plates (some col.)

Subfield $a is repeatable when alternate or additional forms of extent data are entered, in parentheses, under *a separate* $a subfield.

300   ##$a1$fvolume$a(463$fpages)

300   ##$a17$fboxes$a(7$flinear ft.)

Subfield $b

Subfield $b specifies other physical characteristics of an item, such as identification of illustrative matter, coloration, groove characteristics, etc.

Note: In records formulated according to ISBD principles, subfield $b contains all data up to and including the next mark of ISBD punctuation e.g., a semicolon.

300   ##$a11 v. : $bill. ;

300   ##$a1 map : $bcol. ;

Subfield $c

Subfield $c contains the dimensions of an item, usually in centimetres. For materials printed in one of the regular sizes, only the height of the item is given. A parenthetical qualifier giving the printer format of the item e.g., *(fol.)*, *(8 vo)* may be recorded as part of dimension in subfield $c.

300   ##$c23 cm.

300   ##$c10 x 27 cm.

300   ##$c200 x 350 cm., folded to 20 x 15 cm., in plastic case 25 x 20 cm.

300   ##$cimage 33 x 41 cm., on sheet 46 x 57 cm.

300   ##$c20 cm. (8vo)

300   ##$c21 cm. +$eatlas (37 p., 19 leaves of plates : 19 col. maps ; 37 cm.)

310 CURRENT PUBLICATION FREQUENCY (NR)

Field 310 contains the currently *stated* publication frequency of an item.

Note: In records having field 008 (Fixed-Length Data Elements), the data in 008/18 and 008/19 are determined based on information provided in field $310and field 362.

The date(s) of the current publication frequency is given *when the beginning date of the current publication frequency is not the same as the beginning date of the publication.*

For a ceased publication, current frequency date is closed with last appearance date.

Indicator		
1st	Undefined	
2nd	Undefined	
Subfield code		
$a	Current publication frequency	NR
$b	Date of current publication frequency	NR
$6	Linkage	NR
$8	Field link and sequence number	R

Scope & Examples

Subfield $a

The subfield contains the *complete statement* about frequency of the current publication.

310   ##$aMonthly

310   ##$aBimonthly, with a special issue in December

310   ##$aMonthly (except July and Aug.)

310   ##$aAnnual, with quinquennial cumulations

Subfield $b

This is an optional subfield that contains the beginning date, typically the year, of current publication frequency:

- when it is different from the beginning date of the publication, *and*
- When a former publication frequency is given in field 321.
- Field 310 gives frequency also when publication of a serial ceased.

310   ##$aAnnual,$b1983-

310   ##$aMonthly,$bJan. 1984

310   ##$aMonthly,$b1958-

310   ##$a5 no. a year,$b1946-1948

362 Dates of Publication/ Sequential Designation (r)

Field 362 contains the beginning/ending date(s) of an item and/ or the sequential designations used on each part. Dates to be used in this field are chronological designations that identify individual issues of the serial.

The information may be formatted or unformatted. If the date information has been obtained from a source other than the first and/or last issue of the item published, the information is given in an unformatted note and the source of the information is usually cited.

Dates in this field may be identical to the information in fields 008/07-10 (Date 1) and/or 008/11-14 (Date 2).

Note: Incomplete, approximate or questionable dates are not recorded in this field.

Indicator	
1st	Format of date
0	Formatted style
1	Unformatted note
2nd	Undefined

Subfield code		
$a	Dates of publication and/or sequential designation	NR
$z	Source of information	NR
$6	Linkage	NR
$8	Field link and sequence number	R

SCOPE & EXAMPLES

Indicators

First Indicator Value 0

Value **0** indicates that the date is formatted and designed to be displayed following the title and edition statements. The numeric and/or alphabetic, chronological or other designation is customarily recorded as appeared on the piece.

362 0#$aVol. 1, no. 1 (Apr. 1981)-

362 0#$a1968-

362 0#$aVol. 1, no. 1 (Apr. 1983)-v. 1, no. 3 (June 1983).

First Indicator Value 1

Value **1** indicates that the date is given in an unformatted note style. Unformatted date information is designed to be displayed as a note. This value is used when the first and/or last piece is not in hand, but the information is known from other pieces or sources.

362 1#$aBegan with 1930 issue.$zCf. Letter from Ak. State Highway Dept., Aug. 6, 1975.

362 1#$aBegan with vol. 4, published in 1947.

362 1#$aCeased with 2 (1964).

Subfields

Subfield $a

The subfield contains the sequential designation and/or dates of publication. Sequential designators and dates are recorded as given on the item:

- The *sequential designation* may consist of volume number, edition number, issue number, series of volume numbers, or other sequential designations according to the publication policy.

- The *date* may consist of the year, month, or day; month or season and year; or year alone, depending upon the frequency of publication and publication policy.

- When both a numeric designation and a chronological designation are given, the chronological designation is enclosed in parentheses. The ending designation is recorded following the beginning designation.

362   0#$aVol. 1 (Mar. 1980)-

362   0#$aVol. 77, num. 1 (enero-abr. 1981)-

362   0#$aVol. 85B, no. 1 (Jan./Feb. 1945)-v. 92, no. 6 (Nov. Dec. 1952).

362   0#$a1962-1965.

Subfield $z

Subfield **$z** contains a citation of the source of the information contained in subfield **$a**. It is used *only when the first indicator position contains <u>value 1</u>*. The title of the publication cited is preceded by the abbreviation *Cf.*

362 1#$z Cf. New serial titles.

362 1#$z Cf. Letter from Ak. State Highway Dept., Aug. 6, 1975.

440 SERIES STATEMENT/ADDED ENTRY - TITLE (R)

Field 440 contains a series title statement that serves dual purpose:

- a series statement and
- a series added entry *(title is searchable)*.

When a 440 field is present, no corresponding 8XX field is used.

Note: Field 440 is under authority control. Its content designation supports series-title search, but *not* by names associated with the series or by a variant form of the series-title. Neither does the field provide a subfield $h for medium designator which is an important component for series identification at times. To meet any of these special requirements, field 490 is used along with corresponding 8XX field(s) for the series added entry.

Indicator:		
1st	Undefined	
2nd	Nonfiling characters	
0	No nonfiling characters	
1-9	Number of nonfiling characters	
Subfield code:		
$a	Title	NR

$n	Number of part/section of a work	R
$p	Name of part/section of a work	R
$v	Volume #/sequential designation	NR
$x	ISSN	NR
$6	Linkage	NR
$8	Field link and sequence number	R

SCOPE & EXAMPLES

Subfields

Subfield $a

Subfield **$a** contains the title portion of the series alone. Its rendering follows ISBD principles.

440   #0$aPraeger *series* in political communication

440   #4$aThe Jossey-Bass business & management series

440   #0$aJournal for the study of the New Testament $p Supplement series

440   #0$aSage series in modern Indian history

440   #0$aIFLA publications

440   #0$aLand reforms in India

440   #0$aSouth Asia ephemera collection.

Subfield $n

Subfield **$n** contains a *number* designation for a part or section of a series title that indicates sequencing in any form, e.g., *Part 1, Supplement A, Book two, no.7.*

440   #0$aVital and health statistics. **$n***Series* 11

440   #0$aJournal of polymer science.$nPart C

440   #0$aNCHS CD-ROM. $n*Series* 20

Subfield $p

Subfield **$p** contains a *name* designation of a part or section of a series title.

440   #0$aSouth Asia ephemera collection. $pIndia

440   #0$aVital and health statistics. $nSeries 11, $pData from the National Health Survey

440   #0$aJournal for the study of the *New* Testament $p Supplement series

Subfield $v

Subfield **$v** contains the volume number or other *sequential* designation used in a series statement.

440   #0$aDHHS publication ; $vno. (PHS) 2002-1696

440   #0$aSage series in modern Indian history ; $v6

440   #0$aIFLA publications ; $v 95

Subfield $x

Denotes ISSN of the serial

440   #0$aPraeger *series* in political communication, $x1062-5623

440   #0$aISODEC advocacy *series*, $x0855-4986

440   #0$aDrug statistics *series*, $x1442-7230

490 SERIES STATEMENT (R)

Field 490 contains a series statement. It does not serve as series added entry.

When a series added entry is desired, the series statement (field 490) and one or more corresponding series added entries (800-830 fields) are separately recoded.

This field is particularly needed when a series statement includes volume(s) and/or date(s) during which the publication was issued.

Note: Field 490 is used when a *series statement,* as given, is considered unimportant for search; or, found ineffective as a search key. However, if it is considered important for search, the statement may be recorded in field 830 with a qualifier to make the statement an authority controlled access point. Field 490 is not under authority control, when field 830 is. Besides uniform series title (field 830), personal and corporate names associated with the series may serve as added entries (field 800, field 810, and field 811).

Indicator:	
1st	Specifies whether series is traced
0	Series not traced
1	Series traced differently

2nd	Undefined	
Subfield code:		
$a	Series statement	R
$l	Library of Congress call number	NR
$v	Volume #/sequential designation	R
$x	ISBN	NR
$6	Linkage	NR
$8	Field link and sequence number	R

SCOPE & EXAMPLES

Subfields

Subfield $a

Subfield **$a** contains the title of the series. It may also contain a statement of responsibility, other title information, dates, or volume numbers. Volume number may be preceding or appearing as part of the title.

490   1#$aWorcestershire Historical Society

490   1#$aBulletin / U.S. Department of Labor, Bureau of Labor Statistics

490   1#$av. 9-<10>: MPCHT art and anthropological monographs

490   1#$a2004: Woman's day premier *series*

490   1#$a2005-: Woman's day *new* ideas *series*

490   1#$aMonograph series

490   1#$aMP

490   0#$aAddison-Wesley series in computer science and information processing

Note: Subfield $a is repeatable when:

- a subseries is separated from the main series by the numbering of the main series in subfield **$v** or by the ISSN in subfield **$x**, or when
- a series has a parallel title.

490 1#$aPerspectives on Christianity = $aPerspektiewe op die Christendom. *Series* 5 ; $vv. 1

490 1#$aDepartment of State publication ; $v7846. $a Department and Foreign Service series ; $v128

Subfield $v

Subfield $v contains the volume number or other sequential designation used in conjunction with a Series Statement.

490 1#$v37

490 1#$vnew ser., v. 18

490 1#$vno. 73

Note: Alternate numbering systems, preceded by an equal sign (=), are not separately subfielded.

490 **1#$a** Perspectives on Christianity = **$a** Perspektiewe op die Christendom. Series 5 ; **$v**v. 1

490 0#$aForschungen zur Geschichte Vorarlbergs ; $v6. Bd. = der ganzen Reihe 13 Bd.

Subfield $x

Subfield $x contains ISSN for a series title given in a series statement.

490 1#$aPragmatics & beyond new series, $x0922-842X

490 1#$aWorcestershire Historical Society, $x0141-4577

490 0#$aLife series$x0023-6721

490 First indicator: Value 1 - Series traced differently

Value **1** indicates that the form of entry for the series in the series added entry differs from that in the series statement. When value **1** is used, *an 800-830 field is included* in the bibliographic record to provide the appropriate series added entry.

Examples for Field 800 (Series Added Entry - Personal Name):

490   1#$aThe James Joyce archive

800   **1#$a**Joyce, James,**$d**1882-1941.**$t**James Joyce archive.

490   1#$aLouie Armstrong ; $v6.

800   **1#$a**Armstrong, Louis,**$d**1900-1971.**$4**prf**$t**Louie Armstrong (Universal City Studios) ; $v6.

Examples for Field 810 (Series Added Entry - Corporate Name):

490   1#$aCIIL linguistic atlas series ; $v1

810   **2#$a**Central Institute of Indian Languages.**$t**CIIL linguistic atlas series ; **$v**1.

490   1#$aBulletin / U.S. Department of Labor, Bureau of Labor Statistics

810   **2#$a**United States. Bureau of Labor Statistics**$t**Bulletin

Examples for Field 811 (Series Added Entry - Meeting Name):

490   1#$aNutrition and food science ; $vv.1

811   **2#$a**International Congress of Nutrition**$n**(11th : **$d**1978: **$c**Rio de Janeiro, Brazil).**$t**Nutrition and food science ; $vv. 1.

490   1#$aDelaware symposia on language studies ; $v4

811   **2#$a**Delaware Symposium on Language Studies.**$t**Delaware symposia on language studies ; **$v**4.

Examples for Field 830 (Series Added Entry - Uniform Title)

490   1#$aWorcestershire Historical Society

830   **#0$a**Worcestershire Historical Society (Series) ; **$v**new ser., v 18.

490   1#$aDia Art Foundation, New York ; $vno. 2

830   **#0$a**Dia Center for the Arts, New York (Series) ; **$v**no.2.

490   1#$aMonograph series

830   **#0$a**Asiatic Society monograph series ; **$v**no. 33.

490	1#$aMP
830	#0$aMP (Series) (Ontario Genealogical Society. Kawartha Branch) ; $v37.

490	1#$aLanguage and literacy series
830	#0$aLanguage and literacy series (New York, N.Y.)

Note: Field 830 is the most commonly found among series linking fields representing series-titles in standardized search forms.

500 GENERAL NOTE (R)

Field 500 is used for general information for which a specialized 5XX note field has not been defined.

Field 500 ends with a period unless another mark of punctuation is present. MARC records carry punctuation within note (e.g., quotation marks).

Note: The text of the note needs to be short and discrete. The field is repeated to present information in a distinctive manner for different aspect of an object. The examples relating to former title notes show the way it is done.

Indicator		
1st	Undefined	
2nd	Undefined	
Subfield code:		
$a	General note	NR
$3	Materials specified	NR
$5	Institution to which field applies	NR
$6	Linkage	NR
$8	Field link and sequence number	R

Subfields

Subfield $a

Subfield **$a** contains the entire text of the note.

245	04$aThe Calcutta municipal gazette : **$b**Tagore memorial special supplement.
500	##$aOriginally published : Calcutta, 1941.

245	00$aBengal famine of 1943. $h[microform].
500	##$aA collection of pamphlets published during 1943-1945.
500	##$aContents list arranged alphabetically by title.
500	##$aCollected and organized by the Library of Congress Office, New Delhi.

245	10$aUtopia and history in Mexico
500	##$aTranslated into English from the Spanish translation of the French original.

245	10$aContemporary India : $b*Journal* of Nehru Memorial Museum and *Library)*
500	##$a Title from cover.
500	##$a Latest issue consulted: v. 1, no. 4 (Oct.-Dec. 2002).

245	00$a1948 plus fifty years
500	##$a"An IMER Publication".

245	10$aMap & guide, ALA/CLA Annual Conference, June 19-25, 2003.
500	##$aPerspective tourist map.
500	##$aTitle from panel.
500	##$a"GIS map data [copyright] 2003 DMTI Special, Inc."
500	##$aIncludes conference schedules and indexes to hotels and restaurants.
500	##$aIndex to exhibitors, 2 floor plans, and advertisement on verso.

Note: Field 500 also includes reference notes relating to former title of an item. In pre-AACR2 environment, fields 247 and 547 were available to serve that purpose.

245	00$Foreign tax law bulletin.
362	0#$aVol. 2004, no. 1 (Mar. 9, 2004)-
500	**##$a**_Title varies_ slightly.

245	00$aTravel holiday.
362	0#$av. 151, no. 2-v. 186, no. 5; Feb. 1979-June 2003.
500	**##$a**"The magazine that roams the globe."
500	**##$a**Imprint varies: Floral Park, N.Y., Travel Magazine, 1979-
500	**##$a**_Title_ from cover.
500	**##$a**_Formerly_ issued as a regional publication. In winter 1998 began publication as a national edition.
500	**##$a**"Formerly known as Supreme Court journal."
500	**##$a**"... update of the manual, which was rewritten in September 1997 ... The manual, _formerly_ entitled General appraisal manual was originally written in 1960 ..."—Foreword.
500	**##$a**"This revision ... is a complete rewrite of the original manual (formerly titled The income Approach to Value) written in 1988"—Pref.

501 WITH NOTE (R)

Field 501 contains a note indicating that more than one bibliographical work is contained in the physical item when published, released, or issued. The works contained in the item usually have distinctive titles.

The field, however, may be used to describe separate works *bound together locally*, in which case subfield $5 contains a code that indicates the institution to which the note applies.

Punctuation

Field **501** ends with a period unless another mark of punctuation is present. In records formulated according to AACR 2, a space-hyphen-hyphen-space (- -), or a space-dash-space (—), is entered between items in the *with note*.

Display constants

There is no display constant generally associated with the **501** field. Terms such as **With:** and **Issued with:** are *carried in the MARC record as part of the data* in the field.

Note: The field is hardly used in recent time.

Indicator		
1st	Undefined	
2nd	Undefined	
Subfield code		
$a	With note	NR
$5	Institution to which field applies	NR
$6	Linkage	NR
$8	Field link and sequence number	R

Scope & Examples

Subfields

Subfield $a

Subfield **$a** contains the entire text of the note, including the introductory phrase (e.g., **With:**, **On reel with:**, **Issued with:**, etc.). The titles of the separate parts in field 501 are **not** separately subfield coded.

501 ##$a*Issued with* (as second section): Big game odds report.

501 ##$aWith: A dialogue on beauty / George Stubbes. New York : Garland Pub., 1970 — A discourse concerning ridicule and irony in writing / Anthony Collins. New York : Garland Pub., 1970 — Reflections on Dr. Swift's letter to the Earl of Oxford, about the English tongue / John Oldmixon. New York : Garland Pub., 1970.

501 ##$aWith: The reformed school / John Dury. London : Printed for R. Wasnothe, [1850]

501 ##$aWith: Peer Gynt (Suite) no. 1-2 / Edvard Grieg — Till Eulenspiegels lustige Streiche / Richard Strauss.

502 Dissertation Note (R)

Field 502 is defined to record notes on dissertation or thesis *in original form*. It includes the designation of an academic dissertation or thesis, and the institution to which it was presented. The field may also include the degree for which the author was a candidate and the year it was granted.

Punctuation

Field ends with a period unless another mark of punctuation is present. The reference to award of the degree for which the dissertation was presented may be recorded in parentheses following convention.

Indicator		
1st	Undefined	
2nd	Undefined	
Subfield code		
$a	Dissertation note	NR
$6	Linkage	NR
$8	Field link and sequence number	R

Scope & Examples

Subfield $a

Subfield $a contains the entire text of the note.

245 10$aHealth management information systems in lower income countries : $ban analysis of system design, implementation and utilization in Ghana and Nepal / $cBruce Benner Campbell.

502 ##$aThesis (doctoral) — Universiteit van Amsterdam, 1997.

245 10$aBeyond the noise of time : $breadings of Marina Tsvetaeva's memories of childhood / $cKarin Grelz.

502 ##$aThesis (doctoral) — Stockholms universitet, 2004.

245 14$aThe nature of nature tourism / $cAlain A. Grenier.

502 ##$aThesis (Ph.D.) — University of Lapland, 2004.

245 14$aThe new pattern of industrial relations in India : $brestructuring and social insecurity : a case-study of Kothur, a new township in Andhra Pradesh / $ca *thesis* submitted by Vijay Gudavarthy.

502 ##$aThesis (doctoral) — Institute of Social Studies, The Hague, 2004.

Note: Notes are recorded in field 500 (General Note) if the item is not a dissertation/thesis *in original form*. Such notes mostly relate the published target item to the author's dissertation / thesis, such as, *Originally presented as [Theses title]*. Notes about abstracts, abridgements, or revisions of theses are also recorded in field 500.

500 ##$aOriginally presented as author's *thesis* (Ph. D.) — Yale University, 1962.

500 ##$aEnlargement of author's *thesis* (doctoral) — University of Manchester, 1999.

500 ##$aPresented as the author's *thesis* (doctoral) — University of Goettingen.

500 ##$aBased on the author's *thesis* (Ph. D. — University of Chicago, 1992) presented under the title: Invisible cities, Touba Turin, Sengalese transnational migrants in northern Italy.

504 Note: Bibliography, etc. (R)

Field 504 contains a note indicating the presence or absence of a bibliography, discography, filmography, and/or other bibliographic references in an item, or in an accompanying material. For multipart items, including *serials*, the note may pertain to all parts or to a single part or issue. Field 504 is used :

- Only when the bibliography is considered *sufficiently extensive to warrant a separate note.*
- Even when there is a doubt as to whether the note is bibliographical in nature or not.

Note: There is no display constant associated with the **504** field. Introductory terms such as *Bibliography:, Discography:, etc.* are carried in the MARC record as part of the data in the field.

Indicator:		
1st	Undefined	
2nd	Undefined	
Subfield code		
$a	Bibliography, etc. note	NR
$b	Number of references	NR
$6	Linkage	NR
$8	Field link and sequence number	R

Subfields

Subfield $a

Subfield $a contains the text of the note entirely on bibliographic references when sufficiently extensive to warrant use of this separate note field. The field may also include information about presence of an index, provided that accompanies bibliographic references.

245   00$aCavan
504   ##$aIncludes bibliographical references (p. 197-230) and index.

245   04$aThe vampyre
504   ##$aIncludes bibliographical references (p. [195]-197).

245   10$aJodie Foster
504   ##$aIncludes bibliographical references (p. 32) and index.
504   ##$aFilmography: p. 31.

245   10$aBenjamin Britten
504   ##$aIncludes bibliographical references (p. [159]-252), lists of works, and index.
504   ##$a"Discography: Britten on Compact Disc": p. [121]-157.

Note: From the view-point of data manipulation a particular occurrence of field 504 may not include notes on more than one type of reference materials. The following two are examples of using mixed types of reference notes.

245   10$aPhotography and the making of the American West
504   ##$aIncludes bibliographical references (p. 112-114), webography (p. 115-118), and index.

245   14$aThe unauthorized Jackie Chan encyclopedia
504   ##$aIncludes bibliographical references (p. 206-207).
504   ##$aIncludes filmography (p. 201-203) and discography (p. 232-239).

Subfield $b

Subfield **$b** contains the number of references contained in the bibliography. Generally it is used as a way to determine the significance of a bibliography. *A simple numerical count* of references is given in this subfield, following the bibliography note.

504   ##$a"Literature cited": p. 67-68.$b19

Note: The subfield **$b** is hardly used in recent time.

505 FORMATTED CONTENTS NOTE (R)

Field 505 contains *contents note* in a predefined format. The note *usually* contains:

- Titles of separate volumes in a multi-volume item, *or* analytic parts of a single-volume item
- Statements of responsibility
- Volume numbers and other sequential designations

Content note may also include the number of pages, pieces, frames of each part, if desired. Chapter numbers are generally omitted.

Punctuation

- Between descriptions of items a space-hyphen-hyphen-space (- -), or a space-dash-space (—), is recorded unless a delimiter/subfield code follows, in which case no ending space is required.
- Contents notes may contain prescribed ISBD punctuation [e.g., statements of responsibility are preceded by a space-slash-space (/)].
- Field 505 ends with a period when it contains complete or partial contents, *unless* another mark of punctuation or a

closing angle bracket (<>) is present, or the contents continue in another occurrence of field 505.

- For *incomplete contents*, no period is recorded, *unless* the last word, initial/letter, or abbreviation ends in a period.

Indicators		
1st	**Display constant controller**	
0	Contents	
1	Incomplete contents	
2	Partial contents	
8	Machine-generated contents	
2nd	**Level of content designation**	
#	Basic	
0	Enhanced	
Subfield code		
$a	Formatted contents note	NR
$g	Miscellaneous information	R
$r	Statement of responsibility	R
$t	Title	R
$u	Uniform Resource Identifier	R
$6	Linkage	NR
$8	Field link and sequence number	R

Scope & Examples

Indicators

First indicator

Value 0 - Contents

Value **0** indicates a contents note that represents the complete contents of an item. It is used to generate the display constant '**Contents:**' before the text.

505   0#$av. 1. From the origins of civilization to the age of absolutism — v. 2. From the scientific revolution to the present.

505 0#$aThe lost civilization — The women warriors — The lord of battles — The saint and the prince — The popess — The outlaw — The city of gold.

505 0#$aTable of contents:http://www.loc.gov/catdir/tocfy0452003108093.htmlLsInd holdsfortegnelseonline.

[Hyperlinked electronic contents page.]

Value 1 - Incomplete contents

The value 1 indicates that the contents note is incomplete, as because all parts of a multipart item are not available. Either they have not been published, or not yet been acquired by the cataloging agency. Value 1 is used to generate the display constant 'Incomplete contents:'.

505 1#$aINCOMPLETE CONTENTS: 1. Pro-Othomanika phyla sten Asia kai sta Valkania.

505 1#$apt. 1. General observations — pt. 2. Methodology — pt. 3. Initial phase

[Parts to be added after pt. 3; note left open *(no final period)*]

Value 2 - Partial contents

Value 2 indicates a partial contents note that *describes only selected parts* of an item even *though all parts are available* for analysis. Value 2 is used to generate the display constant 'Partial contents:'.

505 2#$aPartial contents : Chelovek — mashina — zhivotnoe / A. Zalygin.

505 2#$aPartial contents : Whispering shadows.

Value 8 - Machine generated contents

The use of this systems generated contents note is steadily increasing. Libraries with IT support opt for this type of contents note with customization, whenever needed.

505 8#$aMachine generated contents note: Introduction — Prescription Drug Index — Prescription Drugs — Natural

Alternatives — Allergies — Anxiety — Arthritis — Asthma — Back Pain — Bronchitis — Bursitis — Cancer — Colds, Coughs, and Flu — Dandruff — Depression — Diabetes — Dry Skin — Gout — Headache — Heartburn — High Blood Pressure — High Cholesterol — Hyperthyroidism — Impotence — Insomnia — Irritable Bowel Syndrome — Menopause — Nail Care — Narcolepsy — Osteoporosis — PMS (Premenstrual Syndrome) — Psoriasis — Ulcers — Urinary Tract Infections — Weight Loss.

Second indicator

Value # - Basic

Value # (blank) indicates that all contents information is recorded in a single occurrence of subfield $a.

505   0#$av. 1. From the origins of civilization to the age of absolutism — v. 2. From the scientific revolution to the present.

505   0#$a*Contents:* Historical setting ; The society and its environment / [Said S. Samatar] — The economy / [David D. Laitin] — Government and politics / [Eric Hooglund] — National security / [Thomas Ofcansky].

Note: This is the most popular way of presenting descriptions of bibliographic contents.

Value 0 - Enhanced (Not often used in recent time barring few European countries)

Value 0 indicates that enhanced content designation is supplied, that is, all relevant subfield codes, not the subfield $a alone, are used for describing parts of the item.

505   00$tAcknowledgments — $g1. The$tmetaphysics of copyright — $g2. The $thistory of an idea — $g3.$tFifty dollars to collect ten — $g4.$tPrivate copies — $g5. The$ttwo cultures of copyright — $g6 "The$tanswer to the machine is in the machine" — $g7. The$tcelestial jukebox — $tNotes — $tIndex.

505   00$tQuark models /$rJ. Rosner — $tIntroduction to gauge theories of the strong, weak, and electromagnetic

interactions /$rC. Quigg — $tDeep inelastic leptognnucleon scattering /$rD.H. Perkins — $tJet phenomena /$rM. Jacob — $tAn accelerator design study /$rR.R. Wilson — $tLectures in accelerator theory /$rM. Month.

Subfields

Subfield $a

Subfield $a contains the formatted contents note, whether complete, incomplete, or partial when the second indicator value is **blank** (#). The text of the contents note may include titles, statements of responsibility, volume numbers and sequential designations, etc. For records formulated according to AACR rules, these elements are separated by ISBD punctuation.

505   0#$aDemography/Nirmala Banerjee and Mukul Mukherjee — Health and nutrition/ Maitreya Ghatak — Education Jasodhara Bagchi and Jaba Guha — Economic empowerment/ Ishita Mukhopadhyay — Political participation/Vidya Munshi — Culture/Malini Bhattacharya — Law and violence against women/Manjari Gupta and Ratnabali Chattopadhyay — Tribal women/Anuradha Chanda.

The following Subfields are used with Enhance Contents:

Subfield $g

Subfield $g contains any information *other than the statement of responsibility or title,* used in a coding-enhanced note (second indicator value is 0). It may include *volume, part, page* numbering or other *extent information* such as *dates.*

Subfield $r

Subfield $r contains the statement of responsibility of the article or part in the coding-enhanced contents note (second indicator value is 0). The author itself may be a personal or corporate name.

Subfield $t

Subfield **$t** contains a title used in the coding-enhanced contents note. (second indicator value is *usually 0*).

Note: Contents formatted using subfields, **$t**, **$r** and **$g**, provide the system with a programming handle to generate keyword index to the analytic titles and authors.

505   00$tAcknowledgments — $g1. The$tmetaphysics of copyright — $g2. The $thistory of an idea — $g3.$tFifty dollars to collect ten — $g4.$tPrivate copies — $g5. The$ttwo cultures of copyright — $g6 "The$tanswer to the machine is in the machine" — $g7. The$tcelestial jukebox — $tNotes — $tIndex.

505   10$gNr. 1.$tRegion Neusiedlersee — $gNr. 2.$tRegion Rosalia/Lithagebirge — $gNr. 3.$tRegion Mettelburgenland — $gNr. 4.$tRegion südliches Burgenland — $gNr. 5.$tRegion Südburgland

505   20$tBaptisms, 1816-1872 — $tChurch members, 1816-1831 — $tHistory of the Second Presbyterian Church of West Durham /$rby L. H. Fellows.

Subfield $u

Subfield **$u** contains the Uniform Resource Identifier (URI), for example a URL or URN, which provides electronic access data in a standard syntax. This data can be used for automated access to an electronic item using one of the Internet protocols. The field is repeated if more than one URI needs to be recorded.

505   0#$uhttp://lcweb.loc.gov/catdir/toc/99176484.html

Display: Contents: http://lcweb.loc.gov/catdir/toc/99176484.html

520 Summary, etc. (R)

Field 520 contains unformatted information about the scope and broad description of the contents of the item. This could be in the form of a summary, abstract, annotation, review, or only a phrase describing the material.

The level of detail may vary depending on the audience for a particular product. However, the text needs to be invariably in discrete, brief and clear language. The text may be displayed and/or printed with an introductory term generated as a *display constant* based on the *first indicator value*. Now a day, the use of display constants is less.

Indicator:	
1st	Display constant controller
#	Summary
0	Subject
1	Review
2	Scope and content
3	Abstract
8	No display constant generated
2nd	Undefined

Subfield code:		
$a	Summary, etc	NR
$b	Expansion of summary note	NR
$u	Uniform Resource Identifier	R
$3	Materials specified	NR
$6	Linkage	NR
$8	Field link and sequence number	R

SCOPE & EXAMPLES

Indicators

First Indicator

Value # - Summary

Value # (blank) is used to generate the display constant **Summary**.

520   ##$aSummary: Pull of Novgorod : the reasons for the Orthodox migration from Käkisalmi province to Russia in the 17th century.

520   ##$aSummary of lectures presented at the Meeting on Luminescent Assays: Perspectives in Endocrinology and Clinical Chemistry, held in Florence, July 1981, organized by the Post-Graduate School of Endocrinology, University of Florence.

Note: Recent trend is to do away with the display constant in field 520, and to put a separate note instead in field 500 specifying the source of the note provided in Field 520.

520   ##$aThe life, work, and times of American painter and sculptor Frederic Remington is described. Known for his scenes of Western life, numerous examples of his work are shown.

500   ##$a*Summary* adapted from Art on screen — a directory of films and videos about the visual arts, p. 75.

Value 0 - Subject [Not in use]

Value 0 is used to generate the display constant **Subject**.

520   0#$aTwo head-and-shoulder portraits in separate ornamental oval frames, one frame held by eagle.

Value 1 - Review [Rarely used]

Value 1 is used to generate the display constant **Review**.

520   1#$a"Important historical analysis of 16th-century accounts concerning indigenous people. Examines context in which chronicles - considered among the earliest ethnographies- were written (and censured and ignored), and Franciscan beliefs about the Indians' future within the millennial kingdom. First English translation"—Handbook of Latin American Studies, v. 57. $u http://www.loc.gov/hlas/

520   1#$a"Combines the most frequently asked questions regarding AIDS with the most prominent US physician, former Surgeon General C. Everett Koop, resulting in an informative 38-minute production"—Cf. Video rating guide for libraries, winter 1990.

Value 2 - Scope and content [Not in use]

Value 2 is used to generate the display constant **Scope and content**.

520   2#$aSeries consists of minutes of meetings of the Board together with correspondence and other documents referred to in the minutes. The records reflect.

Value 3 - Abstract [Less used than Indicator-value #]

Value 3 is used to generate the display constant **Abstract** [Rarely used constant].

520   3#$aThe study examines the fertility history of American couples in metropolitan America and the motivational connections between the environment and fertility decisions and behavior.$bPhase I looks at the social and psychological factors thought to relate to differences in fertility. Phase II focuses on why some couples stopped at two children while others had a third or fourth child during

the first and second phase. Phase III examines how well attitudes and events of the early marriage determined the record of the later years of child bearing.

Subfields

Subfield $a

Subfield $a contains the text of the summary, abstract, review, etc. The extent of the subfield content varies depending on the levels of description policy. In 2-level description subfield $b is used to record the extended part of information given in subfield $a. When subfield $b does not occur, subfield $a contains the entire text.

520   ##$aDescribes associations made between different animal species for temporary gain or convenience as well as more permanent alliances formed for mutual survival.

520   2#$aFonds consists of minutes of meetings, research files relating to the delivery of health case services in Nova Scotia, recorded ...

520   ##$aThe research reported here had five main aims. 1. To review the current literature on the combined effects of occupational hazards on health and safety. 2. Conduct secondary analyses of self-report data from randomly selected community samples to examine the impact of combinations of workplace factors on health and safety. 3. To investigate the effects of combinations of workplace factors on accidents at work in a sample attending Accident and Emergency units in Wales. 4. To investigate using measures taken before and after work at the start and end of the working week and effects of combinations of workplace factors on performance efficiency and physiology. Finally, to assess the utility of the approach to other current topics of interest and review the implications of the results for policy issues such as stress management standards. Contents: Executive summary; Background; The investigation of combined occupational stressors; The negative occupational factors (NOF) score; Community survey samples; A & E survey; Summary from survey methodologies utilised so far; Mood, objectively

measured performance and physiology; Overall summary; Combined effects of occupation health hazards; Literature review; Secondary analyses of the Bristol and Cardiff community samples, methodology and descriptive statistics; Negative occupational factors scores; Further analysis of negative occupational factors, NOF score components; Summary of effects, NOF score, JDCS, ERI and hazards working hours; Analysis of longitudinal data; Accident and emergency (A & E) study; Work-accidents; The impact of occupational stressors on objective measures of performance, mood and physiology; Conclusions and recommendations for further research; Recent applications of the combined effects approach and implications for policy; References; Appendix.

Subfield $b

Subfield $b contains an expansion of the brief summary recorded in subfield $a.

520   ##$aPublic release motion pictures, 1915-37.$bIncludes films on control of rats, prairie dogs and porcupines; fish culture in the United States and pearl culture in Japan; inspection trip to Alaska by Service officials; life in a Boy Scout camp and Air Service bombing techniques in 1921.

520   ##$aMiscellaneous cartographic records with an emphasis on biogeography of the United States and Alaska, 1872-1941.$bIncludes published and photoprocessed maps of Alaska and coastal waters,1888-90, many of which were compiled from surveys made on the "Albatross";-maps, 1908-19, annotated by the Alaskan Fisheries Division ...

520   ##$aA literary journal and review. $bPublished with the objectives of documenting the history and culture of the Pubna district and its people.

520   ##$aA significant literary journal and review appeared for the readership of Muslim women. $bThis was the first amongst the periodicals brought out by Muslim women.

525 Supplement Note (r)

Field 525 contains a note that describes the nature and scope of a supplement, or special issue, which has neither been cataloged as a separate record nor recorded in a linking entry field 770 (Supplement/Special Issue Entry) . Generally, this note field is used *only* for unnamed supplements and/or special issues.

Indicator		
1st	Undefined	
2nd	Undefined	
Subfield code:		
$a	Supplement note	NR
$6	Linkage	NR
$8	Field link and sequence number	R

Scope & Examples

Subfield

Subfield $a

Subfield $a contains the text of the note.

245 00$aProceedings of the American catholic philosophical association

525 ##$aA partir de 1991, devient un supplément du périodique : American catholic philosophical quarterly

525 ##$aKept up to date by occasional supplement with same title. Issued with SuDoc no. LC 3.4/2: FL-4 A-2 (showing only the table of fees); issued <2004-> as SL-04.

525 ##$aUpdating supplement issued annually with title: Bibliographic data additions and revisions for Congressional publications abstracted in the ... CIS annuals.

245 00$aCommento tematico della legge marchi / $c[testi di] Giorgio Marasà ... [et al.].

525 ##$aSupplement: "Addendum al Commento tematico della legge marchi" (7 p.) inserted.

245 00$aCommercial transactions : $ba systems approach/$c Lynn M. LoPucki ... [et al.].

525 ##$aAccompanied by: Revised article 9 supplement (xi, 692 p.).

600 SUBJECT ADDED ENTRY - PERSONAL NAME (R)

Field 600 contains a personal name used as a subject added entry. Personal names as subject added entries are created to provide access to the bibliographic information of the relevant items. The names are rendered according to established subject cataloging principles and guidelines. The content designators identify the sub-elements occurring in personal name fields constructed according to the generally accepted cataloging and thesaurus-building rules e.g., AACR 2, LCSH.

Field 600 may be used by any institution assigning subject headings based on the lists and authority files identified in the second indicator position or in subfield $2 (Source of heading).

Note: Personal names used in phrase subject headings (e.g., *John, the Baptist, saint, in the Koran*) are contained in field 650 for Subject Added Entry - Topical Term.

Indicator	
1st	
0	Forename
1	Surname
3	Family name

2nd		
0	Library of Congress Subject Headings	
1	LC subject headings for children's literature	
2	Medical Subject Headings	
3	National Agricultural Library subject authority file	
4	Source not specified	
5	Canadian Subject Headings	
6	Répertoire de vedettes-matière	
7	Source specified in subfield $2	
Subfield code		
$a	Personal name	NR
$b	Numeration	NR
$c	Titles and other associated words	R
$d	Dates associated with a name	NR
$e	Relator term	R
$f	Date of a work	NR
$g	Miscellaneous information	NR
$h	Medium	NR
$j	Attribution qualifier	R
$k	Form subheading	R
$l	Language of a work	NR
$m	Medium of performance for music	R
$n	Number of part/section of a work	R
$o	Arranged statement for music	NR
$p	Name of part/section of a work	R
$q	Fuller form of name	NR
$r	Key for music	NR
$s	Version	NR
$t	Title of a work	NR
$u	Affiliation	NR
$v	Form subdivision	R
$x	General subdivision	R
$y	Chronological subdivision	R

$z	Geographic subdivision	R
$2	Source of heading or term	NR
$3	Materials specified	NR
$4	Relator code	R
$6	Linkage	NR
$8	Field link and sequence number	R

SCOPE & EXAMPLES

Indicators

Indicator-1 values indicate the access-part of a personal name.

Forename

600	00$aAlexander,$cthe Great,$d356-323 B.C.
600	00$aIbn Batuta,$d1304-1377.
600	00$aGautama Buddha$vBiography$vEarly works to 1800.
600	00$aJesus Christ$xHistory of doctrines$yEarly church, ca. 30-600.
600	00$aZacchaeus$c(Biblical character)
600	00$aElijah,$c(Biblical prophet)

Surname

600	10$aPushkin, Aleksandr Sergeevich, $d1799-1837 $xMuseums $zRussia (Federation) $zMoscow$vMaps.
600	10$aNixon, Richard M.$q (Richard Milhouse),$d1913-$xPsychology.
600	10$aKennedy, John F.$q (John Fitzgerald),$d1917-1963$xAssassination.
600	11$aMagellan, Ferdinand,$dd 1521.

Family name

600	30$aClark family$vFiction.
600	30$aDunlop family.

600 34$aStrachey family.

600 30$aNorfolk, Dukes of.

Indicator-2 values indicate the source of name authority followed.

The most common name authority used in MARC cataloguing is LCSH with indicator-2 value 0. A cataloguing agency, however, may prefer to use another authority control for which no indicator-2 value is assigned. Then two possibilities are there: either use 7 (source specified in $2) combined with $2 (coded name); or, use 4 (source not specified, [may be local]).

Note: In field 600, *use of 2ⁿᵈ indicator value 7 is rare*; whereas value 4 is commonly found in national databases.

Authority : LCSH

600 10$aStrachey, Lytton,$d1880-1932.$xFamily.

Authority : Medical Subject Heading

600 12$aStephanopoulos, George,$d1961-

600 12$aMoynihan, Berkeley Moynihan, Baron, 1865-1936
650 12$aSurgery$vbiography.

Authority : Source *not* specified

600 14$aFoucauld, Charles de,$d1858-1916.

600 14$aDostoevskij, Fedor Michajlovich,$d1821-1881.

600 14$aGoethe, Johann Wolfgang von, $d1749-1832
$x Aesthetics.

Authority : Répertoire de vedettes-matière

600 16$aMontgomery, L. M. $q(Lucy Maud), $d1874-1942
$xAmis et relations.

Subfields

Besides subfield $a, there are quite a few subfields used frequently in field 600 to provide data essentially needed for relating the name with the item catalogued meaningfully. Among those $c, $d, $q, $v, $x, $y and $z are found more often than other subfields.

Subfield $a

600   10$aEinstein, Albert

600   14$aGoethe, Johann Wolfgang von

600   14$aFoucauld, Charles de

Subfield $c

600   00$aAlexander,$cthe Great, $d356-323 B.C.

600   12$aSimpson, James Young,$cSir,$d1811-1870.

600   00$aZacchaeus$c(Biblical character)

600   00$aElijah,$c(Biblical prophet)

Subfield $d

600   11$aMagellan, Ferdinand,$dd 1521.

600   14$aBorn, Max,$d1882-1970

600   12$aStephanopoulos, George,$d1961-

600   00$aAlexander,$cthe Great,$d356-323 B.C.

Subfield $q

600   10$aMontgomery, L. M.$q(Lucy Maud)

600   10$aKennedy, John F.$q(John Fitzgerald)

Subfield $v

600   10$aWoolf, Leonard,$d1880-1969$vCorrespondence.

600   10$aMcNamara, Robert S.,$d1916-$vInterviews.

610   10$aUnited States.$bDept. of Defense$vBiography.

Subfield $x

600   10$aWoolf, Virginia,$d1882-1941$xFriends and associates.

600 10$aMcNamara, Robert S.,$d1916-$xPolitical and social views.

600 00$aJesus Christ$xHistory of doctrines$yEarly church, ca. 30-600.

Subfield $y

600 00$aJesus Christ$xHistory of doctrines$yEarly church, ca. 30-600.

Subfield $z

600 10$aMartí, José,$d1853-1895$xTravel$zUnited States.

610 Subject Added Entry - Corporate Name (R)

Subject added entries are assigned to a bibliographic record to provide access. The defined content designators *identify the sub-elements* occurring in corporate name fields constructed according to the generally accepted cataloging and thesaurus-building rules [e.g., AACR 2, LCSH].

The general guidelines for using Field 610 are:

- Enter a corporate name, a form subheading, a title of a work,and/or a city section name under the name of a jurisdiction.

- A name of a jurisdiction that represents an ecclesiastical entity is an X10 corporate name.

- For *subject purposes*, other names of jurisdictions *used alone or followed by subject subdivisions* are geographic names and are contained in field 651.

- A named meeting, entered under a corporate name, is contained in the X10 fields.

- A meeting entered directly under its own name is contained in the X11 fields.

- Corporate names used in *phrase subject headings* (e.g., *Catholic Church in art*) are contained in field 650 (Subject Added Entry - Topical Term).

Indicator			
1st	Type of corporate name entry element		
0	Inverted name		
1	Jurisdiction name		
2	Name in direct order		
2nd	Subject heading system/thesaurus		
0	Library of Congress Subject Headings		
1	LCSH for children's literature		
2	Medical Subject Headings		
3	National Agri. Lib. subject authority file		
4	Source not specified		
5	Canadian Subject Headings		
6	Répertoire de vedettes-matière		
7	Source specified in subfield $2		
Subfield code:			
$a	Corporate name or jurisdiction name	NR	
$b	Subordinate unit	R	
$c	Location of meeting	NR	
$d	Date of meeting or treaty signing	R	
$e	Relator term	R	
$f	Date of a work	NR	
$g	Miscellaneous information	NR	
$h	Medium	NR	
$k	Form subheading	R	
$l	Language of a work	NR	
$m	Medium of performance for music	R	
$n	Number of part/section/meeting	R	
$o	Arranged statement for music	NR	
$p	Name of part/section of a work	R	
$r	Key for music	NR	
$s	Version	NR	
$t	Title of a work	NR	
$u	Affiliation	NR	

$v	Form subdivision	R
$x	General subdivision	R
$y	Chronological subdivision	R
$z	Geographic subdivision	R
$2	Source of heading or term	NR
$3	Materials specified	NR
$4	Relator code	R
$6	Linkage	NR
$8	Field link and sequence number	R

Scope & Examples

Indicators

First Indicator

Value 1: Jurisdiction - indicates that the entry element is a name of a jurisdiction (but *not an integral part of the name*).

610   10$aAustralia. $bParliament $xElections, 2001.

610   10$aBritish Airways $xHistory.

610   10$aUnited States. $bArmy. $bInfantry Regiment, 347th. $bF Company

610   10$aUnited States. $bArmy $xNon-commissioned officers.

Value 2: Name in direct order - indicates that the name is in direct order. The heading may contain a parenthetical qualifier or may be an acronym or initialism.

610   20$aJ.L.B. Smith Institute of Ichthyology $xHistory.

610   20$aPeerless General Finance & Investment Company Limited $vBiography.

610   20$aAgricultural Society of Kenya $xHistory.

610   20$aSony Computer Entertainment $xManagement.

610   20$aRoyal College of Surgeons of Edinburgh. $xHistory.

610   20$aArt in Cinema Society $xHistory $vSources.

Jurisdiction as an integral part of the name or qualified by a jurisdiction name :

610 20$aBritish Overseas Airways Corporation.

610 20$aAmerican Airlines, inc.

610 20$aIntellectual Property Office of New Zealand $v Periodicals.

610 20$aAmerican Society of Civil Engineers $bIllinois Section $xHistory.

Second Indicator: Subject Heading System

See examples cited under Field 600

Subfields

Subfield $a

Contains a name of a corporate body or the first entity *when subordinate units are present*; a jurisdiction name under which a corporate body, city section, or a title of a work is entered; or a jurisdiction name that is also an ecclesiastical entity

610 20$aPeerless General Finance & Investment Company Limited $vBiography.

610 20$aRoyal College of Surgeons *of* Edinburgh. $xHistory.

610 10$aUnited States.$bDept. of Defense$vBiography.

610 10$aAustralia. $bParliament $xElections, 2001.

A parenthetical qualifying term, jurisdiction name, or date (other than the date of a meeting) is not separately subfield coded.

610 20$aMorris & Co. (London, England)

610 20$aLion Brewery (W.A.)$xHistory.

610 20$aUniversity Boat Club (W.A.)$xHistory.

610 20$aCinema 16 (Society : New York, N.Y.) $xHistory.

Subfield $b

Contains a name of a subordinate corporate unit, a name of a city section, or a name of a meeting entered under a corporate or a jurisdiction name.

610 24$aRoyal Society of Edinburgh. $bMuseum.

610 10$aUnited States.$bDept. of Defense$vBiography.

610 10$aAustralia. $bParliament $xElections, 2001

610 20$aVisvabharati$bSantiniketan (Bolpur).

610 10$aUnited States. $bArmy. $bInfantry Regiment, 347th. $bF Company $xHistory.

Meeting entered under a corporate or a jurisdiction name

610 20$aUnited Church of Christ. $bNew Hampshire Conference $xHistory.

610 20$aCatholic Church $bCanadian Conference of Catholic Bishops $xHistory.

Subfield $g

Contains a data element that is not more appropriately contained in another defined subfield. *In a heading for a meeting, entered under a corporate body*, subfield $g also contains sub-element that is less appropriate for subfields $c, $d, or $n.

610 10$aGreat Britain.$tTreaties, etc.$gIreland,$d1985 Nov. 15.

Subfield $k

Contains a form subheading. A form subheading may occur in either the name or the title portion of an **X10** field. Form subheadings used with corporate names include: *Manuscript*; *Protocols, etc.*; *and Selections*.

610 20$aBritish Library.$kManuscript.$nArundel 384.

Subfield $n

Contains number of a meeting entered under a corporate name

110 1#$aUnited States.$bCongress$n (97th, 2nd session : $d1982).$bHouse.

Subfield **$n** also contains a *number* designation for a part or section of a work used with a title in a name/title field. *Numbering* is defined as an indication of sequencing in any form (e.g., *Part 1, Supplement A, Book two*). For music, the serial, opus, or thematic index number, or date used as a number, is contained in subfield **$n**.

610   20$aBritish Library.$kManuscript.$nArundel 384.

Subfield $x

Subfield **$x** contains a subject subdivision that is not more appropriately contained in subfields $v (Form subdivision), $y (Chronological subdivision), or $z (Geographic subdivision). Subfield **$x** is appropriate only when a general topical subdivision is added to a name or a name/title.

610   10$aAustralia. $bParliament $xElections, 2001.

610   20$aSony Computer Entertainment $xManagement.

Subfield $v

Subfield **$v** contains a form subdivision that designates a specific kind or genre of material as defined by the thesaurus being used. Subfield **$v** is appropriate only when a form subject subdivision is added to a corporate name or name/title to form an extended subject heading. A form subdivision in subfield **$v** is generally the last subfield in the field.

610   10$aFrance.$bBibliothèque nationale$vCatalogs.

610   10$aUnited States.$bDept. of Defense$vBiography.

610   20$aBritish Airways $xEvaluation $vPeriodicals.

Subfield $u

Subfield **$u** contains the affiliation or address of the name.

110   1#$aUnited States.$bNational Technical Information Service.$u5205 Port Royal Road, Springfield, VA 22161.

611 SUBJECT ADDED ENTRY - MEETING NAME (R)

Field 611 contains a meeting or conference name used as a subject added entry. Subject added entries are assigned to a bibliographic record to provide access. The content designators identify the sub-elements occurring in meeting name fields constructed according to the generally accepted cataloging and thesaurus-building rules e.g. AACR 2, LCSH.

Field 611 may be used by any institution assigning subject headings based on the lists and authority files identified in the second indicator position or in subfield $2 (Source of heading or term).

Note: A named meeting that is entered under a corporate name is contained in the X10 fields. Corporate names that include such words as *conference* or *congress* are also contained in the X10 fields. For example, *the Congress of Neurological Surgeons*, a professional group, is a corporate name.

Indicator	
1st	Type of meeting name entry element
0	Inverted name
1	Jurisdiction name
2	Name in direct order
2nd	Subject heading system/thesaurus

0	Library of Congress Subject Headings	
1	LCSH for children's literature	
2	Medical Subject Headings	
3	NAL subject authority file	
4	Source not specified	
5	Canadian Subject Headings	
6	Répertoire de vedettes-matière	
7	Source specified in subfield $2	

Subfield code:

$a	Meeting/jurisdiction name	NR
$c	Location of meeting	NR
$d	Date of meeting	NR
$e	Subordinate unit	R
$f	Date of a work	NR
$g	Miscellaneous information	NR
$h	Medium	NR
$k	Form subheading	R
$l	Language of a work	NR
$n	Number of part/section/meeting	R
$p	Name of part/section of a work	R
$q	Meeting Name following jurisdiction	NR
$s	Version	NR
$t	Title of a work	NR
$u	Affiliation	NR
$v	Form subdivision	R
$x	General subdivision	R
$y	Chronological subdivision	R
$z	Geographic subdivision	R
$2	Source of heading or term	NR
$3	Materials specified	NR
$4	Relator code	R
$6	Linkage	NR
$8	Field link and sequence number	R

Scope & Examples

Indicators

First indicator: Value 1 - Jurisdiction name

Note: Not used in AACR2 environment.

First indicator: Value 2 - Name in direct order

Value **2** indicates that the name is in direct order. The heading may contain a parenthetical qualifier or may be an acronym or initialism.

611   24$aConference of European Ministers responsible for Local Government $n(10th : $d1993 : $cThe Hague)

611   24$aConference of Foreign Ministers$d(1959 : $cGeneva)

Meeting names with a jurisdiction name as its integral part or qualified by a place name.

611   20$aParis Peace Conference $d(1919-1920) $vBibliography.

Second Indicator: Subject Heading Systems

See Examples cited under Field 600

Subfields

The subfield codes specified in MARC21 documentation are defined for possible applications in X11 fields; many of those may not be relevant to the requirements of a particular instance of X11 fields. Examples provided here are only for those subfields which are relevant and commonly found in international databases.

Subfield $a

Contains name of a meeting, or the first entity when subordinate units are present; or a jurisdiction name under which a meeting name is entered.

611   24$aConference for the Reduction and Limitation of Armaments$d(1932-1934 : $cGeneva, Switzerland)

Subfield $c

Contains a place name or a name of an institution where a meeting was held.

611   20$cGustavus Adolphus College.

611   24$cGeneva, Switzerland.

611   20$cTaipei, Taiwan.

611   20$cHuntsville, Ala.

611   20$cDhaka, Bangladesh.

Note: A place name added parenthetically to a meeting name to distinguish between identical names is not separately subfield coded.

Subfield $d

611   24$d1993

611   24$d1932-1934

611   20$d(1919-1920)

Note: Parenthesis may be used as per cataloging rules adopted.

Subfield $n

A number of a meeting or a number designation for a part or section of a work.

611   24$aOlympics$n(25th : $d1992 : $cBarcelona, Spain) $xPolitical aspects.

611   20$aAsian Writers' Conference $n(3rd : $d1970 : $cTaipei, Taiwan)

Note: Parenthesis may be used as per cataloguing rules adopted. Subfield $n also contains a number designation for a part or section of a work. Numbering is defined as an indication of sequencing.

Subfield $v

611   20$vBibliography.

611   20$vPeriodicals.

Subfield $x

611   **20$xHistory $xSources.**

611   **20$xPolitical aspects**

611   **20$xPolitics and government**

630 SUBJECT ADDED ENTRY - UNIFORM TITLE (R)

Field 630 contains a uniform title used as a subject added entry. Subject added entries are assigned to a bibliographic record to provide access according to established subject cataloging principles and guidelines. Institutions assigning subject headings are at liberty to use any thesaurus, or authority files, of their choice for subject access control. If, however, the thesaurus is MARC coded, the code should be entered in subfield $2 and value 7 in the second indicator position; otherwise, value 4 to be entered in the second indicator suggesting source not specified.

The content designators identify the sub-elements occurring in uniform or conventional title, and construct the headings according to the generally accepted cataloging and thesaurus-building rules e.g. AACR 2, LCSH.

Indicator:	
1st	filing characters
0	No nonfiling characters present
1-9	Number of nonfiling characters
2nd	thesaurus
0	LCSH
1	LCSH for children's literature

2	Medical Subject Headings	
3	NAL subject authority file	
4	Source not specified	
5	Canadian Subject Headings	
6	Répertoire de vedettes-matière	
7	Source specified in subfield $2	
Subfield code		
$a	Uniform title	NR
$d	Date of treaty signing	R
$f	Date of a work	NR
$g	Miscellaneous information	NR
$h	Medium	NR
$k	Form subheading	R
$l	Language of a work	NR
$m	Medium of performance for music	R
$n	Number of part/section of a work	R
$o	Arranged statement for music	NR
$p	Name of part/section of a work	R
$r	Key for music	NR
$s	Version	NR
$t	Title of a work	NR
$v	Form subdivision	R
$x	General subdivision	R
$y	Chronological subdivision	R
$z	Geographic subdivision	R
$2	Source of heading or term	NR
$3	Materials specified	NR
$6	Linkage	NR
$8	Field link and sequence number	R

Subfields

The subfield codes specified in MARC21 documentation are defined for possible applications in X11 fields; many of those may not be relevant to the requirements of a particular instance of X11 fields. Examples provided here are only for those subfields which are relevant and commonly found in international databases.

Subfield $a

Note: This subfield $a definition applies to the X30 fields, field 240, and field 243. Parenthetical information added to make a title distinctive is not separately subfield coded *except in the case of the date of a treaty (see description of subfield $d)*.

245   00$aNine Homeric *papyri* from Oxyrhynchos / $cedited by Joseph Spooner.

630   00$aOxyrhynchus papyri.

630   00$aSouthern *review* (Baton Rouge, La.)

Note: A date added parenthetically to distinguish between identical uniform titles is not separately subfield coded.

630   00$aEdinburgh *review* (1802)

Subfield $l

Subfield $l contains the name of a language(s) (or a term representing the language, e.g., *Polyglot*) used in a uniform title field.

630   00$aBible.$lEnglish$xVersions.

Subfield $p

Indicates name of part/section.

630   00$a*Veda*. $pRgveda $xCriticism, interpretation, etc.

630   00$aValmiki. $pRamayana $xIllustrations.

630 00$a*Bible*. $pN.T. $pCorinthians $xCommentaries.

630 00$a*Bible*. $pO.T. $pPsalms XXIII $xJuvenile literature.

Subfield $v

630 00$aUkrainian weekly$vIndexes$vPeriodicals.

630 00$aNew York times$vIndexes.

Subfield $x

630 00$xTheology.

630 00$xCriticism, interpretation, etc.

630 00$xCommentaries.

630 00$xJuvenile literature.

Subfield $y

630 00$aBerliner revue$xHistory$y20th century.

650 Subject Added Entry - Topical Term (R)

Field 650 contains a topical subject used as a subject added entry. Topical subject added entries may consist of general subject terms *including names of events or objects.*

Subject added entries are assigned to a bibliographic record to provide access according to generally accepted thesaurus-building rules [e.g., LCSH, MeSH]. Field 650 may be used by any institution assigning subject headings based on the lists and authority files identified in the second indicator position or in subfield $2 (Source of heading or term) .

Note: A title (e.g., *Bible and atheism*), a geographic name (e.g., *Iran in the Koran*), or the name of a corporate body (e.g., *Catholic Church in motion pictures*) used in a phrase subject heading are also recorded in field 650.

Indicator	
1st	Level of subject
#	No information provided
0	No level specified
1	Primary
2	Secondary

2nd	Subject heading system	
0	Library of Congress Subject Headings	
1	LCSH for children's literature	
2	Medical Subject Headings	
3	NAL subject authority file	
4	Source not specified	
5	Canadian Subject Headings	
6	Repertoire de vedettes-matière	
7	Source specified in subfield $2	

Subfield code:
Main term portion

$a	Topical term/geographic name	NR
$b	Topical term following geographic name	NR
$c	Location of event	NR
$d	Active dates	NR
$e	Relator term	NR

Subject subdivision portion

$v	Form subdivision	R
$x	General subdivision	R
$y	Chronological subdivision	R
$z	Geographic subdivision	R

Control subfields

$2	Source of heading or term	NR
$3	Materials specified	NR
$6	Linkage	NR
$8	Field link and sequence number	R

SCOPE & EXAMPLES

Indicators

Indicator-2 Subject heading system

In field 650, the use of Indicator-2 with value 4 is almost rare in international databases. In some cases, value 7 is used without subfield $2 to suggest unspecified status of authority control file. To avoid anomaly it is desirable to use value 4 and value 7 whenever needed without deviating from MARC 21 specifications.

Subfields

The subfield codes specified in MARC21 documentation are defined for all possible applications; many of those may be relevant only to very limited instances, as the current usage reveals. Examples provided here are only for those subfields which are relevant and commonly found in international databases.

Subfield $a

Subfield $a contains a topical subject or a geographic name used as an entry element for a topical term. Parenthetical qualifying information associated with the term is not separately subfield coded.

650   #0$aSecurity, International.

650   #0$aEuropean cooperation.

650   #0$aRelativity (Physics)$xHistory.

650   #0$aChristian literature, Early $x*Greek* authors.

650   #0$aKalmyk cattle.

650   #0$aAstronauts.

650   #0$aBull Run, 2d Battle, 1862.

650   #0$aSurbahar(String instrument)$zIndia$xHistory.

Subfield $b

Note: This construction is not used in AACR 2 formulated records.

Subfield $v

Subfield $v contains a form subdivision that designates a specific kind or genre of material as defined by the thesaurus being used. Subfield $v is appropriate only when a form subject subdivision is added to a main term.

650   #0$aExcavations (Archaeology) $vJuvenile literature.

650 #0$aMotion picture actors and actresses $zUnited States $vBiography $vDictionaries.

650 #0$aInformation visualization $vCongresses.

650 #0$aHouseholds $zIndia $zWest Bengal $vStatistics.

650 #0$aMeteorology $zCanada $vCongresses.

650 #0$aArt in Industry $vPeriodicals.

650 #0$aVomiting $xTreatment $vHandbooks, manuals, etc.

650 #0$aElectronic games industry $xManagement $vCase studies.

Subfield $x

Subfield $x contains a subject subdivision that is not more appropriately contained in subfields $v (Form subdivision), $y (Chronological subdivision), or $z (Geographic subdivision). Subfield $x is appropriate only when a general topical subdivision is added to a main term.

650 #0$aSony video games $xHistory.

650 #0$aElectronic games industry $xManagement $vCase studies.

650 #0$aLibrary users $xEffect of technological innovations on $zIndia $vCongresses.

650 #0$aConsumer goods $xEvaluation $vPeriodicals.

650 #0$aIndians of Mexico $xHistory $xSources.

650 #0$aLand titles $zIndia $xData processing.

650 #0$aRacetracks (Horse-racing)$zUnited States$xHistory.

650 #0$aVedic literature $xHistory and criticism.

650 #0$aPhilosophy, Hindu.

650 #0$aSanskrit language $xGrammar.

650 #0$aNumismatics$xCollectors and collecting.

Subfield $y

Subfield $y contains a subject subdivision that represents a period of time. Subfield $y is appropriate only when a chronological subject subdivision is added to a main term.

650 #0$aArt, Modern $y21st century.

650 #0$aNovelists, English $y20th century $vBiography.

650 #0$aArchitecture $zIndia $zBengal $y17th century.

650 #0$aMusic $y500-1400.

Subfield $z

Subfield $z contains a geographic subject subdivision. Subfield $z is appropriate in field 650 only when a geographic subject subdivision is added to a main term.

650 #0$aWorld War, 1939-1945 $xCampaigns $zTunisia.

650 #0$aReal property $zMississippi $zTippah County $vMaps.

650 #0$aMiniature painting, Indic $zIndia $zKangra (District)

650 #0$aWomen $zIndia $zWest Bengal.

650 #0$aRiots $zBangladesh $zNoakhali District $xHistory.

651 Subject Added Entry - Geographic Name (R)

Subject added entries are assigned to a bibliographic record to provide access according to generally accepted cataloging and thesaurus-building rules. Field 651 may be used by any institution assigning subject headings based on the lists and authority files identified in the second indicator position or in subfield $2 combined with value 7 in indicator-2. Jurisdiction names alone or followed by subject subdivisions are contained in 651 fields.

A name of a jurisdiction that represents an ecclesiastical entity is contained in a 610 field. A corporate name, a form subheading, a title of a work, and/or a city section name entered under the name of a jurisdiction are contained in 610 fields. Geographic names used in phrase (e.g., *Iran in the Koran*) are contained in 650 fields.

Indicator	
1st	Undefined
2nd	Subject heading system/thesaurus
0	Library of Congress Subject Headings
1	LCSH for children's literature
2	Medical Subject Headings
3	NAL subject authority file

4	Source not specified	
5	Canadian Subject Headings	
6	Repertoire de vedettes-matière	
7	Source specified in subfield $2	
Subfield code:		
$a	Geographic name	NR
	Subject subdivision portion	
$v	Form subdivision	R
$x	General subdivision	R
$y	Chronological subdivision	R
$z	Geographic subdivision	R
	Control subfields	R
$2	Source of heading or term	NR
$3	Materials specified	NR
$6	Linkage	NR
$8	Field link and sequence #	R

Scope & Examples

Subfields

The subfield codes specified in MARC21 documentation are defined for all possible applications; many of those may be relevant only to very limited instances, as the current usage reveals. Examples provided here are only for those subfields which are relevant and commonly found in international databases.

Subfield $a

Subfield $a contains a geographic name. Parenthetical qualifying information is not separately subfield coded.

651   #0$aAmazon River.

651   #0$aAjanta Cave (India)

651   #0$aPompeii (Ancient city)

651   #0$aAntietam National Battlefield (Md.)

651   #0$aKing Ranch (Tex.)

651   #0$aMing Tombs (China)

651   #0$aKenwood (Chicago, Ill.)

651   #0$aChelsea (London, England)

651   #0$aClear Lake (Iowa : Lake)

Subfield $v

Subfield $v contains a form subdivision that designates a specific kind or genre of material as defined by the thesaurus being used. Subfield $v is appropriate only when a form subject subdivision is added to a geographic name.

651   #0$aRajmahal(India)$vFiction.

651   #0$aRussia$xHistory$vMaps.

651   #0$aCanterbury (England)$vPoetry.

651   #0$aGreat Britain$xCharters, grants, privileges$vIndexes.

651   #0$aNorfolk (England)$xSocial life and customs$vSources.

Subfield $x

Subfield $x contains a subject subdivision that is not more appropriately contained in subfield $v (Form subdivision), $y (Chronological subdivision), or $z (Geographic subdivision). Subfield $x is appropriate only when a general topical subdivision is added to a geographic name.

651   #0$aBerlin (Germany)$xDescription and travel.

651   #0$aTexas$xGovernors$xStaff.

651   #0$aAix-en-Provence (France) $xSocial life and customs $vEarly works to 1800.

651   #0$aIndia$xCensus, 1991.

Subfield $y

Subfield $y contains a subject subdivision that represents a period of time. Subfield $y is appropriate only when a chronological subject subdivision is added to a geographic name.

651   #0$aUruguay$xHistory$yGreat War, 1843-1852.

651   #0$aGermany$xHistory$y1933-1945.

651   #0$aGreece$xHistory$yGeometric period, ca. 900-700
B.C.

651   #0$aSicily (Italy)$xHistory$y1194-1282.

Subfield $z

Subfield $z contains a geographic subject subdivision. Subfield
$z is appropriate only when a geographic subject subdivision is
added to a geographic name.

651   #0$aUnited States$xBoundaries$zCanada.

651   # 0$aFrance$xRelations$zGermany.

651   #0$aUnited States$xRelations$zGermany.

651   #0$aIndia$xStudy and teaching$zGermany.

653 Index Term - Uncontrolled (R)

Field 653 contains index terms that are not derived from a controlled subject heading system/thesaurus. The field may be appropriately used for system-generated index terms extracted from major access fields. The cataloguing agency may decide on this issue in consultation with system administrator.

Note: Uncontrolled terms may not be used without having support of effective editing software to deal with the inaccuracies, inconsistencies, duplications.

Punctuation

An uncontrolled term followed by a subsequent term does not end with a mark of punctuation unless the term ends with punctuation as part of the data.

Indicator:	
1st	Level of index term
#	No information provided
0	No level specified
1	Primary
2	Secondary

2nd	Undefined	
Subfield code:		
$a	Uncontrolled term	R
$6	Linkage	NR
$8	Field link/sequence #	R

SCOPE & EXAMPLES

First indicator

Value 1 - Primary

An index term is considered primary if it covers only the main focus or subject content.

Value 2 - Secondary

An index term is considered *secondary* if it represents an aspect less important than the content of the field created for the same item with first indicator value 1.

653 1#$aOriental art

653 2#$aMiniature painting

Subfields

Subfield $a

653   1#$afuel cells$amolten carbonate$apower generation

653   ##$aMan$aEyes$aDiseases

653   1#$aIce, Sculpture, moulds, etc.$aChildren's games

653   ##$aStamp collecting (United States)

653   ##$5Gm$aMedicin: historia: Finland

69X LOCAL SUBJECT ACCESS FIELDS (R)

Fields 690-699 are reserved for local subject use and local definition. For interchange purposes, documentation of the structure of the 69X fields and input conventions should be provided to exchange partners by the organization initiating the exchange.

MARC 21 field group 6XX may serve as a framework for developing specs for subject headings to meet local needs, which cannot be accommodated in regular subject field designations. Field group 69X may be defined locally as:

690 Subject AE Personal Name

691 Subject AE Corporate Name

693 Subject AE Uniform Title

695 Subject AE Topical Term etc., etc.

Subfield codes **a**, **x**, **y**, and **z** may follow the definitions used in regular subject fields, for example:

$a Key element

$x Sub-element

$y Chronological sub-division

$z Geographical sub-division
For more information *see* Part-1: MARC cataloguing elements

700 Personal Name - Added Entry (R)

Field 700 contains a personal name used *as an added entry*. Added entries are assigned to give access to the bibliographic record from personal name headings which may not be suitable for 600 (Subject Added Entry - Personal Name) or 800 (Series Added Entry - Personal Name) fields.

The content designators identify the sub-elements occurring in personal name fields constructed according to the generally accepted cataloging and thesaurus-building rules e.g., AACR 2, LCSH.

Note: Personal names used in phrase subject headings (e.g., *John, the Baptist, saint, in the Koran*) are contained in field 650 (Subject Added Entry - Topical Term).

Indicator:	
First	Type of personal name entry element
0	Forename
1	Surname
3	Family name
Second	Type of added entry

#	No information provided	
2	Analytical entry	
Subfield code:		
$a	Personal name	NR
$b	Numeration	NR
$c	Titles and other words associated with a name	R
$d	Dates associated with a name	NR
$e	Relator term	R
$f	Date of a work	NR
$g	Miscellaneous information	NR
$h	Medium	NR
$j	Attribution qualifier	R
$k	Form subheading	R
$l	Language of a work	NR
$m	Medium of performance for music	R
$n	Number of part/section of a work	R
$o	Arranged statement for music	NR
$p	Name of part/section of a work	R
$q	Fuller form of name	NR
$r	Key for music	NR
$s	Version	NR
$t	Title of a work	NR
$u	Affiliation	NR
$x	International Standard Serial Number	NR
$3	Materials specified	NR
$4	Relator code	R
$5	Institution to which field applies	NR
$6	Linkage	NR
$8	Field link and sequence number	R

SCOPE & EXAMPLES

Subfields

The subfield codes specified in MARC21 documentation are defined for possible applications in X00 fields; many of those may not be relevant to the requirements of a particular instance of X00 fields. Field 100 and Field 700 both concern personal name elements. Examples provided under Field 100 are applicable in Field 700 too. Examples include only for those subfields which are relevant and commonly found in international databases.

$a - Personal name:

Subfield $a contains a personal name. The name may be a surname and/or forename; letters, initials, abbreviations, phrases, or numbers used in place of a name; or a family name.

Subfield $a

700   1#$aArrow, Kenneth Joseph, $d1921-$eeditor

700   1#$aSen, Amartya Kumar, $d1933-$4spk

700   1#$aSuzumura, Kotaro, $d1944-

700   1#$aDube, R. P. $q(Rajendra Prasad), $d1950-

700   0#$aRajendra Prasad,$d1884-1963

See examples of other subfield contents under Field 100

710 Corporate Name - Added Entry (R)

Field 710 contains a corporate name used as an added entry. Added entries are assigned according to various cataloging rules to give access to the bibliographic record from corporate name headings which may not be more appropriately assigned as 610 (Subject Added Entry - Corporate Name) or 810 (Series Added Entry - Corporate Name) fields.

Indicator		
1st		
1	Jurisdiction	
2	Corporate Name in Direct order	
2nd	Undefined	
Subfield		
$a	Corporate/Jurisdiction name	NR
$b	Subordinate unit	R
$c	Location of meeting	NR
$d	Date of meeting or treaty signing	R
$e	Relator term	R
$f	Date of a work	NR

$g	Miscellaneous information	NR
$h	Medium	NR
$k	Form subheading	R
$l	Language of a work	NR
$m	Medium of musical performance	R
$n	Number of part/section/meeting	R
$p	Name of part/section of a work	R
$r	Key for music	NR
$s	Version	NR
$t	Title of a work	NR
$u	Affiliation	NR
$x	International Standard Serial Number	NR
$3	Material specified	NR
$4	Relator code	R
$5	Institution to which field applies	NR
$6	Linkage	NR
$8	Field link and sequence number	R

SCOPE & EXAMPLES

Subfields

The subfield codes specified in MARC21 documentation are defined for possible applications in X10 fields; many of those may not be relevant to the requirements of a particular instance of X10 fields. Field 110 and Field 710 both concern corporate name elements. Examples provided under Field 110 are applicable in Field 710 too.

Examples include only for those subfields which are relevant and commonly found in international databases.

Subfield $a

Subfield $a contains a corporate name.

710   2#$aNational Bureau of Economic Research.

710 2#$aSociety of Photo-optical Instrumentation Engineers.

710 2#$aOhio Genealogical Society. $bSouthwest Cuyahoga Chapter.

710 2#$aIndian Council of Historical Research. $esponsor

710 2#$aFederal Reserve Bank of Minneapolis. $bResearch Dept.

710 2#$aWorld Bank. $4clb

See examples of other subfield contents under Field 110

711 MEETING NAME - ADDED ENTRY (R)

Field 711 contains a meeting or conference name used as an added entry. Added entries are assigned according to various cataloging rules to give access to the bibliographic record from meeting or conference name headings which may not be more appropriately entered in field 611 or field 811.

A meeting entered directly under its own name is contained in the X11 fields.

Indicators		
1st	Type of meeting name entry element	
0	Inverted name	
1	Jurisdiction name	
2	Name in direct order	
2nd	Undefined; contains a blank	
Subfield code		
$a	Meeting name or jurisdiction name	R
$c	Location of meeting	N
$d	Date of meeting	NR
$e	Subordinate unit	R
$f	Date of a work	NR

$g	Miscellaneous information	NR
$h	Medium	NR
$k	Form subheading	R
$l	Language of a work	NR
$n	Number of part/section/meeting	R
$p	Name of part/section of a work	R
$q	Name of meeting following jurisdiction name	NR
$s	Version	NR
$t	Title of a work	NR
$u	Affiliation	NR
$x	International Standard Serial Number	NR
$3	Material specified	NR
$4	Relator code	R
$5	Institution to which field applies	NR
$6	Linkage	NR
$8	Field link and sequence number	R

SCOPE & EXAMPLES

Subfields

The subfield codes specified in MARC21 documentation are defined for possible applications in X11 fields; many of those may not be relevant to the requirements of a particular instance of X11 fields. Field 111 and Field 711 both concern corporate name elements. Examples provided under Field 111 are applicable in Field 711 too.

Examples include only for those subfields which are relevant and commonly found in international databases.

Subfield $a

Subfield $a contains name of a *temporary* corporate body which may be a conference, meeting, symposium, workshop, exhibition, etc.

711   2#$a International Conference on Information Visualisation $d(2003 : $cLondon., England)

711   2#$aIFLA General Conference $n(65th : $d1999 : $cBangkok, Thailand)

711   2#$aRound Table Conference on Business-led HR Strategies $d(1997 : $cNew Delhi, India)

711   2#$aConference of Public Sector Bank Economists $n(17th : $d1994 : $cGoa, India)

711   2#$aTwo Day National Conference on "Child Labour, Retrospect and Prospect" $d(1995 : $cCuttack, India)

711   2#$aMostly Mozart Festival.$eOrchestra.

711   2#$aICES Symposium on 100 Years of Science under ICES $d(2000 : $cHelsinki, Finland)

711   2#$aSymposium on Advanced Characterization Techniques for Data Storage Materials $d(2003 : $cBoston, Mass.)

711   2#$aInternational Symposium on Advanced Display Technologies $n(9th : $d2000 : $cMoscow, Russia)

711   2#$aInternational Symposium of Dynamic Games and Applications. $n(8th : $d1998 : $cMaastrich, Netherlands)

711   2#$aInternational Architectural Exhibition $n(7th : $d1999 : $cVenice, Italy)

711   2#$aIndo-Austrian Seminar and Exhibition of Picture Books from Austria and SAARC Countries $d(2001 : $cNew Delhi?, India)

711   2#$aInternational Conference on Environmental Problems in Coastal Regions $n(3rd : $d2000)

711   2#$aInternational Workshop on Advanced Internet Services and Applications $n(1st : $d2002 : $cSeoul, Korea)

711   2#$aNATO Advanced Research Workshop on Source Control Measures for Stormwater Runoff $d(2000 : $cSt. Marienthal-Ostritz, Germany)

711   2#$aAmerican Physical Society Topical Conference on Atomic Processes in Plasmas $n(14th : $d2004 : $cSanta Fe, N.M.)

See examples of various subfield contents under Field 111

740 Analytical Title - Added Entry (R)

Field 740 is *uncontrolled*, that is, not dependent on any authority file or thesaurus. It is used for providing additional access to:

- one or more titles related to the item recorded, or
- the analytical title(s) of the work(s) contained in the item recorded.

To record a collection *lacking a collective title*, where the title first appeared in a work takes place in field 245 (Title Statement), subsequent title(s), may enter in field 740.

Field 740 entries are recorded on the basis of data available in the item, without consulting any external authority file for validation. The 740 is used for uncontrolled analytical titles of independent works *contained within the item* and for titles of related items.

Indicator:	
1st	Nonfiling characters
0	No nonfiling characters present
1-9	Number of nonfiling characters present
2nd	Type of added entry
#	No information provided
2	Analytical entry

Subfield code:		
$a	Uncontrolled related/analytical title	N
$h	Medium	NR
$n	Number of part/section of a work	R
$p	Name of part/section of a work	R
$5	Institution to which field applies	NR
$6	Linkage	NR
$8	Field link and sequence number	R

Scope & Examples

Second indicator

Value # - No information provided

Value # (blank) is used when the added entry is not for an analytic or when no information is provided as to the type of added.

740 0#$aManual del adivino.

Value 2 - Analytical entry

Value 2 indicates that the item in hand contains the work that is represented by the added entry.

```
100     1#$aChekhov, Anton Pavlovich,$d1860-1904.
245     14$aThe cherry orchard ;$bUncle Vanya /$cAnton Chekhov.
740     02$aUncle Vanya.
```

Subfields

Subfield $a

Subfield $a contains the uncontrolled related/analytical title. Parenthetical data which may appear as part of the title should not be separately subfield coded.

```
245     04$aThe Buddhism omnibus /$cwith an introduction by
        Matthew T. Kapstein.
505     0$aGautama Buddha / Iqbal Singh — The Dhammapada /
        with introductory essays, Pali text, English translations
```

and notes, edited by S. Radhakrishnan — The philosophy of religion: a Buddhist perspective / Arvind Sharma.

740   02$aGautama Buddha.
740   02$aDhammapada.
740   02$aPhilosophy of religion.

245   10$aPuerto Rico, 2000.$p[Population and housing unit counts] :$b2000 census of population and housing = Puerto Rico, 2000.$pCifras de población y de unidades vivienda : censo 2000 de población y vivienda.
246   30$a2000 census of population and housing
246   30$aCenso 2000 de población y vivienda
546   ##$aParallel texts in English and Spanish bound together back to back and inverted, each with its own title page.
740   0#$aCifras de población y de unidades de vivienda.

Subfield $p

Subfield $p contains a **name** designation of a part or section of a work in a title.

245   10$aLaw and the family, New York /$c[by] Henry H. Foster and Doris Jones Freed.
500   ##$a"Joint Legislative Committee on Matrimonial and Family Laws, proposed statute":8 p. (inserted in pocket of v. 1).
505   1#$av.1. Dissolution of the family unit. Divorce, separation, and annulment — v. 2. Dissolution of the family unit. Economic aspects, custody, taxes.
740   02$aJoint Legislative Committee on Matrimonial and Family Laws, proposed statute.
740   02$aDissolution of the family unit.$pDivorce, separation, and annulment.

770 SUPPLEMENT/SPECIAL ISSUE ENTRY (R)

Field 770 contains information concerning supplements or special issues associated with the target item but cataloged as separate records (vertical relationship).

When a note is generated from this field, it is displayed /printed with a *display constant* based on the second indicator value.

Indicator:		
1st	Note controller	
0	Display note	
1	Do not display note	
2nd	Display constant controller	
#	Has supplement	
8	No display constant generated	
Subfield code:		
$a	Main entry heading	NR
$b	Edition	NR
$c	Qualifying information	NR
$d	Place, publisher, and date of publication	NR
$g	Relationship information	R

$h	Physical description	NR
$i	Display text	NR
$k	Series data for related item	R
$m	Material-specific details	NR
$n	Note	R
$o	Other item identifier	R
$r	Report number	R
$s	Uniform title	NR
$t	Title	NR
$u	Standard Technical Report Number	NR
$w	Record control number	R
$x	International Standard Serial Number	NR
$y	CODEN designation	NR
$z	International Standard Book Number	R
$6	Linkage	NR
$7	Control subfield	NR

Scope & Examples

Indicators

Second indicator

Display constant controller

Values in the second indicator position control generation of a *display constant* preceding the data in the linking entry field. The display constant **Has supplement** is not carried in the MARC record. It may be system generated based on the second indicator value.

Value # - Has supplement

Value # (blank) is needed to generate the display constant **Has supplement**:

Subfields

Subfield $a

The subfield codes specified in MARC21 documentation are defined for possible applications in 73X -8XX fields; many of those may not be relevant to the requirements of a particular field within that range. Field 770 and Field 730 both concern supplement title from two angles, as shown in *Example A,* and *Example B.*

Example A : The target item is a supplement. Field 730 links the parent publication.

245   04$aThe Calcutta municipal gazette : $bTagore memorial special supplement.

730   0#$aCalcutta Municipal Gazette.

Example B : Field 770 describes the supplement issued by the target item.

245   04$aThe Calcutta municipal gazette.

770   0#$tThe Calcutta municipal gazette. Tagore memorial special supplement.$w13081708

Note: Qualifying information is generally parenthetical information supplied by the cataloger, instead of using separate subfield designator $c.

770   0#$tThe Statesman. Weekly Supplement(Bengali)$w34652

Subfield $t

Subfield $t contains the title of the physically separate part of the item being catalogued.

245   00$aNews of the Cooperative Health Statistics System.

770   0#$tDirectory: United States, territories, and Canada $w(DLC)###78646712 $w(OCoLC)4579783

245   04$aThe Times magazine.

770   0#$tGuide to military installations in the U.S. $w(DLC) 91643451 $w(OCoLC)17834262

245   00$aVending times.

770   1#$tVending times. Census of the industry $w (OCoLC)12417128 $w(DLC) 2004257145

Subfield $g

Relationship information/Publication year(s)

770   0#$g1910-

770   0#$g1902-1968

Subfield $x

ISSN

770   0#$x0040-7887

770   0#$x0040-7895

770   0#$x0307-661X

Subfield $w

Record control number

770   0#$w(DLC) 91643451

770   0#$w(OCoLC)17834262

770   0#$w(DLC)###78646712

Examples of many 770 fields related to a single target record:

245   14$aThe times.

770   0#$tTimes educational supplement $g1910- $x0040-7887 $w(DLC) 18006784 $w(OCoLC)2239057

770   0#$tTimes educational supplement. Scotland $g1965-

770   0#$tTimes literary supplement $g1902-1968 $x0040-7895 $w(DLC)sn 89007753 $w(OCoLC)1767078

770   0#$tTLS, the Times literary supplement $g1969- $x0307-661X $w(DLC) 75644287 $w(OCoLC)2241740

800 Series Added Entry - Personal Name (R)

Field 800 contains an author/title series added entry in which the author portion is a personal name. It is used when the series' added entry form is different from that in the corresponding series statement. An 800 field is usually justified by a series statement(field 490) or a general note (field 500) relating to the series.

The content designators identify the sub-elements occurring in personal name fields constructed according to the generally accepted cataloging and thesaurus-building rules [e.g. *Anglo-American Cataloguing Rules* (AACR 2).

Indicator:		
1st	Type of personal name entry element	
0	Forename	
1	Surname	
3	Family name	
2nd	Undefined; contains a blank	
Subfield code:		
$a	Personal name	NR
$b	Numeration	NR

$c	Titles and other words associated with a name	R
$d	Dates associated with a name	NR
$e	Relator term	R
$f	Date of a work	NR
$g	Miscellaneous information	NR
$h	Medium	NR
$j	Attribution qualifier	R
$k	Form subheading	R
$l	Language of a work	NR
$m	Medium of performance for music	R
$n	Number of part/section of a work	R
$o	Arranged statement for music	NR
$p	Name of part/section of a work	R
$q	Fuller form of name	NR
$r	Key for music	NR
$s	Version	NR
$t	Title of a work	NR
$u	Affiliation	NR
$v	Volume/sequential designation	NR
$4	Relator code	R
$6	Linkage	NR
$8	Field link and sequence number	R

Scope & Examples

Subfields

The subfield codes specified in MARC21 documentation are defined for possible applications in X00 fields; many of those may not be relevant to the requirements of a particular instance of X00 fields. All of them concern personal name elements. Examples include only for those 800 Subfields which are relevant and commonly found in international databases.

Subfield $a

245 10$aLegends or lies? / $cby Gary L. Blackwood.
490 1#$aUnsolved history
800 1#$aBlackwood, Gary L. $tUnsolved history.

490 1#$aGesammelte Werke / Edgar Allan Poe ; $v1. Bd.
800 1#$aPoe, Edgar Allan,$d1809 1849.$tWorks.$lGerman. $f1922.$sRosl ; $v1. Bd.

490 1#$aThe James Joyce archive
800 1#$aJoyce, James,$d1882-1941.$tJames Joyce archive.

490 1#$aLouie Armstrong ; $v6.
800 1#$aArmstrong, Louis,$d1900-1971.$4prf$tLouie Armstrong (Universal City Studios) ; $v6.

Subfield $d

Dates associated with a name

800 1#$d1882-1941.

800 1#$d1932-

Subfield $t

800 1#$tJames Joyce archive.

800 1#$tWorks.

Subfield $l

800 1#$lGerman.

Subfield $f

Date of a work

800 1#$f1922.

Subfield $s

Version

800 1#$sRosl

Subfield $v

800   1#$v1. Bd.

Subfield $4

Relator code

800   1#$sprf

See under Field 100 for more examples of personal name elements.

830 SERIES ADDED ENTRY - UNIFORM TITLE (R)

Field 830 contains a title series added entry in which the entry of the series is *under uniform title*. It is used when the added entry form of a series title is different from that in the corresponding series statement. An 830 field is usually justified by a series statement (field 490) or a general note (field 500) relating to the series.

The content designators identify the sub-elements occurring in uniform or conventional title, title page title, or series title headings that are not entered under a name in a name/title heading. The subfield-contents are constructed according to the generally accepted cataloging and thesaurus-building rules, e.g. AACR2, LCSH.

Uniform titles used in phrase subject headings (e.g. *Bible and atheism*) are contained in field 650 (Subject Added Entry - Topical Term).

Indicator:	
1st	Undefined; contains a <u>blank</u>
2nd	Nonfiling characters
0	No nonfiling characters present
1-9	Number of nonfiling characters present

Subfield code:		
$a	Uniform title	NR
$d	Date of treaty signing	R
$f	Date of a work	NR
$g	Miscellaneous information	NR
$h	Medium	NR
$k	Form subheading	R
$l	Language of a work	NR
$m	Medium of performance for music	R
$n	Number of part/section of a work	R
$o	Arranged statement for music	NR
$p	Name of part/section of a work	R
$r	Key for music	NR
$s	Version	NR
$t	Title of a work	NR
$v	Volume/sequential designation	NR
$6	Linkage	NR
$8	Field link and sequence number	R

SCOPE WITH EXAMPLES

Subfields

The subfield codes specified in MARC21 documentation are defined for possible applications in X30 fields; many of those may not be relevant to the requirements of a particular instance of X30 fields. Examples provided here are only for those subfields which are relevant and commonly found in international databases.

Subfield $a

Subfield $a contains a uniform title. Parenthetical information added to make a title distinctive is not separately subfield coded [except in the case of the date of signing added to a uniform title of a treaty].

490　1#$aMesoamerican worlds : from the Olmecs to the Danzantes
830　#0$aMesoamerican worlds.

490　1#$a2004: Woman's day premier series
830　#0$aWoman's day premier series.

490　1#$a2005-: Woman's day new ideas series
830　#0$aWoman's day new ideas series.

490　1#$aEvents that changed the world series
830　#0$aEvents that changed the world.

Note: Parenthetical information with no separate subfield

245　00$aSocial theories of Jacksonian democracy : $b representative writings of the period 1825-1850 / edited, with an introduction, by Joseph L. Blau.
500　##$aOriginally published: Indianapolis : Bobbs-Merrill, c1954. (The American heritage series).
830　#0$aAmerican heritage series (New York, N.Y.)

490　1#$aLanguage and literacy *series*
830　#0$aLanguage and literacy series (New York, N.Y.)
830　#0$aEnvironmental studies (Southampton, England) ; $vv. 5.
830　#0$aSelect papers (University of Chicago. Center for East Asian Studies) ; $v no. 9.
830　#0$aMiddle East studies (Routledge (Firm))

Subfield $n

This is generally applicable in identifying a series within a series.

490　1#$aPerspectives on Christianity = $aPerspektiewe op die Christendom. Series 5 ; $v v. 1
830　#0$aPerspectives on Christianity. $nSeries 5, $vv. 1.

Subfield $v

490　1#$aMonograph series ; $vno. 33
710　2#$a**Asiatic Society** (Calcutta, India)
830　#0$a**Asiatic Society** monograph series ; $vno. 33.

830	#0$aParimala Samskrta granthamala ; $vsankhya 73.
490	1#$aPeleus : Studien zur Archäologie und Geschichte Griechenlands und Zyperns ; $vBd. 24
830	#0$aPeleus (Series) ; $v24.
490	1#$aDia Art Foundation, New York ; $vno. 2
830	#0$aDia Center for the Arts, New York (Series) ; $vno. 2.
490	1#$aWorcestershire Historical Society, $x0141-4577 ; $v new ser., v. 18
830	#0$aWorcestershire Historical Society (Series) ; $vnew ser., v 18.
490	1#$aPragmatics & beyond new series, $x0922-842X ; $vv. 127
830	#0$aPragmatics & beyond ; $vnew ser. 127.

850 HOLDING INSTITUTION (R)

The field contains the *MARC code* of the institution that holds the item recorded. The main purpose of the field content is to locate the resources. Cataloguing agencies record here their codes to provide the online viewer with minimum level holding data, i.e. the holding institution's name. The provision is particularly helpful for shared databases and online union catalogue.

Note: Organization codes can be used only if those are included in MARC Code List; otherwise, full name of the organizations may be entered in Field 850.

Indicator:		
1st	Undefined	
2nd	Undefined	
Subfield code:		
$a	Holding institution	R
$8	Field link and sequence number	R

Subfield $a

Subfield $a contains the MARC code or the name of the institution holding the item.

850	##$aAAP$aCU$aDLC$aMiU
850	##$aIiCaINL
850	##$aQGU
850	##$aNMQU
850	##$aWU

852 Location (r)

Field 852 provides information about physical location where copy of the target item may be available; whereas, the Field 850 provides only the identity of the host organization.

Field 852 is repeated when holdings are reported for multiple copies of an item and the location data elements vary.

Note: According to MARC guidelines, Field 852 may be used flexibly for identifying the host organization or for locating the item physically on shelf. Institutions have begun to increasingly use the MARC Holdings Format, as they attempt to gain better control of their collections.

It is, however, more helpful to use both the fields, 850 and 852, and treat identity and physical location at two levels in searching.

Indicator:	
1st	Shelving scheme
#	No information provided
0	Library of Congress classification
1	Dewey Decimal classification
2	National Library of Medicine classification
3	Superintendent of Documents classification

4	Shelving control number
5	Title
6	Shelved separately
7	Source specified in subfield $2
8	Other scheme
2nd	Shelving order
#	No information provided
0	Not enumeration
1	Primary enumeration
2	Alternative enumeration

Subfield code:

Location

$a	Location	NR
$b	Sub-location or collection	R
$c	Shelving location	R
$e	Address	R
$f	Coded location qualifier	R
$g	Non-coded location qualifier	R

Shelving designation

$h	Classification part	NR
$i	Item part	R
$j	Shelving control number	NR
$k	Call number prefix	NR
$l	Shelving form of title	NR
$m	Call number suffix	NR

Numbers/codes

$n	Country code	NR
$s	Copyright article-fee code	R
$t	Copy number	NR

Descriptors

$p	Piece designation	NR
$q	Piece physical condition	NR

Notes		
$x	Nonpublic note	R
$z	Public note	R
Control subfield		
$2	Source of classification or shelving scheme	NR
$3	Materials specified	NR
$6	Linkage	NR
$8	Link and sequence number	NR

SCOPE & EXAMPLES

Subfields

Subfield $a

Subfield **$a** identifies the institution or person holding the item or from which access is given. The field contains a MARC code of the holding institution or the name of the institution or person. The name contained in the subfield to be in a form suitable for external communications

852 ##$aDelhi University

852 ##$aUniversity of Calcutta$bDepartment of Radiophysics $eRajabazar Campus, Kolkata, India.

Subfield $b

Subfield **$b** may be repeated to indicate the organizational hierarchy of the sub location.

852 ##$aCSf$bSci$t1

852 ##$aNational Geographic Society$bPersonnel Dept.$e17th & M St., N.W., Washington, D.C. USA

852 81$aB.C. Roy Memorial Library$bLevel 2$bWest Wing $gCorporate Report Collection

Subfield $f

Subfield $f contains a two- or three-character code that identifies the specific issues of the item that are housed in a location different from that of the main holdings of the same item. A two-character alphabetic code is composed of Qualifier type and Unit type codes; a three-character code is composed of Qualifier type, Number of units, and Unit type codes. If the location qualifier cannot be expressed in coded form, or its units exceed 9, it may be described in subfield $g (Non-coded location qualifier).

The designation may be an identification number such as a bar code number or an accession number.

Subfield $g

Non-coded location qualifier

852   81$a<location identifier>$gRA$p1100064014 [*RA = Rare Book Collections*]

Subfield $h

Subfield $h contains the classification portion of the call number used as the shelving scheme for an item.

852   01$aNvLN$hZ67$i.L7

852   81$aFrPALP$hPer$iREF

[Reference periodicals all shelved together, unclassified.]

852   00$a<location qualifier>$kR$h301.15$i.H59$j25$k$m(3)

Note: A cataloging agency may like to adopt the same content designations for shelving organization in a local field *cf.* 9XX.

856 ELECTRONIC LOCATION AND ACCESS (R)

Field 856 contains details of electronic access to the item recorded for establishing online communications. The field may be used in a bibliographic record of a resource when that resource or a subset of it is accessible electronically. In addition, it may be used to locate and access an electronic version of a non-electronic resource described in the bibliographic record or a related electronic resource. Field 856 is repeated when the location data elements vary.

Indicators	
First	Access method
#	No information provided
0	Email
1	FTP
2	Remote login (Telnet)
3	Dial-up
4	HTTP
7	Method specified in subfield $2
Second	Relationship
#	Electronic resource

0	Electronic Resource	
1	Electronic Version	
2	Related electronic resource	
8	No display constant generated	
Subfield code:		
$a	Host name	R
$b	Access number	R
$c	Compression information	R
$d	Path	R
$f	Electronic name	R
$h	Processor of request	NR
$i	Instruction	R
$j	Bits per second	NR
$k	Password	NR
$l	Logon	NR
$m	Contact for access assistance	R
$n	Name of location of host in subfield $a	NR
$o	Operating system	NR
$p	Port	NR
$q	Electronic format type	NR
$r	Settings	NR
$s	File size	R
$t	Terminal emulation	R
$u	Uniform Resource Identifier	R
$v	Hours access method available	R
$w	Record control number	R
$x	Nonpublic note	R
$y	Link text	R
$z	Public note	R
$2	Access method	NR
$3	Materials specified	NR
$6	Linkage	NR
$8	Field link and sequence number	R

Scope & Examples

The data in field 856 may be a Uniform Resource Identifier (URI), which is recorded in subfield $u. An access method, or protocol used, is given as a value in the first indicator position; or if the access method is anything else in subfield $2. The access method is the first element of a URL. The field may also include a Uniform Resource Name or URN, e.g. a DOI (Digital Object Identifier) or handle.

Commonly used data elements

The most used data elements in field 856 are as follows:

- 1st indicator   = 4 for HTTP (earlier records may use blank)
- Subfield $u   = [HTTP URL]
- Subfield $3   : data specifying to what the URI refers, if applicable
- Subfield $z   : data relating to the electronic location of the source that is adequate for public display Indicators

Indicators

First Indicator (Access Method)

The first indicator contains information about the access method to the resource and has values defined for Email, FTP, Remote login (Telnet), Dial-up, and HTTP. Access methods *without defined values* may contain a *first indicator value 7* with the method indicated in *subfield $2*.

Value 7 and subfield $2 is used for electronic access to host-specific file names (i.e., files stored locally) with the access method, 'file.' This designation is also a defined URL scheme.

Second indicator (Relationship)

A second indicator is provided to show the relationship between the information in field 856 and the resource described in the record. This may be used for the generation of a display constant or for ordering multiple 856 fields.

Subfields

Subfield $3

Subfield $3 is used to specify to what portion or aspect of the resource the electronic location and access information applies. Specific situations may be:

- A portion or subset of the item is electronic

  $3table of contents; $3v. 2-5; $3abstract; $3b&w copy negative

- A related electronic resource is being linked to the record

  $3author's self-portrait

Subfield $q

Subfield $q was originally defined as File transfer mode to include 'binary' or 'ascii'. It was redefined in June 1997, as Electronic format type to accommodate an Internet Media Type (MIME type), such as text/html. Alternatively, textual information about the electronic format type may also be recorded.

Subfield $u (URI)

Subfield $u may be repeated only if both a URN and a URL or more than one URN are recorded. Field 856 is repeated if more than one URL needs to be recorded. Some institutions may wish to record a persistent name (URN) as well as a resolvable HTTP URL in field 856.

856   7#$dsawmp$f1694$uhttp://hdl.loc.gov/loc.mbrsmi sawmp.1694$uurn:hdl:loc.mbrsmi/sawmp.1694$2http

Subfield $y

Subfield $y contains link text, which is used for display in place of the URL in subfield $u. Often URLs are difficult to read and most systems do not display them to the user.

Subfield $z

Subfield $z may be used for any additional notes about the electronic resource at the specified location. Examples include subscription information or access restrictions. Subfield $z Include desired file format following the hyphen in the filename: EID0ASCII, EID-PDF or EID-PS.

Examples: Field 856 in context of title statement in field 245

Example A

245 10 $aAndré Breton : selections / $cAndré Breton ; edited and with an introduction by Mark Polizzotti.

856 42$3Contributor biographical information $uhttp://www.loc.gov/catdir/bios/ucal052/2003041009.html

856 41$3Table of contents $uhttp://www.loc.gov/catdir/toc/ucal041/2003041009.html

856 42$3Publisher description $uhttp://www.loc.gov/catdir/description/ucal042/2003041009.html

Example B

245 10$aPuerto Rico, 2000.$p[Population and housing unit counts] :$b2000 census of population and housing = Puerto Rico, 2000.$pCifras de población y de unidades vivienda : censo 2000 de población y vivienda.

856 41$3Spanish version$uhttp://purl.access.gpo.gov/GPO/LPS58487

More Examples: Field 856 with URL/URN:

856 42$3Essays from annual reports$uhttp://woodrow.mpls.frb.fed.us/pubs/ar/index.html

856 2#$utelnet://maine.maine.edu$nUniversityof Maine$t3270

856 1#$uftp://wuarchive.wustl.edu/mirrors2/win3/games/atmoids.zip $cdecompress with PKUNZIP.exe$xcannot verify because of transfer difficulty

856 42$3Finding aid$uhttp://lcweb2.loc.gov/ammem/ead/jackson.sgm

856 40$uhttp://lcweb2.loc.gov/ammem/gmdhtml/gmdhome.html

856 4#$3Table of contents $uhttp://www.loc.gov/catdir/toc/93-3471.html

Examples: Field 856 without URL/URN:

856   2#$aanthrax.micro.umn.edu$b128.101.95.23

856   0#$akentvm.bitnet$facadlist file1$facadlist file2$facadlist file3

866 TEXTUAL HOLDINGS - BASIC BIBLIOGRAPHIC UNIT (R)

This field contains a textual description of the holdings of a basic bibliographic unit in the collections of the reporting organization. It may be used self-sufficiently to record and display all or part of the holdings.

Note: A cataloging agency may, however, use in addition the field 863 (Enumeration and Chronology - Basic Bibliographic Unit) and related field 853 (Captions and Pattern - Basic Bibliographic Unit).

1st Indicator	
	Field encoding level
#	No information provided
3	Holdings level 3
4	Holdings level 4
5	Holdings level 4 with piece designation
2nd Indicator	
	Type of notation
0	Non-standard
1	ANSI Z39.44 or ANSI/NISO Z39.57
2	ANSI Z39.42

Subfield Codes	
$a	Textual holdings
$x	Nonpublic note
$z	Public note
$8	Link and sequence number

Scope & Examples

Indicators

First Indicator - Field encoding level:

The first indicator position contains a value that indicates the level of specificity of the enumeration and chronology in the field. Values 3 and 4 reflect requirements of Levels 3 and 4 of *Serial Holdings Statement* (ANSI Z39.44) and *Holdings Statement for Non-Serial Items* (ANSI/NISO Z39.57). Values 3, 4, and 5 correspond to the level of specificity defined for the enumeration and chronology data at the record level by codes 3, 4, and 5 in Leader/17 (Encoding level).

866-868 1st Indicator 3 - Holdings level 3:

Value 3 indicates that the field contains summary enumeration and chronology (that is only at the first level of enumeration and chronology in a compressed form).

866   31$80$a1-86 (1941-1987)$xbound in 2 v. per year$zSome issues missing

866-868 1st Indicator 4 - Holdings level 4:

Value 4 indicates that the field contains detailed enumeration and chronology (that is, at the first level and all subsequent levels and in either itemized or compressed form or a combination of the two).

866   4$80$a1974-1981$zSome issues lost

866-868 1st Indicator 5 - Holdings level 4 (piece designation):

Value **5** indicates that the field contains detailed enumeration and chronology information and an identifying number for the physical piece in subfield **$p** (Piece designation).

Second Indicator - Type of notation:

The second indicator position contains a value that indicates whether the holdings contained in subfield **$a** is formulated according to standard or non-standard notation.

866-868 2nd Indicator 1 - ANSI Z39.44 or ANSI/NISO Z39.57:

Value **1** indicates that the holdings are formulated according to either *Serial Holdings Statement* (Z39.44) or *Holdings Statements for Non-Serial Items* (Z39.57).

Subfields

Subfield $a

Subfield **$a** contains the textual form of the holdings.

866   31$60$a1-86 (1941-1987)

Subfield $x

Subfield **$x** contains a note relating to the field. The note is not written in a form that is adequate for public display. A note adequate for public display is contained in subfield **$z** (Public note).

866   31$60$a1-86 (1941-1987)$xbound in 2 v. per year$zbound in one volume

Subfield $z

Subfield **$z** contains a note relating to the field. The note is written in a form that is adequate for the public display. It contains information that cannot be contained in subfield **$a.** For example, it may be used to specifically record missing issues or numbering irregularities. A note for public display is contained in subfield **$x** (Nonpublic note).

866　　31$82$av. 37-52$zBound; some issues missing

866　　31$80$av. 36-49 (1961-1974)$xincomplete vols. unbound
　　　　$zsome issues missing

Subfield **$5** contains the MARC code of the institution or organization that holds the copy to which the data in the field applies. Data in the field may not apply to the universal description of the item or may apply universally to the item but be of interest only to the location cited.

880 Multiscript Records & Alternate Graphic Representations (r)

Field 880 contains representation of the data content of another field in the same record in a *different script*. A field 880 may be repeated to hold the same data in more than one script.

Every field 880 is linked to the associated regular field by a linking subfield $6. The alternate data field (Field 880) and the associated field both contain a subfield $6. Field 066 is used in records encoded with characters from sets *other than* ISO 10646 (or Unicode) to specify the character sets for data content that are present in the record. *See* discussion on Vernacular Languages in Part-I: Frequently asked questions, page 46.

When there is no general field associated in the record, field 880 is provided with a reserved *occurrence number* (00) to indicate its stand-alone status.

Indicator:						
1st	Same as associated field					
2nd	Same as associated field					

Subfield code:		
$6	Linkage	NR
$a-z, $0-5, 7-9	Same as associated field	

SCOPE & EXAMPLES

Multi-script Record Models

A multi-script record may be of two types, which are defined under Model A and Model B in MARC documentation.

MODEL A

Fields 880 are used *when data needs to be duplicated* to express it in *both* the original vernacular script and transliterated form. Records contain vernacular or transliterated text in a *regular field*. The texts are reproduced in the alternate field 880 in another script. Each pair of fields, *regular* and *alternate*, is interlinked with subfield $6.

245   1#$6880-03$aSanchayita:$bRabindranath Thakur
880   1#$6245-03/(B$aসঞ্চয়িতা$bরবীন্দ্রনাথ ঠাকুর

Subfield $6

It is always the first subfield in a field 880, and contains data that links fields with representations of different scripts. Subfield $6 may contain the tag number of an associated field, an occurrence number, a code that identifies the first script encountered, and the orientation for a display of the field data. Subfield $6 is structured as follows:

$6<linking tag>-<occurrence number>/<script identification code>/<field orientation code>

Linking tag and occurrence number

The *linking* part contains the tag number of the associated field, followed immediately by a hyphen. A two-digit *occurrence number* is assigned to each set of associated fields, which permits matching of the associated fields. It may be assigned *at random* for each set of associated fields. An *occurrence number* of less than two digits is right justified and the unused position contains a zero. Example:

100   1#$6800-01

245   10$6800-02

800   1#$6100-01

800   10$6245-02

Script identification code

The *occurrence number* is followed immediately by a slash (/) and the *script identification code*. This code identifies the alternate script found in the field. The following codes are used:

Code	Script
(3	Arabic
(B	Latin
$1	Chinese, Japanese, Korean
(N	Cyrillic
(2	Hebrew

Note: The Indic characters fall within the range of Latin-1 characters.

If more than one script is present in the field, subfield **$6** will contain the identification of the *first* alternate script encountered in a left-to-right scan of the field.

Orientation code

In a MARC record, the contents of field 880 are recorded in their logical order, from the first character to the last, regardless of field orientation. For a display of the field, the default field orientation is left-to-right. When the field contains text, e.g. Arabic, that has a right-to-left orientation, the *script identification code* is followed by a slash (/) and then the field *orientation code*. The MARC field *orientation code* for right-to-left scripts is the letter **r**, but it needs no mention as because left-to-right is default orientation in field 880. (See *MARC 21*

Specifications for Record Structure, Character Sets, and Exchange Media for a detailed description of field orientation). Example:

880   **10$6245-03/(B**$a<Title in Bengali script> : $b<Subtitle on Bengali script>.

[Primary script is Latin; alternate script is Bengali]

100   1#$6100-01$aরায়, অন্নদাশঙ্কর

245   10$6100-01$aবিনুর বই$Cঅন্নদাশঙ্কর রায়

880   **1#$6100-01**(B$aRay, Annadashankar

880   **10$6245-02**(B$a Binur Boi$cAnnadashankar Ray

880   **1#$6100-01**(B$aRay, Annadashankar

880   **10$6245-02**(B$a Binur Boi$cAnnadashankar Ray

100   1#$6880-01$a<Heading in Devanagari script>

880   10$6110-01/(2/r$a<Heading in Latin script linked to associated field>

100   1#$6800-01/(B$a शर्मा, विनय कुमार, $d 1960-

245   10$6800-02/(B$a उपनिशद योग तत्त्व दर्शन/$c विनय कुमार शर्मा

260   #$6800-03/(B$a दिल्ली : भारतीय विद्वान प्रकाशना, $c2004

800   1#$6100-01/(B$aSarmā, Vinaya Kumāra, $d1960-

800   10$6245-02/(B$a"Upanishad Yoga tattva darsana"/$c Vinaya Kumāra Sarmā.

800   ##$6260-03/(B$aDillī : $bBhāratiya Vidyā Prakāsana, $c2004.

Regular fields contain English texts and transliterated Japanese in Latin; Alternate fields contain texts in Japanese:

000 01613cam a2200409 a 450
001 5253176
005 19940928070206.0
008 940816s1993 ja 001 0 jpn d
035 __ |9 (DLC) 94465524
906 __ |a 7 |b cbc |c copycat |d u |e ncip |f 19 |g n-rlinjack
955 __ |a NS
010 __ |a 94465524
020 __ |a 4311700288 : |c Y1748
035 __ |a (CStRLIN)DCLP94-B16906
040 __ |a CU |c CU |d DLC-R
041 0_ |a jpneng
042 __ |a lccopycat
043 __ |a a-ja---
050 00 |a DS805 |b .S47 1993

066 __ |c $1

245 00 |6 880-01 |a Nihon, sono sugata to kokoro = |b Nippon, the land and its people / |c [kanshū] Shin Nihon Seitetsu Kabushiki Kaisha Nōryoku Kaihatsushitsu ; [chosha] Nittetsu Hyūman Deberopumento.

250 __ |6 880-02 |a Dai 4-han.

260 __ |6 880-03 |a Tōkyō : |b Gakuseisha, |c 1993.

300 __ |a 475 p. ; |c 18 cm.

500 __ |a Maps on lining papers.

500 __ |a Includes index.

500 __ |a Errata slip inserted.

651 _0 |a Japan |x Handbooks, manuals, etc.

710 2_ |6 880-04 |a Nittetsu Hyūman Deberopumento, Kabushiki Kaisha.

740 0_ |a Nippon, the land and its people.

880 00 |6 245-01/$1 |a 日本・その 姿 と 心 = |b Nippon, the land and its people / |c [監修] 新 日本 製鐵 株式 会社 能力 開発室 ; [著者] 日鉄 ヒューマン デベロプメント.

880 __ |6 250-02/$1 |a 第 4版.

880 __ |6 260-03/$1 |a 東京 : |b 学生社, |c 1993.

880 20 |6 710-04/$1 |a 日鉄 ヒューマン デベロプメント, 株式 会社.

922 __ |a ap

952 __ |a 09/28/94 T;08/16/94 T

991 __ |b c-Asian |h DS805 |i .S47 1993 |m Japan |w JACKPHY

Model B

A vernacular library requires its bibliographic records transcribed in native script, and may be some of the fields in Latin or other script. The records then comprises simple multiscript records with all data in *regular fields*. Field 880 is *not* involved since reproduction of text does not take place. This model of multi-script recording is found much more popular than Model A.

Multi-script Record consists of regular fields holding texts in Hebrew and Latin.

001   001607765

005   20030811113422.0

008   030806s200u——|||a||||r ||||000|| heb||

041   0#$a HEB

090   ##$a 901

100   1#$a עשוהי, ילאירא.

245   0$a היירוטסיה-הטמו הירוטסיה / $c רא עשוהי
           הנחוא דוד היפרגוילביבו

260   ##$a שורילי : $b מוסד ביאליק, $c תש"ג

300   ##$a ע' 598

590   ##$a לי-נל

651   0#$a United States $x History

650   0#$a Historians

650   0#$a History, Modern

700   1#$a דוד, הנחוא.

Multi-script Record consists of regular fields holding texts in Devanagari and Latin

001   xxxxxxxx

008   xxxxxxmxxxxxxxxxx000 0 hino

020   ## $a 8121701813

040   ## $a xxx $c xxx

041   0# $a hin $a san

100   1#

245   10

100   1#$a शर्मा, विनय कुमार, $d1960-
245   10$a उपनिषद योग तत्व दर्शन/$c विनय कुमार शर्मा
260   #$a दिल्ली : भारतीय विद्वान प्रकाशना, $c2004
800   1#$6100-01/(B$aSarma, Vinaya Kumara, $d1960-520
           ## $aStudy of Yoga *philosophy* as described in Upanishads, Hindu philosophical classic.

504   ## $aIncludes bibliographical references (p. [249]-253).

630   00 $aUpanishads $x Criticism, interpretation, etc.

650   #0 $aYoga.

Complete List of MARC Fields

The List covers all assigned and unassigned tags, including obsolete ones. For the usage of the tagged fields, the MARC21 Bibliographic Data Format and Holding Data Format are required to be consulted.

Variable Control Fields:

001   Control Number (NR)

002   unassigned

003   Control Number Identifier (NR)

004   unassigned

005   Date and Time of Latest Transaction (NR)

006   Fixed-Length Data Elements - Additional Material Characteristics (R)

007   Physical Description Fixed Field (R)

008   Fixed-Length Data Elements (NR)

009   Physical Description Fixed-Field for Archival Collection **[obsolete]** *Currently reserved for local use.*

Variable Data Fields:

Numbers and Codes:

010	Library of Congress Control Number (NR)
011	Linking Library of Congress Control Number [obsolete]
012	unassigned
013	Patent Control Information (R)
014	unassigned
015	National Bibliography Number (NR)
016	National Bibliographic Agency Control Number (R)
017	Copyright Registration Number (R)
018	Copyright Article-Fee Code (NR)
019	unassigned
020	International Standard Book Number (R)
021	unassigned
022	International Standard Serial Number (R)
023	Standard Film Number [deleted]
024	Other Standard Identifier (R)
025	Overseas Acquisition Number (R)
026	unassigned
027	Standard Technical Report Number (R)
028	Publisher Number (R)
029	unassigned
030	CODEN Designation (R)
031	unassigned
032	Postal Registration Number (R)
033	Date/Time and Place of an Event (R)
034	Coded Cartographic Mathematical Data (R)
035	System Control Number (R)

036	Original Study Number for Computer Data Files (NR)
037	Source of Acquisition (R)
038	unassigned
039	Level of Bibliographic Control and Coding Detail [obsolete]
040	Cataloging Source (NR)
041	Language Code (NR)
042	Authentication Code (NR)
043	Geographic Area Code (NR)
044	Country of Publishing/Producing Entity Code (NR)
045	Time Period of Content (NR)
046	Special Coded Dates (NR)
047	Form of Musical Composition Code (NR)
048	Number of Musical Instruments or Voices Code (R)
049	Local Holdings (NR)
050	Library of Congress Call Number (R)
051	Library of Congress Copy, Issue, Offprint Statement(R)
052	Geographic Classification (R)
053–054	unassigned
055	Call Numbers/Class Numbers Assigned in Canada (R)
056–059	unassigned
060	National Library of Medicine Call Number (R)
061	National Library of Medicine Copy Statement (R)
062–065	unassigned
066	Character Sets Present (NR)
067–069	unassigned
070	National Agricultural Library Call Number (R)
071	National Agricultural Library Copy Statement (R)
072	Subject Category Code (R)

073   unassigned

074   GPO Item Number (R)

075–079 unassigned

080   Universal Decimal Classification Number (R)

081   unassigned

082   Dewey Decimal Call Number (R)

083   unassigned

084   Other Call Number (R)

085   unassigned

086   Government Document Call Number (R)

087   Report Number **[obsolete]** [CAN/MARC only]

088   Report Number (R)

089   unassigned

090–099 Local Call Numbers

Main Entries:

100   Main Entry - Personal Name (NR)

101–109 unassigned

110   Main Entry - Corporate Name (NR)

111   Main Entry - Meeting Name (NR)

112–129 unassigned

130   Main Entry - Uniform Title (NR)

131–199 unassigned

Titles:

200–209 unassigned

210   Abbreviated Title (R)

211   Acronym or Shortened Title **[obsolete]**

212   Variant Access Title **[obsolete]**

213   unassigned

214   Augmented Title [**obsolete**]

215–221 unassigned

222   Key Title (R)

223–239 unassigned

240   Uniform Title (NR)

241   Romanized Title [**obsolete**]

242   Translation of Title by Cataloging Agency (R)

243   Collective Uniform Title (NR)

244   unassigned

245   Title Statement (NR)

246   Varying Form of Title (R)

247   Former Title or Title Variations (R)

248–249 unassigned

Edition, Imprint, Etc.:

250   Edition Statement (NR)

251–253 unassigned

254   Musical Presentation Statement (NR)

255   Cartographic Mathematical Data (R)

256   Computer File Characteristics (NR)

257   Country of Producing Entity for Archival Films (NR)

258–259 unassigned

260   Publication, Distribution, Etc. (Imprint) (NR)

261   Imprint Statement for Films (Pre-AACR 1 Revised) (NR) *(USA only)*

262   Imprint Statement for Sound Recordings (Pre-AACR 2) (NR) *(USA only)*

263   Projected Publication Date (NR)

264   unassigned

265   Source for Acquisition/Subscription Address [**obsolete**]

266–269 unassigned

270   Address (R)

271–299 unassigned

Physical Description, Etc.:

300   Physical Description (R)

301   Physical Description for Films (Pre-AACR 2) [obsolete]

302   Page Count [obsolete]

303   Unit Count [obsolete]

304   Linear Footage [obsolete]

305   Physical Description for Sound Recordings (Pre-AACR 2) [obsolete]

306   Playing Time (NR)

307   Hours, Etc. (R)

308   Physical Description for Films (Archival) [obsolete]

309   unassigned

310   Current Publication Frequency (NR)

311–314 unassigned

315   Frequency [obsolete]

316–320 unassigned

321   Former Publication Frequency (R)

322–339 unassigned

340   Physical Medium (R)

341   unassigned

342   Geospatial Reference Data (R)

343   Planar Coordinate Data (R)

344–349 unassigned

350   Price [obsolete]

351   Organization and Arrangement of Materials (R)

352   Digital Graphic Representation (R)

353–354 unassigned

355   Security Classification Control (R)

356   unassigned

357   Originator Dissemination Control (NR)

358   unassigned

359   Rental Price [obsolete]

360–361 unassigned

362   Dates of Publication and/or Sequential Designation (R)

363–399 unassigned

Series Statements:

400   Series Statement/Added Entry - Personal Name (R) *(USA only)*

401–409 unassigned

410   Series Statement/Added Entry - Corporate Name (R) *(USA only)*

411   Series Statement/Added Entry - Meeting Name (R) *(USA only)*

412–439 unassigned

440   Series Statement/Added Entry - Title (R)

441–489 unassigned

490   Series Statement (R)

491–499 unassigned

Notes:

500   General Note (R)

501   With Note (R)

502   Dissertation Note (R)

503   Bibliographic History Note [obsolete]

504   Bibliography, Etc. Note (R)

505	Formatted Contents Note (R)
506	Restrictions on Access Note (R)
507	Scale Note for Graphic Material (NR)
508	Creation/Production Credits Note (NR)
509	unassigned
510	Citation/References Note (R)
511	Participant or Performer Note (R)
512	Earlier or Later Volumes Separately Cataloged Note [obsolete]
513	Type of Report and Period Covered Note (R)
514	Data Quality Note (NR)
515	Numbering Peculiarities Note (R)
516	Type of Computer File or Data Note (R)
517	Categories of Films Note (Archival) [obsolete]
518	Date/Time and Place of an Event Note (R)
519	unassigned
520	Summary, Etc. (R)
521	Target Audience Note (R)
522	Geographic Coverage Note (R)
523	Time Period of Content Note [obsolete]
524	Preferred Citation of Described Materials Note (R)
525	Supplement Note (R)
526	Study Program Information Note (R)
527	Censorship Note [obsolete]
528–529	unassigned
530	Additional Physical Form Available Note (R)
531–532	unassigned
533	Reproduction Note (R)
534	Original Version Note (R)

535	Location of Originals/Duplicates Note (R)
536	Funding Information Note (R)
537	Source of Data Note [obsolete]
538	System Details Note (R)
539	unassigned
540	Terms Governing Use and Reproduction Note (R)
541	Immediate Source of Acquisition Note (R)
542	unassigned
543	Solicitation Information Note [obsolete]
544	Location of Other Archival Materials Note (R)
545	Biographical or Historical Data (R)
546	Language Note (R)
547	Former Title Complexity Note (R)
548–549	unassigned
550	Issuing Body Note (R)
551	unassigned
552	Entity and Attribute Information Note (R)
553–554	unassigned
555	Cumulative Index/Finding Aids Note (R)
556	Information About Documentation Note (R)
557–560	unassigned
561	Ownership and Custodial History (R)
562	Copy and Version Identification Note (R)
563–564	unassigned
565	Case File Characteristics Note (R)
566	unassigned
567	Methodology Note (R)
568–569	unassigned

570	Editor Note [**obsolete**]
571–579	unassigned
580	Linking Entry Complexity Note (R)
581	Publications About Described Materials Note (R)
582	Related Computer Files Note [**obsolete**]
583	Action Note (R)
584	Accumulation and Frequency of Use Note (R)
585	Exhibitions Note (R)
586	Awards Note (R)
587–589	unassigned
590–599	Local Notes (R)

Subject Access:

600	Subject Added Entry - Personal Name (R)
601–609	unassigned
610	Subject Added Entry - Corporate Name (R)
611	Subject Added Entry - Meeting Name (R)
612–629	unassigned
630	Subject Added Entry - Uniform Title (R)
631–649	unassigned
650	Subject Added Entry - Topical Term (R)
651	Subject Added Entry - Geographic Name (R)
652	Subject Added Entry - Reversed Geographic [**obsolete**]
653	Index Term - Uncontrolled (R)
654	Subject Added Entry - Faceted Topical Terms (R)
655	Index Term - Genre/Form (R)
656	Index Term - Occupation (R)
657	Index Term - Function (R)
658	Index Term - Curriculum Objective (R)

659-679 unassigned

680   PRECIS Descriptor String [**obsolete**, 1991] [CAN/MARC only]

681   PRECIS Subject Indicator Number (SIN) [**obsolete**, 1991] [CAN/MARC only]

682   unassigned

683   PRECIS Reference Indicator Number (RIN) [**obsolete**, 1991] [CAN/MARC only]

684-689 unassigned

690-699 Local Subject Access Fields (R)

Add Entries:

700   Added Entry - Personal Name (R)

701-704 unassigned

705   Added Entry - Personal Name (Performer) [**obsolete**]

706-709 unassigned

710   Added Entry - Corporate Name (R)

711   Added Entry - Meeting Name (R)

712-714 unassigned

715   Added Entry - Corporate Name (Performing Group) [**obsolete**]

716-719 unassigned

720   Added Entry - Uncontrolled Name (R)

721-729 unassigned

730   Added Entry - Uniform Title (R)

731-739 unassigned

740   Added Entry - Uncontrolled Related/Analytical Title (R)

741-750 unassigned

751   Geographic Name/Area Name Entry [**obsolete**] [CAN/MARC only]

752   Added Entry - Hierarchical Place Name (R)

753   System Details Access to Computer Files (R)

754   Added Entry - Taxonomic Identification (R)

755   Added Entry - Physical Characteristics [**obsolete**]

756–759 unassigned

Linking Entries:

760   Main Series Entry (R)

761   unassigned

762   Subseries Entry (R)

763–764 unassigned

765   Original Language Entry (R)

766   unassigned

767   Translation Entry (R)

768–769 unassigned

770   Supplement/Special Issue Entry (R)

771   unassigned

772   Parent Record Entry (R)

773   Host Item Entry (R)

774   Constituent Unit Entry (R)

775   Other Edition Entry (R)

776   Additional Physical Form Entry (R)

777   Issued With Entry (R)

778–779 unassigned

780   Preceding Entry (R)

781–784 unassigned

785   Succeeding Entry (R)

786   Data Source Entry (R)

787   Nonspecific Relationship Entry (R)

788–799 unassigned

Series Added Entries:

800   Series Added Entry - Personal Name (R)

801–809 unassigned

810   Series Added Entry - Corporate Name (R)

811   Series Added Entry - Meeting Name (R)

812–829 unassigned

830   Series Added Entry - Uniform Title (R)

831–839 unassigned

840   Series Added Entry - Title [obsolete]

Holdings, Alternate Graphics, Etc.:

841   Holdings Coded Data Values (NR) *Holdings Data Format*

842   Textual Physical Form Designator (NR) *Holdings Data Format*

843   Reproduction Note (R) *Holdings Data Format*

844   Name of Unit (NR) *Holdings Data Format*

845   Terms Governing Use and Reproduction Note (R) *Holdings Data Format*

846–849 unassigned

850   Holding Institution (R)

851   Location [obsolete]

852   Location (R)

853   Captions and Pattern - Basic Bibliographic Unit (R) *Holdings Data Format*

854   Captions and Pattern - Supplementary Material (R) *Holdings Data Format*

855   Captions and Pattern - Indexes (R) *Holdings Data Format*

856   Electronic Location and Access (R)

857–862 unassigned

863   Enumeration and Chronology - Basic Bibliographic Unit (R) *Holdings Data Format*

864	Enumeration and Chronology - Supplementary Material (R) *Holdings Data Format*
865	Enumeration and Chronology - Indexes (R) *Holdings Data Format*
866	Textual Holdings - Basic Bibliographic Unit (R) *Holdings Data Format*
867	Textual Holdings - Supplementary Material (R) *Holdings Data Format*
868	Textual Holdings - Indexes (R) *Holdings Data Format*
869	unassigned
870	Variant Personal Name [obsolete]
871	Variant Corporate Name [obsolete]
872	Variant Conference or Meeting Name [obsolete]
873	Variant Uniform Title Heading [obsolete]
874–875	unassigned
876	Item Information - Basic Bibliographic Unit (R) *Holdings Data Format*
877	Item Information - Supplementary Material (R) *Holdings Data Format*
878	Item Information - Indexes (R) *Holdings Data Format*
879	unassigned
880	Alternate Graphic Representation (R)
881–885	unassigned
886	Foreign MARC Information Field (R)
887–899	unassigned

Locally Defined Fields:

| 9XX | Locally-Defined Fields |

PART

3

Cataloging Resources

Contents

PART 3

MARC 21 Record Examples

The records belonging to the Library of Congress database are presented in this section in tagged display format as necessary input for learning MARC 21. The records are recent, and of assorted types representing content designations following current norms and principles.

The blank positions in indicators are displayed here as underscores (_). A vertical bar (I) is displayed for sub-Field delimiter.

Record # 1

```
000    01526cam 22003378a 450
001    13797762
005    20041217152205.0
008    041123s2005 nyu b 001 0 eng
906    __  |a 7 |b rix |c orignew |d 1 |e ecip |f 20 |g y-gencatlg
925    0_  |a acquire |b 2 shelf copies |x policy default
955    __  |a sf03 2004-11-23 |c sf03 2004-11-23; |a sd13 2004-11-26
            |d sf12 200 4-12-01 |e sf04 2004-12-02 to Dewey |a aa08
            2004-12-06
010    __  |a 2004027933
020    __  |a 0761418911
040    __  |a DLC |c DLC |d DLC
042    __  |a pcc
050    00  |a GR78 |b .B53 2005
```

| 082 | 00 |a 398.2/09 |2 22 |

100   1_ |a Blackwood, Gary L.

245   10 |a Legends or lies? / |c by Gary L. Blackwood.

260   __ |a New York : |b Marshall Cavendish Benchmark, |c c2005.

263   __ |a 0510

300   __ |a p. cm.

490   1_ |a Unsolved history

520   __ |a "Describes several legends that have intrigued people for centuries: the lost civilization of Atlantis, the Amazons, King Arthur, St. Brendan, Pope Joan, and El Dorado"—Provided by publisher.

504   __ |a Includes bibliographical references and index.

505   0_ |a The lost civilization — The women warriors — The lord of battles — The saint and the prince — The popess — The outlaw — The city of gold.

650   _0 |a Legends.

650   _0 |a Geographical myths.

800   1_ |a Blackwood, Gary L. |t Unsolved history.

856   41 |3 Table of contents |u http://www.loc.gov/catdir/toc/ ecip054/2004027933.html

963   __ |a Marilyn Mark; phone: 914-3328888; email: mmark@marshallcavendish.com; bc: mmark@marshallcavendish.com

Record # 2

000   01028cam 22002654a 450

001   12408969

005   20021001113039.0

008   010515s2001 enk b 001 0 eng

906   __ |a 7 |b cbc |c orignew |d 1 |e ecip |f 20 |g y-gencatlg

925   0_ |a acquire |b 2 shelf copies |x policy default

955   __ |a sb17 05-15-01; sb11 5/16/01; sb31 to Dewey 05-16-01; aa19 05-16-2001 |a ps11 2001-11-21 bk rec'd, to CIP ver. |a sb00 2001-11-26 |f sb21 2001-11-30 |g sb21 2001-11-30; |a Copy 2 to BCCD sp55 2002-10-01

010   __ |a 2001002917

020   __ |a 0714652288 (cloth)

040   __ |a DLC |c DLC |d DLC

042   __ |a pcc

050   00 |a JA71 |b .D76 2001

082   00 |a 320/.01 |2 21

100   1_ |a Dror, Yehezkel, |d 1928-

245	14	a The capacity to govern :	b a report to the Club of Rome /	c Yehezkel Dror.
260	__	a London ;	a Portland, OR :	b F. Cass,	c 2001.
300	__	a xvi, 264 p. ;	c 25 cm.
504	__	a Includes bibliographical references (p. 224-251) and index.
650	_0	a Political science.
650	_0	a Public administration.
710	2_	a Club of Rome.

Record # 3

000	01565cam 22003018a 450
001	13667907
005	20050225163045.0
008	040727s2004 cau b 001 0 eng
906	__ |a 7 |b rix |c orignew |d 1 |e ecip |f 20 |g y-gencatlg
925	0_ |a acquire |b 2 shelf copies |x policy default
955	__ |a sc21 2004-07-27 |c sc21 2004-07-27 (rev sc19) |d sc05 2004-08-02 |e sc02 2004-08-03 to Dewey |a aa20 2004-08-05 |a CAD uf22 2005-02-25
010	__ |a 2004017646
020	__ |a 0761932429 (hard back)
040	__ |a DLC |c DLC |d DLC
042	__ |a pcc
043	__ |a a-ii—
050	00 |a HQ1744.W47 |b C42 2004
082	00 |a 305.4/0954/14 |2 22
245	04 |a The changing status of women in West Bengal, 1970-2000 : |b the challenge ahead / |c edited by Jasodhara Bagchi.
260	__ |a Thausand Oaks, Calif : |b Sage Publications, |c 2004.
263	__ |a 0409
300	__ |a p. cm.
504	__ |a Includes bibliographical references and index.
505	0_ |a Demography / Nirmala Banerjee and Mukul Mukherjee — Health and nutrition / Maitreya Ghatak — Education / Jasodhara Bagchi and Jaba Guha — Economic empowerment / Ishita Mukhopadhyay — Political participation / Vidya Munshi — Culture / Malini Bhattacharya — Law and violence against women / Manjari Gupta and Ratnabali Chattopadhyay — Tribal women / Anuradha Chanda.
650	_0 |a Women |z India |z West Bengal.

700   1_ |a Bagchi, Jasodhara.
856   41 |3 Table of contents |u http://www.loc.gov/catdir/toc/
        ecip0421/2004017646.html

Record # 4

000   01233cam 2200349 a 450
001   13699372
005   20050302162755.0
008   040617r20031968ii ab b 000 0 eng
035   __ |a (DLC) 2004328424
906   __ |a 7 |b cbc |c origode |d 3 |e ncip |f 20 |g y-gencatlg
925   0_ |a acquire |b 1 shelf copy |x policy default
955   __ |a wd36 2004-07-06 to RCCD |e yk00 2005-03-02 to Dewey
010   __ |a 2004328424
020   __ |a 8172361440
025   __ |a I-E-2004-328424; 60-91
037   __ |b Library of Congress — New Delhi Overseas Office |c
        Rs450.00 ($45.00 U.S.)
040   __ |a DLC |c DLC
041   0_ |a eng |a per
042   __ |a lcode
043   __ |a a-ii—- |a a-bg—
050   00 |a DS485.B47 |b B6 2003
100   1_ |a Blochmann, H. |q (Henry), |d 1838-1878.
245   10 |a Contributions to the geography and history of Bengal
        : |b Muhammedan period / |c H. Blochmann.
260   __ |a Kolkata : |b Asiatic Society, |c 2003.
300   __ |a iv, 170 p. : |b ill., 1 folded map ; |c 24 cm.
500   __ |a Originally published: 1968.
546   __ |a Includes passages in Persian.
504   __ |a Includes bibliographical references.
651   _0 |a Bengal (India) |x History.
710   2_ |a Asiatic Society (Calcutta, India)

Record # 5

000   01235cam 22003258a 450
001   13909492
005   20050401103900.0
008   050323s2005 cau b 001 0 eng
906   __ |a 7 |b cbc |c orignew |d 1 |e ecip |f 20 |g y-gencatlg
925   0_ |a acquire |b 2 shelf copies |x policy default

955   __ |a sc21 2005-03-23 |c sc21 2005-03-23 |d sc17 2005-03-30 |e sc02 2005-03-30 to Dewey |a aa08 2005-04-01

010   __ |a 2005007840

020   __ |a 0761933476 (hard back)

040   __ |a DLC |c DLC

042   __ |a pcc

043   __ |a a-ii—

050   00 |a HD876 |b .C66 2005

082   00 |a 333.3/0285 |2 22

245   00 |a Computerisation of land records in India / |c edited by Wajahat Habibullah, Manoj Ahuja.

246   3_ |a Computerization of land records in India

260   __ |a Thousand Oaks, Calif. : |b Sage Publications, |c 2005.

263   __ |a 0505

300   __ |a p. cm.

440   _0 |a Land reforms in India ; |v v. 10

504   __ |a Includes bibliographical references and index.

650   _0 |a Land tenure |z India |x Data processing.

650   _0 |a Land titles |z India |x Data processing.

700   1_ |a Habibullah, Wajahat, |d 1945-

700   1_ |a Ahuja, Manoj, |d 1964-

Record # 6

000   01890cam 22003977a 450

001   13690887

005   20050225111440.0

008   040818s2004 abc 101 0 eng d

906   __ |a 7 |b cbc |c copycat |d 2 |e ncip |f 20 |g y-gencatlg

925   0_ |a acquire |b 2 shelf copies |x policy default

955   __ |a nb28 2004-08-18 Preprocessor Copy 1 to ASCD |a jp00 2004-09-14 |d jp18 2005-02-17 to SL |e jp14 2005-02-25 to Dewey

010   __ |a 2004444746

020   __ |a 0973281219

035   __ |a (OCoLC)ocm55985778

040   __ |a SCA |c SCA |d DLC

041   0_ |a eng |f fre

042   __ |a lccopycat

043   __ |a n-cn—

050   00 |a QC851 |b .C24 2004

110   2_ |a Canadian Meteorological and Oceanographic Society. |b Congress |n (38th : |d 2004 : |c Edmonton, Alberta, Canada)

245	10 |a Human dimensions of weather and climate : |b program and abstracts : 38th CMOS Congress, 31 May-03 June, 2004, Edmonton, Alberta = La dimension humaine de la météo et du climat : programme et résumés / |c editorial team, Geoff Strong ... [et al.].
246	30	a Human dimensions of weather and climate
246	31	a Dimension humaine de la métò et du climat
246	30	a Program and abstracts
246	30	a Programme et résumés
246	14	a 38th Congress of the Canadian Meteorological and Oceanographic Society
246	14	a 38ième congrès de la société canadienne de mé
260	__ |a Edmonton, Alberta, Canada : |b Canadian Meteorological and Oceanographic Society, |c [2004]
300	__ |a xlvi, 182 p. ; |c 28 cm.
546	__	a In English; table of contents also in French.
500	__	a At head of title: Canadian Meteorological and Oceanographic Society; La Société Canadienne de Météorologie et d'Océanographie.
500	__	a Includes index.
650	_0 |a Meteorology |z Canada |v Congresses.
651	_0 |a Canada |x Climate |v Congresses.
700	1_	a Strong, Geoff.
710	2_	a Canadian Meteorological and Oceanographic Society.

Record # 7

000	01422cam 2200289 a 450
001	12193692
005	20010314121918.0
008	001003s2001 cau b 001 0 eng
906	__ |a 7 |b cbc |c orignew |d 1 |e ocip |f 20 |g y-gencatlg
925	0_ |a acquire |b 1 shelf copy |x policy default
955	__ |a to HLCD pc05 10-03-00; AA3d lk50 received for descriptive Oct 5, 2000; AA3s lk29 received for subject Oct 6, 2000; to SL 10-06-00; lj05 to Dewey 10-20-00; aa19 10-20-2000 ; vols 1-2 rec'd, to CIP ver. ps17 03/06/01; CIP ver. lh04 to SL 03-14-01; lj05 sent copy 1, v. 1-2 to BCCD 03-14-01
010	__ |a 00050339
020	__ |a 1565109899 (v. 1 : lib. bdg. : alk. paper)
020	__ |a 1565109880 (v. 2 : pbk. alk. paper)
020	__ |a 1565109910 (v. 2 : lib. bdg. : alk. paper)
020	__ |a 1565109902 (v. 2 : pbk. : alk. paper)

040	__	a DLC	c DLC
050	00	a CB245	b .W475 2001
082	00	a 909/.09821	2 21
245	00	a Western civilization :	b original and secondary source readings /	c Benjamin C. Sax, book editor.
260	__	a San Diego, Calif. :	b Greenhaven Press,	c c2001.
300	__	a 2 v. ;	c 26 cm.
440	_0	a Perspectives on history
504	__	a Includes bibliographical references and index.
505	0_	a v. 1. From the origins of civilization to the age of absolutism − v. 2. From the scientific revolution to the present.
650	_0	a Civilization, Western	x History.
700	1_	a Sax, Benjamin C.,	d 1950-

Record # 8

000	01871cam a2200397 a 450
001	13799352
005	20050411095046.0
008	040918s2004 ii b s f000 0 eng
035	__ |a (DLC) 2004329970
906	__ |a 7 |b cbc |c origode |d 2 |e ncip |f 20 |g y-gencatlg
925	0_ |a acquire |b 1 shelf copy |x policy default
955	__ |a wd32 2004-10-07 to RCCD |e yj12 2005-04-11 to BCCD
010	__ |a 2004329970
025	__ |a I-E-2004-329970
037	__ |b Library of Congress − New Delhi Overseas Office |c Rs815.00 ($44.00 U.S. : set)
040	__ |a DLC |c DLC
041	0_ |a eng |a hin
042	__ |a lcode
043	__ |a a-ii−
050	00 |a HD7361.W47 |b C46 2004
245	00 |a Census of India, 2001. |n Series 20, West Bengal : |b tables on houses, household amenities, and assets / |c [compiled by] Viktam Sen = Bharata ki janaganòana, 2001. Sìr.nkhala 20, Paoscima Banògala : makanomò, parivaromò ko upalabdha suvidhaomò, tatha parisampatti sambandhita saraniyam / [compiled by] Vikrama Sena.
246	31 |a Bharata ki janaganòana, 2001. Sìr.nkhala 20,Pasìcima Banògala : makanomò, parivaromò ko upalabdha suvidhaomò, tatha parisampatti sambandhita saraniyam

260	__	|a Delhi : |b Controller *of* Publications, |c 2004.
300	__	|a 798 p. : |b col. map ; |c 30 cm.
546	__	|a English and Hindi.
500	__	|a Issued by Director *of Census* Operations, West Bengal.
500	__	|a "PRG-224 (W.B.)/750-2004 (DSK-II)"—P. 4 *of* Cover.
500	__	|a Chiefly statistical tables.
650	_0	|a Housing |z *India* |z West Begal |v Statistics.
650	_0	|a Households |z *India* |z West Bengal |v Statistics.
651	_0	|a West Bengal (India) |v *Census, 2001.*
651	_0	|a *India* |v *Census, 2001.*
700	1_	|a Sen, Vikram.
710	1_	|a *India.* |b Director *of Census* Operations, West Bengal.
985	__	|e ODE-nd
991	__	|b c-GenColl |o am |p 00131061535

Fields 245, 246 and 700 show some discrepancies in Indic names.

Record # 9

000		01233cam 2200349 a 450
001		13699372
005		20050302162755.0
008		040617r20031968ii ab b 000 0 eng
035	__	|a (DLC) 2004328424
906	__	|a 7 |b cbc |c origode |d 3 |e ncip |f 20 |g y-gencatlg
925	0_	|a acquire |b 1 shelf copy |x policy default
955	__	|a wd36 2004-07-06 to RCCD |e yk00 2005-03-02 to Dewey
010	__	|a 2004328424
020	__	|a 8172361440
025	__	|a I-E-2004-328424; 60-91
037	__	|b Library of Congress — New Delhi Overseas Office |c Rs450.00 ($45.00 U.S.)
040	__	|a DLC |c DLC
041	0_	|a eng |a per
042	__	|a lcode
043	__	|a a-ii—- |a a-bg—
050	00	|a DS485.B47 |b B6 2003
100	1_	|a Blochmann, H. |q (Henry), |d 1838-1878.
245	10	|a Contributions to the geography and history of Bengal : |b Muhammedan period / |c H. Blochmann.
260	__	|a Kolkata : |b Asiatic Society, |c 2003.
300	__	|a iv, 170 p. : |b ill., 1 folded map ; |c 24 cm.
500	__	|a Originally published: 1968.

546	__	|a Includes passages in Persian.
504	__	|a Includes bibliographical references.
651	_0	|a Bengal (India) |x History.
710	2_	|a Asiatic Society (Calcutta, India)
985	__	|e ODE-nd
991	__	|b c-GenColl |o am |p 0011633690A

Record # 10

000	01028cam 22002654a 450
001	12408969
005	20021001113039.0
008	010515s2001 enk b 001 0 eng
906	__ |a 7 |b cbc |c orignew |d 1 |e ecip |f 20 |g y-gencatlg
925	0_ |a acquire |b 2 shelf copies |x policy default
955	__ |a sb17 05-15-01; sb11 5/16/01; sb31 to Dewey 05-16-01; aa19 05-16-2001 |a ps11 2001-11-21 bk rec'd, to CIP ver. |a sb00 2001-11-26 |f sb21 2001-11-30 |g sb21 2001-11-30; |a Copy 2 to BCCD sp55 2002-10-01
010	__ |a 2001002917
020	__ |a 0714652288 (cloth)
040	__ |a DLC |c DLC |d DLC
042	__ |a pcc
050	00 |a JA71 |b .D76 2001
082	00 |a 320/.01 |2 21
100	1_ |a Dror, Yehezkel, |d 1928-
245	14 |a The capacity to govern : |b a report to the Club of Rome / |c Yehezkel Dror.
260	__ |a London ; |a Portland, OR : |b F. Cass, |c 2001. 300 __ |a xvi, 264 p. ; |c 25 cm.
504	__ |a Includes bibliographical references (p. 224-251) and index.
650	_0 |a Political science.
650	_0 |a Public administration.
710	2_ |a Club of Rome.

Record # 11

000	01565cam 22003134a 450
001	13233218
005	20040423100749.0
008	030610s2003 njua b 101 0 eng
035	__ |a (DLC) 2003108222

906	__	|a 7 |b cbc |c orignew |d 2 |e epcn |f 20 |g y-gencatlg
925	0_	|a acquire |b 2 shelf copies |x policy default
955	__	|a pc14 2003-06-10 |a pv21 2004-02-05 two copies to ASCD |a ja00 marcadia 2004-02-14 |a jf00 2004-03-02; |c jf03 2004-04-07 to Subj. |e jf12 2004-04-09 to Dewey |a aa07 2004-04-23
010	__	|a 2003108222
020	__	|a 0769520014 (pbk.)
040	__	|a DLC |c DLC |d DLC
042	__	|a pcc
050	00	|a TK7882.I6 |b I65 2003
082	00	|a 006.6 |2 220
111	2_	|a International Conference on Coordinated & Multiple Views in Exploratory Visualization |d (2003 : |c London, England)
245	10	|a Proceedings, International Conference on Coordinated & Multiple Views in Exploratory Visualization : |b CMV 2003, 15 July 2003, London, England / |c edited by Jonathan Roberts.
246	30	|a CMV 2003
246	18	|a International Conference on Coordinated & Multiple Views in Exploratory Visualization
260	__	|a Piscataway, NJ : |b IEEE Computer Society, |c 2003.
300	__	|a viii, 134 p. : |b ill. ; |c 28 cm.
500	__	|a "Associated and co-located with International Conference on Information Visualisation (IV03)."
504	__	|a Includes bibliographical references and index.
650	_0	|a Information visualization |v Congresses.
700	1_	|a Roberts, Jonathan |q (Jonathan C.)
711	2_	|a International Conference on Information Visualisation |d (2003 : |c London., England)

Record # 12

000	00914cam 22002771 450
001	7519750
005	20040423064927.0
008	711227s1963 enk 000 0 eng
035	__ |9 (DLC) 64054589
906	__ |a 7 |b cbc |c oclcrpl |d u |e ncip |f 19 |g y-gencatlg
010	__ |a 64054589
015	__ |a GB64-2017
035	__ |a (OCoLC)187247
040	__ |a DLC |c OAU |d OCoLC |d Uk |d DLC

050	00		a Z3501	b .S8
110	2_		a Standing Conference on Library Materials on Africa.
245	14		a The Scolma directory of libraries and special collections on Africa.
250	__		a [1st ed.
260	__		a Cambridge, Eng.,	b Distributed by W. Heffner]	c 1963.
300	__		a 101, 18 p.	c 18 cm.
500	__		a Cover title.
500	__		a "Five hundred copies ... produced."
651	_0		a Africa	x Library resources.
650	_0		a Library resources	z Great Britain.
985	__		e OCLC REPLACEMENT
991	__	|b c-GenColl |h Z3501 |i .S8 |t Copy 1 |w OCLCREP

Record # 13

000	01479cas 2200349 a 450
001	13871720
005	20050217133105.0
008	950522u1992uuuunyu x i0 0eng d
906	__	|a 7 |b cbc |c serials |d 3 |e ncip |f 20 |g n-oclcserc
925	0_	|a Acquire |b 1 shelf copy |x Policy default 02-15-05
955	__	|i db44 2005-02-15 to Cat. Tech. |g db21 2005-02-17 to BCCD
010	__	|a 2005204679
035	__	|a (OCoLC)ocm34168076
040	__	|a ICU |c ICU |d DLC
012	__	|a -3-7-0502110277-p——
042	__	|a lc
050	00	|a HF1428 |b .U48b
110	2_	|a United Nations Conference on Trade and Development. |b Standing Committee on Commodities.
245	10	|a Report of the Standing Committee on Commodities on its ... session / |c United Nations Conference on Trade and Development.
260	__	|a New York ; |a Geneva : |b United Nations,
300	__	|a v. ; |c 30 cm.
310	__	|a Irregular
362	1_	|a Began with: 1st (19 to 23 Oct. 1992).
500	__	|a "TD/B."
500	__	|a "TB/B/CN."
500	__	|a Description based on: 2nd (31 Jan. to 4 Feb. 1994).
500	__	|a Latest issue consulted: 4th (30 OCt. to 3 Nov. 1995).

610	20	a United Nations Conference on Trade and Development.	b Standing Committee on Commodities.
650	_0	a Commodity control.
650	_0	a International trade.
780	00 |a United Nations Conference on Trade and Development. Committee on Commodities. |t Report of the Committee on Commodities on its ... session |w (DLC)sn 85017469 |w (OCoLC)1713918
850	__	a DLC

Record # 14

000	01447nam 22003855a 450
001	13842133
005	20050113190452.0
008	041206s2005 ii b 010 0 eng
035	__ |a (DLC) 2004309352
906	__ |a 7 |b ibc |c origode |d 3 |e ncip |f 20 |g y-gencatlg
925	0_ |a acquire |b 1 shelf copy |x policy default
955	__ |a wd24 2004-12-16 to RCCD
010	__ |a 2004309352
020	__ |a 8177020986
025	__ |a I-E-2004-309352; 06-92; 23
037	__ |b Library of Congress — New Delhi Overseas Office |c Rs1000.00
040	__ |a DLC |c DLC
041	0_ |a eng |a san
042	__ |a lcode
043	__ |a a-ii—
050	00 |a BL1112.26 (BL1)+
245	00 |a Facets of Indology : |b Mahamahopadhyaya Pandit Damodhar Mahapatra Shastri commemoration volume / |c editor, Subash Chandra Dash.
250	__ |a 1st ed.
260	__ |a Delhi : |b Pratibha Prakashan, |c 2005.
300	__ |a xvi, 502 p. ; |c 22 cm.
546	__ |a Includes some articles in Sanskrit.
520	__ |a Festschrift in honor of Damodhar Mahapatra Shastri, 1890-1975, Sanskritist; comprises rsearch articles on Vedic literature, religion, and Sanskrit grammar.
504	__ |a Includes bibliographical references.
650	_0 |a Vedic literature |x History and criticism.
650	_0 |a Philosophy, Hindu.

650	_0	a Sanskrit language	x Grammar.
700	1_	a Shastri, Damodhar Mahapatra,	d 1890-1975.
700	1_	a Dash, Subas Chandra.
985	__	e ODE-nd
991	__	b c-GenColl	o am	p 00131069017

Record # 15

000	01488cam 2200361 a 450
001	13081708
005	20030721123740.0
008	021129r20021941ii a s010 0deng
035	__ |a (DLC) 2002298093
906	__ |a 7 |b cbc |c origode |d 3 |e ncip |f 20 |g y-gencatlg
925	0_ |a acquire |b 1 shelf copy |x policy default
955	__ |a wd34 2002-11-29 to RCCD |e yj12 2003-06-27 to Dewey |a aa05 2003-07-21
010	__ |a 2002298093
025	__ |a I-E-2002-298093; 61-34
037	__ |b Library of Congress — New Delhi Overseas Office |c Rs500.00
040	__ |a DLC |c DLC |d DLC
041	0_ |a engori
042	__ |a lcode
043	__ |a a-ii—
050	00 |a PK1725 |b .C33 2002
082	00 |a 891.4/414 |2 22
245	04 |a The Calcutta municipal gazette : |b Tagore memorial special supplement.
246	3_ |a Tagore memorial special supplement
250	__ |a 3rd ed.
260	__ |a Kolkata : |b Kolkata Municipal Corporation and New Age Publishers Pvt., Ltd., |c 2002.
300	__ |a 199 p. : |b ill. ; |c 33 cm.
500	__ |a Originally published: Calcutta, 1941.
546	__ |a Includes passages in Bengali.
520	__ |a Festschrift reprinted on the occasion of Rabindranath Tagore's, 1861-1941 one hundred and twenty-fifth birth anniversary; contributed articles on his life and works published as part of the Calcutta Municipal Gazette.
600	10 |a Tagore, Rabindranath, |d 1861-1941 |x Criticism and interpretation.
730	0_ |a Calcutta Municipal Gazette.

```
985     __  |e ODE-nd
991     __  |b c-GenColl |o am |p 00089369496
```

Record # 16

```
000     01255cam 22003258a 450
001     13816901
005     20050203182911.0
008     041216s2005 cau b 001 0 eng
906     __  |a 7 |b rix |c orignew |d 1 |e ecip |f 20 |g y-gencatlg
925     0_  |a acquire |b 2 shelf copies |x policy default
955     __  |a yj17 2004-12-16 RCCD/SA |i yj17 2004-12-16 RCCD |a
            aa19 2004-12-16
010     __  |a 2004029996
020     __  |a 0761933352 (hardback)
040     __  |a DLC |c DLC |d DLC
042     __  |a pcc
043     __  |a a-ii— |a a-bg—
050     00  |a DS422.C64 |b B385 2005
082     00  |a 954/.140359 |2 22
100     1_  |a Batabyal, Rakesh, |d 1966-
245     10  |a Communalism in Bengal : |b from famine to Noakhali,
            1943-47 / |c Rakesh Batabyal.
260     __  |a Thousand Oaks, Calif. : |b Sage Publications, |c 2005.
263     __  |a 0501
300     __  |a p. cm.
440     _0  |a Sage series in modern Indian history ; |v 6
504     __  |a Includes bibliographical references and index.
650     _0  |a Communalism |z India |z Bengal |x History.
650     _0  |a Famines |x Political aspects |z India |z Bengal.
650     _0  |a Riots |z Bangladesh |z Noakhali District |x History.
856     41  |3 Table of contents |u http://www.loc.gov/catdir/toc/
            ecip055/2004029996.html
963     __  |a Subir Lahiri; phone: (911) 26491290; email:
            slahiri@indiasage.com
```

Record # 17

```
000     00894cam 22002411 450
001     3590275
005     19990107112747.0
008     740605m19689999maua b 001 0 eng
035     __  |9 (DLC) 67026020
```

906	__	a 7	b cbc	c orignew	d u	e ocip	f 19	g y-gencatlg
010	__	a 67026020
040	__	a DLC	c DLC	d DLC
050	00	a QA76.5	b .K57
082	00	a 651.8
100	1_	a Knuth, Donald Ervin,	d 1938-
245	14	a The art of computer programming	c [by] Donald E. Knuth.
260	__	a Reading, Mass.,	b Addison-Wesley Pub. Co.	c 1968-
300	__	a v.	b illus.	c 25 cm.
490	0_	a Addison-Wesley series in computer science and information processing
504	__	a Includes bibliographical references and index.
505 1	_	a v. 1. Fundamental algorithms.—v. 2. Semi-numerical algorithms.—v. 3. Sorting and searching.
650	_0	a Computer programming.
991	__	b c-GenColl	h QA76.5	i .K57	t Copy 1	w BOOKS

Record # 18

000	01572cam 22003618a 450
001	13654875
005	20040816131748.0
008	040714s2005 inu b 001 0 eng
906	__ |a 7 |b rix |c orignew |d 1 |e ecip |f 20 |g y-gencatlg
925	0_ |a acquire |b 2 shelf copies |x policy default
955	__ |a jh52 2004-07-14 |c jh52 2004-07-14 |d jh34 2004-07-15 to SL |e jh85 200 4-07-16 to Dewey |a aa08 2004-07-19
010	__ |a 2004016533
020	__ |a 0253344875 (cloth : alk. paper)
040	__ |a DLC |c DLC |d DLC
042	__ |a pcc
043	__ |a a-ii—
050	00 |a NA6007.B4 |b G55 2005
082	00 |a 726/1/09541409032 |2 22
100	1_ |a Ghosh, Pika, |d 1969-
245	10 |a Temple to love : |b architecture and devotion in seventeenth-century Bengal / |c Pika Ghosh.
260	__ |a Bloomington : |b Indiana University Press, |c 2005.
263	__ |a 0502
300	__ |a p. cm.
440	_0 |a Contemporary Indian studies
504	__ |a Includes bibliographical references and index.

505	0_	a Desire, devotion, and the double-storied temple — A paradigm shift — Acts of accommodation — Axes and the mediation of worship — New sacred center.
650	_0 |a Temples |z India |z Bengal.
650	_0 |a Architectural terra-cotta |z India |z Bengal.
650	_0 |a Terra-cotta sculpture, Indic |z India |z Bengal.
650	_0 |a Architecture |z India |z Bengal |y 17th century.
650	_0	a Architecture and religion.
856	41 |3 Table of contents |u http://www.loc.gov/catdir/toc/ecip0420/2004016533.html
963	__	a Jane Lyle; phone: 812-855-9686; fax: 812-855-8507; email: jlyle@indiana.edu; bc: jlyle@indiana.edu

Record # 19

000	01432nam 22003495a 450
001	13833202
005	20050106190950.0
008	041026s2005 ii b 001 0 eng
035	__ |a (DLC) 2004309448
906	__ |a 7 |b ibc |c origode |d 3 |e ncip |f 20 |g y-gencatlg
925	0_ |a acquire |b 1 shelf copy |x policy default
955	__ |a wd30 2004-12-06 to RCCD
010	__ |a 2004309448
020	__ |a 8172111770
025	__ |a I-E-2004-309448; 86-32; 70-32
037	__ |b Library of Congress — New Delhi Overseas Office |c Rs500.00
040	__ |a DLC |c DLC
042	__ |a lcode
043	__ |a a-ii—
050	00 |a HD6073.A-ZB.x2A-.x2ZI (H76)+
100	1_ |a Mandal, Amal.
245	10 |a Women workers in brick factory : |b sordid saga from a district of West Bengal / |c Amal Mandal.
260	__ |a New Delhi : |b Northern Book Centre, |c 2005.
300	__ |a xii, 131 p. ; |c 22 cm.
520	__ |a Study on socio-economic conditions and wage structure of women brickworkers of Koch Bihar District of West Bengal.
504	__ |a Includes bibliographical references (p. [123]-128) and index.

650	_0 |a Women brickmakers |z India |z Koch Bihar (District) |x Social conditions.
650	_0 |a Women brickmakers |z India |z Koch Bihar (District) |x Economic conditions.
650	_0 |a Wages |z Brickmakers |z India |z Koch Bihar (District) |x Economic conditions.
650	_0 |a Brick trade |z India |z Koch Bihar (District)
985	__ |e ODE-nd
991	__ |b c-GenColl |o am |p 00131068517

Record # 20

000	01254nam 22003617a 450
001	4992574
005	19990422044544.5
007	he|amb—bacp
007	he|bmb—baap
008	990422s1999 ii b 000 0 eng
035	__ |9 (DLC) 98908002
906	__ |a 7 |b cbc |c origode |d 5 |e ncip |f 19 |g y-genmicro
955	__ |a wd31;08/31/98
010	__ |a 98908002
025	__ |a I-CLR-783
040	__ |a DLC |c DLC
042	__ |a lcode
043	__ |a a-ii—
050	00 |a Microfiche 98/60318 (H)
245	00 |a Bengal famine of 1943. |h [microform].
260	__ |a New Delhi : |b Library of Congress Office ; |a Washington, D.C. : |b Library of Congress Photoduplication Service, |c 1999.
300	__ |a 8 microfiches.
440	_0 |a South Asia ephemera collection. |p India ; |v I-CLR-783
500	__ |a A collection of pamphlets published during 1943-1945.
500	__ |a Contents list arranged alphabetically by title.
500	__ |a Collected and organized by the Library of Congress Office, New Delhi.
500	__ |a Master microform held by: DLC.
650	_0 |a Famines |z India |z Bengal.
650	_0 |a Natural disasters |z India.
650	_0 |a Disaster relief |z India.
922	__ |a ap

985   __ |e ODE-nd
991   __ |b c-Asian |h Microfiche 98/60318 (H) |t Copy 1 |m So Asia |w BOOKS

Record # 21

000   01379cam 2200373 a 450
001   12609308
005   20020618173320.0
008   011031s2001 ii a b 001 0 eng
035   __ |a (DLC) 2001413811
906   __ |a 7 |b cbc |c origode |d 3 |e ncip |f 20 |g y-gencatlg
925   0_ |a acquire |b 1 shelf copy |x policy default
955   __ |a wd14 2001-10-31 to RCCD |e yb40 2002-06-17 to Dewey
010   __ |a 2001413811
020   __ |a 8172361041
025   __ |a I-E-2001-413811; 95-32; 61-91; 48
037   __ |b Library of Congress — New Delhi Overseas Office |c Rs600.00
040   __ |a DLC |c DLC
042   __ |a lcode
043   __ |a a-ii—
050   00 |a BX4705.L242 |b B57 2001
100   1_ |a Biswas, Arun Kumar, |d 1934-
245   10 |a Father Eugene Lafont of St. Xavier's College, Kolkata and the contemporary science movement / |c Arun Kumar Biswas.
246   30 |a Contemporary science movement
260   __ |a Kolkata : |b Asiatic Society, |c 2001.
300   __ |a xxviii, 331 p. : |b ill. ; |c 23 cm.
490   1_ |a Monograph series ; |v no. 33
504   __ |a Includes bibliographical references (p. [152]-158) and index.
600   10 |a Lafont, Eugene, |d 1837-1908.
610   20 |a Jesuits |z India |v Biography.
650   _0 |a Scientists |z India |v Biography.
710   2_ |a Asiatic Society (Calcutta, India)
830   _0 |a Asiatic Society monograph series ; |v no. 33.
985   __ |e ODE-nd
991   __ |b c-GenColl |o am |p 0006215472A

Record # 22

```
000    01526cam 22003378a 450
001    13797762
005    20041217152205.0
008    041123s2005 nyu b 001 0 eng
906    __ |a 7 |b rix |c orignew |d 1 |e ecip |f 20 |g y-gencatlg
925    0_ |a acquire |b 2 shelf copies |x policy default
955    __ |a sf03 2004-11-23 |c sf03 2004-11-23; |a sd13 2004-11-26
       |d sf12 2004-12-01 |e sf04 2004-12-02 to Dewey |a aa08 2004-
       12-06
010    __ |a 2004027933
020    __ |a 0761418911
040    __ |a DLC |c DLC |d DLC
042    __ |a pcc
050    00 |a GR78 |b .B53 2005
082    00 |a 398.2/09 |2 22
100    1_ |a Blackwood, Gary L.
245    10 |a Legends or lies? / |c by Gary L. Blackwood.
260    __ |a New York : |b Marshall Cavendish Benchmark, |c
       c2005.
263    __ |a 0510
300    __ |a p. cm.
490    1_ |a Unsolved history
520    __ |a "Describes several legends that have intrigued people
       for centuries: the lost civilization of Atlantis, the Amazons,
       King Arthur, St. Brendan, Pope Joan, and El Dorado"—Provided
       by publisher.
504    __ |a Includes bibliographical references and index.
505    0_ |a The lost civilization — The women warriors — The lord
       of battles — The saint and the prince — The popess — The
       outlaw — The city of gold.
650    _0 |a Legends.
650    _0 |a Geographical myths.
800    1_ |a Blackwood, Gary L. |t Unsolved history.
856    41 |3 Table of contents |u http://www.loc.gov/catdir/toc/
       ecip054/2004027933.html
963    __ |a Marilyn Mark; phone: 914-3328888; email:
       mmark@marshallcavendish.com;
       bc: mmark@marshallcavendish.com
```

Record # 23

000	01931cam 2200361 a 450
001	2561715
005	20021205202953.0
008	950801s1995 couab b s001 0 eng
035	__ |9 (DLC) 95037781
906	__ |a 7 |b cbc |c orignew |d 1 |e ocip |f 19 |g y-gencatlg
955	__ |a pc14 to la00 08-02-95; lc04 (desc.) 08-02-95; lc07 08-04-95;lc03 to ddc 08-07-95; lc10 (verif) 07-02-96; lc03 07-03-96
010	__ |a 95037781
020	__ |a 087081401X (alk. paper)
040	__ |a DLC |c DLC |d DLC
041	1_ |a eng |h spafre
043	__ |a n-mx—
050	00 |a F1219 |b .B3513 1995
082	00 |a 972/.02 |2 20
100	1_ |a Baudot, Georges.
240	10 |a Utopie et histoire au Mexique. |l English
245	10 |a Utopia and history in Mexico : |b the first chroniclers of Mexican civilization (1520-1569) / |c Georges Baudot ; translated by Bernard R. Ortiz de Montellano and Thelma Ortiz de Montellano.
260	__ |a Niwot : |b University Press of Colorado, |c 1995.
300	__ |a xix, 566 p. : |b ill., map ; |c 24 cm.
490	1_ |a Mesoamerican worlds : from the Olmecs to the Danzantes
500	__ |a Translated into English from the Spanish translation of the French original.
504	__ |a Includes bibliographical references (p. 532-551) and index.
520	1_ |a "Important historical analysis of 16th-century accounts concerning indigenous people. Examines context in which chronicles - considered among the earliest ethnographies - were written (and censured and ignored), and Franciscan beliefs about the Indians' future within the millennial kingdom. First English translation"—Handbook of Latin American Studies, v. 57. |u http://www.loc.gov/hlas/
650	_0 |a Indians of Mexico |x History |x Sources.
651	_0 |a Mexico |x History |y Conquest, 1519-1540 |x Sources.
650	_0 |a Ethnology |z Mexico.
830	_0 |a Mesoamerican worlds.

```
920        __  |a **LC HAS REQ'D # OF SHELF COPIES**
991        __  |b c-GenColl |h F1219 |i .B3513 1995 |p 00035139849
           |t Copy 1 |w BOOKS
```

Record # 24

```
000        01147cam 22003138a 450
001        13816130
005        20050208091757.0
008        041215s2005 cau j b 001 0 spa
906        __  |a 7 |b rip |c orignew |d 1 |e ecip |f 20 |g y-gencatlg
925        0_  |a acquire |b 2 shelf copies |x policy default
955        __  |a jb11 2004-12-15 |c jb11 2004-12-15 |d jb08 2004-12-17
           to sl |e jb18 2004-12-17 to Dewey |a aa07 2004-12-20
010        __  |a 2004029713
020        __  |a 1410306828 (hard cover : alk. paper)
040        __  |a DLC |c DLC |d DLC
041        1_  |a spa |h eng
042        __  |a pcc
043        __  |a a-ii—
050        00  |a QL309 |b .I5818 2005
082        00  |a 591.954 |2 22
130        0_  |a Into wild India. |l Spanish.
245        10  |a Dentro de India salvaje / |c edited by Elaine Pascoe.
260        __  |a San Diego, Calif. : |b Blackbirch Press, |c 2005.
263        __  |a 0509
300        __  |a p. cm.
440        _4  |a The Jeff Corwin experience
504        __  |a Includes bibliographical references and index.
650        _0  |a Animals |z India |v Juvenile literature.
700        1_  |a Pascoe, Elaine.
963        __  |a Brian V. Staples; phone: 858-524-2944; fax: 858-485-9549;
           email: Brian.Staples@thomson.com; bc: Brian.Staples
           @thomson.com
```

Record # 25

```
000        01695cas 2200517 a 450
001        11465298
005        20031130172608.0
008        920527c19929999gw ar m 0 0eng d
010        __  |a 96640284 |z sf 95010893 |z sn 92024224
035        __  |a (OCoLC)ocm25898081
```

040	__		a NNM	c NNM	d OUCA	d GU	d DNAL	d MH	d MiU	d DNAL	d NIC	d DLC	d MH	d OCoLC
012	__		a -3-7-0311291108-p-9211
022	__		a 0942-5225
030	__		a ADVBEX
042	__		a lc
050	00		a QH543	b .A33
070	0_		a QH543.A38
072	_0		a B200
072	_0		a F300
072	_0		a L300
210	0_		a Adv. bioclimatol.
222	_0		a Advances in bioclimatology
245	00		a Advances in bioclimatology.
246	18		a Bioclimatology
260	__		a Berlin ;	a New York :	b Springer-Verlag,	c c1992-
300	__		a v. :	b ill. ;	c 25 cm.
310	__		a Annual
362	0_		a 1-
500	__		a Title from cover.
500	__		a Latest issue consulted: 3, published in 1994.
590	__		a SERBIB/SERLOC merged record
650	_0		a Bioclimatology	v Periodicals.
850	__		a DLC	a DNAL	a GU	a MH-CS	a MiU	a NIC
852	__		x universal pattern
853	00		8 1	a (*)	i (year)
863	40		8 1	a <1>-	i <1992>-	x provisional
890	__		a Advances in bioclimatology.	i 96-640284
906	__		a 7	b cbc	c serials	d u	e ncip	f 19	g n-oclcserc
920	__		a Keep 1
984	__		a srvf
991	__		b c-GenColl	h QH543	i .A33	w SERIALS
991	__		b c-GenColl	h QH543	i .A33	p 00016238016	t Copy 1	v 3

RECORD # 26

000	01249cas 2200313 a 450
001	12859889
005	20030731050642.0
008	020718c20019999enkuu p 0 0eng
010	__ |a 2002202515
035	__ |a (OCoLC)ocm51110921

```
040        __  |a DLC |c DLC
012        __  |a -3-7-0307300434-p——
037        __  |b Dialogue Magazine, 10 Little College St., Westminster,
               London, SW1P 3SH
042        __  |a lc
043        __  |a e-uk—
050     00  |a JN101 |b .D53
130     0_  |a Dialogue (Westminster (London, England))
245     00  |a Dialogue.
246     13  |a Dialogue magazine
260        __  |a Westminster, London : |b Parliamentary Communications
               Ltd., |c [2001]-
300        __  |a v. : |b ill. (chiefly col.) ; |c 30 cm.
362     0_  |a Vol. 1, issue 1 (July 23, 2001)-
500        __  |a Title from cover.
651     _0  |a Great Britain |x Politics and government |y 1997- |v
               Periodicals.
650     _0  |a Political planning |z Great Britain |v Periodicals.
850        __  |a DLC
906        __  |a 7 |b cbc |c serials |d 3 |e ncip |f 20 |g n-oclcserc
925     0_  |a Acquire |b 1 shelf copy |x policy default, 2002-12-04
955        __  |a To Selection Officer, dj11 07-18-02 |a ejm, 2002-08-12
               to SERCAT |a da00 2002-08-21 SERCAT1 |c da40 2002-12-04
               sent to cat. tech. |g da59 2002-12-04 to SSCD |d sf11 2003-
               02-20 |e sf15 2003-07-30 to serials
```

RECORD # 27

```
000        01474cas 2200409 a 450
001        13648495
005        20050429050309.0
008        040708c20049999nyuqr1p 0 a0eng c
010        __  |a 2004212421
035        __  |a (OCoLC)ocm55871691
040        __  |a NSDP |c NSDP |d NN |d NSDP |d DLC
012        __  |a -3-7-0504280064-p—— 11
022     0_  |a 1551-1863
037        __  |b Vitals magazine, Fairchild Publications, 7 W. 34th St.,
               New York, NY 10001
042        __  |a lcd |a nsdp
050     00  |a WMLC 2005/00083
082     10  |a 305 |2 13
130     0_  |a Vitals (New York, N.Y.)
```

222	_0	a Vitals	b (New *York*, N.Y.)
245	10	a Vitals.
246	13	a Vitals *magazine*
260	__	a *New York*, N.Y. :	b Fairchild Publications, Inc.	c 2004-
300	__	a v. :	b ill. (chiefly col.) ;	c 28 cm.
310	__	a Quarterly
362	0_	a Vol. 1, no. 1 (Sept. 2004)-
500	__	a Title from cover.
520	__	a News and information about commercial products for men.
580	__	a Split into: Vitals man; and: Vitals woman.
650	_0	a Consumer goods	x Evaluation	v Periodicals.
650	_0	a Men	v Periodicals.
650	_0	a Men's clothing	v Periodicals.
785	06	t Vitals man	x 1555-8150	w (DLC) 2005212992
785	06	t Vitals woman	x 1553-9822	w (DLC) 2004213483
850	__	a DLC
906	__ |a 7 |b cbc |c serials |d 4 |e ncip |f 20 |g n-oclcserc
925	0_	a acquire	b 1 shelf copy	x policy default
955	__ |a df49 2004-07-08 |j df49 2004-07-08 |c df00 2005-02-03 |c df12 2005-02-13 to cat tech |a df37 2005-04-14 to Ser

RECORD # 28

000	01455cas 2200397 a 450
001	13344622
005	20041115131434.0
008	030915c20029999ii qr p 0 0eng
010	__ |a 2003308351
012	__ |a -3-7-0409130136-p-0903
025	__ |a I-E-E-2003-308351; 56-92
035	__ |a (OCoLC)ocm53022111
037	__ |b Editor, Contemporary India, Nehru Memorial Museum and *Library*, Teen Murti House, New Delhi-110011
040	__ |a DLC |c DLC |d InU |d DLC
042	__ |a lc
043	__ |a a-ii—
050	00 |a DS436.A3 |b C66
130	0_ |a Contemporary India (Nehru Memorial Museum and *Library*)
245	10 |a Contemporary India : |b *journal* of Nehru Memorial Museum and *Library*)

| 260 | __ | a New Delhi : | b Memorial Museum and *Library,* | c 2002-
| 300 | __ | a v. : | b ill. ; | c 25 cm.
| 310 | __ | a Quarterly
| 362 | 0_ | a Vol. 1, no. 1 (Jan.-Mar. 2002)-
| 500 | __ | a Title from cover.
| 500 | __ | a Latest issue consulted: v. 1, no. 4 (Oct.-Dec. 2002).
| 651 | _0 | a India | x History | v Periodicals.
| 710 | 2_ | a Nehru Memorial Museum and *Library.*
| 850 | __ | a DLC
| 852 | __ | x universal pattern
| 859 | 00 | u mailto:nmml@vsnl.net
| 853 | 20 | 8 1 | a v. | b no. | u 4 | v r | i (year) | j (month/month) | w q
| 863 | 41 | 8 1.1 | a 1 | b 1 | i 2002 | j 01/03
| 906 | __ | a 7 | b cbc | c serials | d 3 | e ncip | g n-oclcserc
| 925 | 0_ | a Acquire 1 shelf copy | x New Delhi Field Office
| 955 | __ | a dd77 2004-07-22 to Shelflisting | e dd95 2004-09-10 | g dd95 2004-09-10 to BCCD
| 985 | __ | e eserial 200406

Record # 29

| 000 | 01216cas 22003375a 450
| 001 | 13144984
| 005 | 20050209050858.0
| 008 | 030401c20039999ii qr p 0 0eng
| 010 | __ | a 2003310751
| 035 | __ | a (OCoLC)ocm51951509
| 040 | __ | a DLC | c DLC | d IU | d WaU
| 012 | __ | a -3-7-0502080550-p-0304
| 025 | __ | a I-D-E-2003-310751
| 037 | __ | b Aeronautical Society of *India,* 13-B, Indraprastha Estate, New Delhi 110002, *India*
| 042 | __ | a lc
| 043 | __ | a a-ii—
| 050 | 00 | a IN PROCESS
| 050 | 14 | a TL504 | b .A3556
| 245 | 00 | a *Journal* of aerospace sciences and technologies : | b a quarterly *journal* from the Aeronautical Society of *India.*
| 260 | __ | a New Delhi : | b Aeronautical Society of *India,* | c 2003-
| 300 | __ | a v. : | b ill. (some col.) ; | c 29 cm.
| 310 | __ | a Quarterly
| 362 | 0_ | a Vol. 55, no. 1 (Feb. 2003)-

500	__ |a Title from cover.

500   __ |a Title from cover.

650   _0 |a Aeronautics |z *India* |v Periodicals.

710   2_ |a Aeronautical Society of *India.*

780   00 |a Aeronautical Society of *India.* |t *Journal* of the Aeronautical Society of *India* |w (DLC) 52038044 |w (OCoLC)3189799

852   __ |x universal pattern

853   20 |8 1 |a v. |b no. |u 4 |v r |i (year) |j (month) |w q

863   41 |8 1.1 |a 55 |b 1 |i 2003 |j 02

850   __ |a DLC

Record # 30

000   01312nam 22002657a 450

001   13748001

005   20041009162218.0

008   041008s2004 ja 000 0 jpn

906   __ |a 7 |b cbc |c orignew |d 4 |e ncip |f 20 |g n-rlinjack

925   0_ |a acquire |b 1 shelf copy |x policy default

955   __ |a yf13 2004-10-08 |h yf13 2004-10-08 to shelf

010   __ |a 2004553405

035   __ |a (CStRLIN)DCLP04-B18392

040   __ |a DLC-R |c DLC-R

050   00 |a MLCMJ 2004/00348 (H)

066   __ |c $1

245   00 |6 880-01 |a Chūshō kigyō no IT-ka no hōkō to shiensaku ni kansuru chōsa : |b hōkokusho : Heisei 15-nendo Chūshō Kigyōchō itaku chōsa.

260   __ |6 880-02 |a [Tokyo] : |b Mitsubishi Sōgō Kenkyūjo, |c Heisei 16 [2004]

300   __ |a 138 p. : |b ill. ; |c 30 cm.

653   0_ |a Small buisiness; |a information technology; |a Japan

710   2_ |6 880-03 |a Mitsubishi Sōgō Kenkyūjo.

880   00 |6 245-01/$1 |a 中小 企業 の IT化 の 方向 と 支援策 に 関する 調査 : |b 報告書 : 平成 15年度 中小 企業庁 委託 調査.

880   __ |6 260-02/$1 |a [Tokyo] : |b 三菱 総合 研究所, |c 平成 16 [2004]

880   2_ |6 710-03/$1 |a 三菱 総合 研究所.

923   __ |s NDL

Source: library of Congress
www.loc.gov/marc/countries/cou_home.html

MARC Country Codes: Name Sequence

A Select List

For full list *access* Library of Congress website.

Argentina [ag]

Australia [at]

Austria [au]

Bangladesh [bg]

Belgium [be]

Bhutan [bt]

Brazil [bl]

British Columbia [bcc]

Bulgaria [bu]

Burma [br]

Cambodia [cb]

Canada [xxc]

Chile [cl]

China [cc]

China (Republic : 1949-)[ch]

Cuba [cu]

Cyprus [cy]

Czech Republic [xr]

Denmark [dk]

England [enk]

Fiji [fj]

Finland [fi]

France [fr]

Georgia (Republic) [gs]

Germany [gw]

Ghana [gh]

Greece [gr]

Greenland [gl]

Hungary [hu]

India [ii]

Indonesia [io]

Iran [ir]

Iraq [iq]

Ireland [ie]

Israel [is]

Italy [it]

Japan [ja]

Kenya [ke]

Korea (North) [kn]

Korea (South) [ko]

Luxembourg [lu]

Malaysia [my]

Mexico [mx]

Nepal [np]

Netherlands [ne]

New York (State) [nyu]

New Zealand [nz]

Newfoundland [nfc]

No place, unknown, or
undetermined [xx]

Northern Ireland [nik]

Norway [no]

Pakistan [pk]

Philippines [ph]

Poland [pl]

Portugal [po]

Romania [rm]

Russia (Federation) [ru]

Saudi Arabia [su]

Scotland [stk]

Singapore [si]

South Africa [sa]

Spain [sp]

Sri Lanka [ce]

Sudan [sj]

Swaziland [sq]

Sweden [sw]

Switzerland [sz]

Thailand [th]

Uganda [ug]

United Kingdom [xxk]

United States [xxu]

Uzbekistan [uz]

Various places [vp]

Vatican City [vc]

Venezuela [ve]

Vietnam [vm]

Wales [wlk]

Washington (State) [wau]

Yugoslavia [yu

Source: Library of Congress
www.loc.gov/marc/languages/langascii.html

MARC LANGUAGE CODE

A Select List

For complete code list *access* **Library of Congress website.**

Arabic	ara	Finnish	fin
Assamese	asm	French	fre
Awadhi	awa	Germanic (Other)	gem
Bengali	ben	German	ger
Bhojpuri	bho	Greek, Modern	
Bihari	bih	(1453-)	gre
Chinese	chi	Gujarati	guj
Czech	cze	Hawaiian	haw
Danish	dan	Hebrew	heb
Dravidian (Other)	dra	Himachali	him
English	eng	Hindi	hin
English, Middle		Hungarian	hun
(1100-1500)	enm	Indic (Other)	inc

Italian	ita	Persian	per
Japanese	jpn	Pali	pli
Kannada	kan	Polish	pol
Kashmiri	kas	Portuguese	por
Kanuri	kau	Prakrit languages	pra
Khasi	kha	Rajasthani	raj
Konkani	kok	Romanian	rum
Korean	kor	Russian	rus
Lao	lao	Sanskrit	san
Latin	lat	Santali	sat
Maithili	mai	Sign languages	sgn
Malayalam	mal	Sinhalese	sin
Marathi	mar	Sindhi	snd
Malay	may	Spanish	spa
Miscellaneous		Swedish	swe
languages	mis	Tamil	tam
Manipuri	mni	Telugu	tel
Multiple languages	mul	Thai	tha
Munda (Other)	mun	Tibetan	tib
Marwari	mwr	Turkish	tur
Nepali	nep	Urdu	urd
Norwegian	nor	Vietnamese	vie
Oriya	ori	Welsh	wel

Source: Library of Congress
http://www.loc.gov/marc/organizations/orgshome.html

MARC CODE LIST FOR ORGANIZATIONS: INDIAN ENTRIES

The MARC Code List for Organizations is a well-planned directory and it covers all major countries although the representations of U.S. organizations are much higher than the others. The Library of Congress, who maintains the directory, welcomes proposals to include new codes for unlisted organizations. Since representation of India is most inadequate, the cataloguing agencies may propose for registering new codes; see *Appendix* for procedure.

MARC code: **CaMsICC**
Organization: India Community Center (Milpitas, CA)

MARC code: **DLC-ON**
Organization: United States, Library of Congress, Overseas
Operations   Division, Overseas Field Office-India (New Delhi, India)

MARC code: **IiCaNL**
Organization: National Library of India (Calcutta, India)

MARC code: **IiDaU**
Organization: University of North Bengal, Darjeeling District (West Bengal, India)

MARC code:	**IiNaU**
Organization:	University of Nagpur (Nagpur, India)
MARC code:	**IiNdDKA**
Organization:	D. K. Agencies, Ltd. (New Delhi, India)
MARC code:	**IiNdINS**
Organization:	Indian National Scientific Documentation Center (New Delhi, India)
MARC code:	**IiNdNA**
Organization:	National Archives of India (New Delhi, India)
MARC code:	**IiNdNMM**
Organization:	Nehru Memorial Museum and Library (New Delhi, India)
MARC code:	**IiVaMA**
Organization:	Management Aids (Vadodara, Gujarat, India)
MARC code:	**IN-AzMPH**
Organization:	Mizoram Police Headquarters (Aizawl, India)
MARC code:	**IN-BeDL**
Organization:	Dera Library (Beas, District Amritsar, Punjab, India)
MARC code:	**IN-NdJHU**
Organization:	Jamia Hamdard University - Hakim Mohammed Said Library (New Delhi, India)
MARC code:	**UkCbIIT**
Organization:	Ancient India and Iran Trust, Library (Cambridge, Cambridgeshire, England)
MARC code:	**UkLIO**
Organization:	India Office Library and Records, Foreign and Commonwealth Office (London, England)

Access Library of Congress interface for searching MARC Organization Code:
http://www.loc.gov/marc/organizations/orgshome.html#searches

Source: Library of Congress
www.loc.gov/marc/relators/relaterm.html

MARC Relator Codes: Term Sequence

A Select List

For detailed code list access Library of Congress website.

Adapter [adp]
> Use for a person or organization who 1) reworks a musical composition, usually for a different medium, or 2) rewrites novels or stories for motion pictures or other audiovisual medium.

Annotator [ann]
> Use for a person who writes manuscript annotations on a printed item.

Artist [art]
> Use for a person (e.g., a painter) or organization who conceives, and perhaps also implements, an original graphic design or work of art, if specific codes (e.g., [egr], [etr]) are not desired. For book illustrators, prefer Illustrator [ill].

Associated name [asn]
> Use for a person or organization associated with or found in an item or collection, which cannot be determined to

be that of a Former owner [fmo] or other designated relator indicative of provenance.

Attributed name [att]

Use for an author, artist, etc., relating him/her to a work for which there is or once was substantial authority for designating that person as author, creator, etc. of the work.

Author [aut]

Use for a person or organization chiefly responsible for the intellectual or artistic content of a work, usually printed text. This term may also be used when more than one person or body bears such responsibility.

UF Joint author

Author of introduction, etc. [aui]

Use for a person or organization responsible for an introduction, preface, foreword, or other critical introductory matter, but who is not the chief author.

Bibliographic antecedent [ant]

Use for a person or organization responsible for a work upon which the work represented by the catalog record is based. This may be appropriate for adaptations, sequels, continuations, indexes, etc.

Binder [bnd]

Use for a person or organization responsible for the binding of printed or manuscript materials.

Book producer [bkp]

Use for a person or organization responsible for the production of books and other print media, if specific codes (e.g., [bkd], [egr], [tyd], [prt]) are not desired.

UF Producer of book

Bookseller [bsl]

Use for a person or organization who makes books and other bibliographic materials available for purchase. Interest in the materials is primarily lucrative.

Cartographer [ctg]

Use for a person or organization responsible for the creation of maps and other cartographic materials.

Collaborator [clb]

Use for a person or organization that takes a limited part in the elaboration of a work of another person or organization that brings complements (e.g., appendices, notes) to the work.

Collector [col]

Use for a person or organization who has brought together material from various sources that has been arranged, described, and cataloged as a collection. A collector is neither the creator of the material nor a person to whom manuscripts in the collection may have been addressed.

Commentator for written text [cwt]

Use for a person or organization responsible for the commentary or explanatory notes about a text. For the writer of manuscript annotations in a printed book, use Annotator [ann].

Compiler [com]

Use for a person or organization who produces a work or publication by selecting and putting together material from the works of various persons or bodies.

Contributor [ctb]

Use for a person or organization one whose work has been contributed to a larger work, such as an anthology, serial publication, or other compilation of individual works. Do not use if the sole function in relation to a work is as author, editor, compiler or translator.

Copyright holder [cph]

Use for a person or organization to whom copy and legal rights have been granted or transferred for the intellectual content of a work. The copyright holder, although not necessarily the creator of the work, usually has the exclusive right to benefit financially from the sale and use of the work to which the associated copyright protection applies.

Correspondent [crp]

Use for a person or organization who was either the writer or recipient of a letter or other communication.

Creator [cre]

Use for a person or organization responsible for the intellectual or artistic content of a work.

Dedicatee [dte]

Use for a person or organization to whom a book, manuscript, etc., is dedicated (not the recipient of a gift).

Designer [dsr]

Use for a person or organization responsible for the design if more specific codes (e.g., [bkd], [tyd]) are not desired.

Director [drt]

Use for a person or organization who is responsible for the general management of a work or who supervises the production of a performance for stage, screen, or sound recording.

Dissertant [dis]

Use for a person who presents a thesis for a university or higher-level educational degree.

Distributor [dst]

Use for a person or organization that has exclusive or shared marketing rights for an item.

Donor [dnr]

Use for a person or organization who is the donor of a book, manuscript, etc., to its present owner. Donors to previous owners are designated as Former owner [fmo] or Inscriber [ins].

Dubious author [dub]

Use for a person or organization to which authorship has been dubiously or incorrectly ascribed.

Editor [edt]

Use for a person or organization who prepares for publication a work not primarily his/her own, such as by elucidating text, adding introductory or other critical matter, or technically directing an editorial staff.

Funder [fnd]

Use for a person or organization that furnished financial support for the production of the work.

Honoree [hnr]

Use for a person or organization in memory or honor of whom a book, manuscript, etc. is donated. UF Memorial

Illustrator [ill]

Use for a person or organization who conceives, and perhaps also implements, a design or illustration, usually to accompany a written text.

Interviewee [ive]

Use for a person or organization who is interviewed at a consultation or meeting, usually by a reporter, pollster, or some other information gathering agent.

Interviewer [ivr]

Use for a person or organization who acts as a reporter, pollster, or other information gathering agent in a consultation or meeting involving one or more individuals.

Joint author USE Author

Manufacturer [mfr]

Use for a person or organization that makes an artifactual work (an object made or modified by one or more persons). Examples of artifactual works include vases, cannons or pieces of furniture.

is not possible or desirable to identify the function more precisely.

Narrator [nrt]

Use for a person who is a speaker relating the particulars of an act, occurrence, or course of events.

Originator [org]

Use for a person or organization performing the work, i.e., the name of a person or organization associated with the intellectual content of the work. This category does not include the publisher or personal affiliation, or sponsor except where it is also the corporate author. Includes a person designated in the work as investigator or principal investigator. UF Principal investigator

Other [oth]

Use for relator codes from other lists which have no equivalent in the MARC list or for terms which have not been assigned a code.

Owner [own]

Use for a person or organization that currently owns an item or collection.

Patron [pat]

Use for a person or organization responsible for commissioning a work. Usually a patron means or influence to support the work of artists, writers, etc. This includes those who commission and pay for individual works.

Photographer [pht]

Use for a person or organization responsible for taking photographs, whether they are used in their original form or as reproductions.
printed images and/or text.

Printer [prt]

Use for a person or organization who prints texts, whether from type or plates.

Producer [pro]

Use for a person or organization responsible for the making of a motion picture, including business aspects, management of the productions, and the commercial success of the work.
Producer of book USE Book producer

Publisher [pbl]

Use for a person or organization that makes printed matter, often text, but also printed music, artwork, etc. available to the public.

Publishing director [pbd]

Use for a person or organization who presides over the elaboration of a collective work to ensure its coherence or continuity. This includes editors-in-chief, literary editors, editors of series, etc.

Reporter [rpt]

Use for a person or organization who writes or presents reports of news or current events on air or in print.

Researcher [res]
Use for a person or organization responsible for performing research.

Respondent [rsp]
Use for the party who makes an answer to the courts pursuant to an application for redress, usually in an equity proceeding.

Reviewer [rev]
Use for a person or organization responsible for the review of a book, motion picture, performance, etc.

Speaker [spk]
Use for a person who participates in a program (often broadcast) and makes a formalized contribution or presentation generally prepared in advance.

Sponsor [spn]
Use for a person or organization that issued a contract or under the auspices of which a work has been written, printed, published, etc.

Thesis advisor [ths]
Use for a person under whose supervision a degree candidate develops and presents a thesis, mémoire, or text of a dissertation.
UF Promoter

Translator [trl]
Use for a person or organization who renders a text from one language into another, or from an older form of a language into the modern form.

Writer of accompanying material [wam]
Use for a person or organization who writes significant material which accompanies a sound recording or *other audiovisual material*.

Source: University of Virginia Library
http://www.lib.virginia.edu/cataloging/manual/appendices/appx21.html

FORMAT INTEGRATION-SERIALS

SUMMARY OF CHANGES FOR SERIALS

Note Fields Now Used for Serials

A number of note fields can now be used with Serials. Listed below are some of the ones you are likely to find useful.

1. **With note (tag 501):** This note is used when two separately catalogued publications come bound together.
2. **Systems details note (tag 538):** This field contains information about system requirements. This could be used to describe accompanying diskettes, or to describe requirements for electronic journals.

Changes in Note Fields Already Used

1. **Reproduction Note (tag 533):** Notes about microform reproductions formerly input in 500 fields are now included in subfield |n of tag 533. This subfield is repeatable.

Title Fields

1. **Acronym or Shortened Title (tag 211):** This field is now obsolete. The information formerly included in this tag should instead be placed in a 246 field.

2. **Variant Access Title (tag 212):** This field is now obsolete. The information formerly included in this tag should instead be placed in a 246 field.

3. **Augmented Title (tag 214):** This field is now obsolete. The information formerly included in this tag should instead be placed in a 246 field.

4. **Variant Titles (tag 246):** Field 246 is still used for variant titles of a serial, much as it was before.

A few additions have been made. Variant titles of the kind formerly coded in fields 211, 212, and 214, are now placed in tag 246.

A new subfield, |i has now been defined. It's purpose is to allow the cataloguer to specify the source of a variant title when no second indicator has the appropriate meaning. A new second indicator, [blank] has been defined for use with this subfield, for use when one of the predefined meanings does not apply.

245 00 |a Bulletin of atomic scientists.

246 1 |i At head of title: |a Science and public affairs |f Jan. 1970-Apr. 1974

245 00 |a Library of Congress subject headings.

246 1 |i Also known as: |a LCSH

110 2 |a Media Services Inc.

245 00 |a Report.

246 0 |i Some issues have title: |a Annual report

245 00 |a Chartbook of federal programs on aging.

246 18 |a Chartbook on aging

110 2 |a American Library Association.

245 14 |a ALA bulletin.

246 2 |a American Library Association bulletin

245 00 |a Journal of physics. |n D, |p Applied physics.

246 10 |a Applied physics

More information and examples of this field were included in the section on Format Integration—Books.

Related/Analytical Uniform Titles (tag 730): Use of this field is more restrictive than it was before format integration. This tag is used for the uniform title of a related record. A 740 field is now used for a title added entry for a related work, when the title is not in the form of the established catalog entry. The added entry is still normally justified with a note.

| 500 | | |a Issues for 1922-1931 include: The woman voter : official organ of the League of Women Voters. |
| 730 | 02 | |a Woman voter (Albany, N.Y.) |

Related/Analytical titles (tag 740): This field is used for title added entries of individual works within the publication that have not been published separately, or for title added entries of related works for which no entry has been established. The added entry is still normally justified with a note. (See also Format Integration—Books, tag 740)

| 500 | | |a Includes: Directory of Mexican manufacturers. |
| 740 | 02 | |a Directory of Mexican manufacturers. |

FORMATTING HOLDINGS INFORMATION

A. Use explicitly stated volume designators (v., no., etc.) for enumeration data at all levels of enumeration. When entering volume designators, first identify the volume designator(s) or highest level of enumeration appearing on the piece. Consult the AACR2, rev. standard abbreviations and part V. of this documentation to identify the correct format to use in entering holdings data. For foreign language enumeration designators, use the appropriate abbreviation for that language.

Example:

866 _0|81|av.1-5

866 _0|81|at.1-10

866 _0|81|av.1:no.1-3

866 _0|81|av.1:no.3:pt.A

Record example:

ISSN: 0360-5302 Communications in partial differential equations

Also follow AACR2 rules for capitalization or words.

Example:

866 _0|81|aBd.1-6 (German)

866 _0|81|abd.1-4 (dutch)

B. Volume designators are not repeated before the last unit in a sequence.

Example:

USE: v.6-32 NOT: v.6-v.32

C. When a volume with missing issue(s) is completed, compress the parts as follows:

Example:

When the library adds v.7:no.4

CHANGE FROM:

866_0|81|av.7:no.1-3,5-12

TO:

866_0|81|av.7

NOT:

866_0|81|av.7:no.1-12

Example:

When the library has;

866_0|81|av.5-6

866_0|81|av.7:no.1-3,5-12

866_0|81|av.8-10

Compress to:

866 _0|81|av.5-10 (when v. 7 is complete)

For issues that were not published, compress holdings and add a note about the missing issue.

Ex: v.7|zissue no.8 not published

D. Use only Arabic numerals (0-9) when entering numerical data. Translate all Roman numerals to Arabic numerals.

E. If alphabetic characters are part of the enumeration or chronology data, include these in the transcription.

Example:

866_0|81|a1968A-1969A

866_0|81|apt.A-D

F. When entering months or seasons of the year in chronology data, first identify the chronology as it appears on the piece. Consult the AACR2, rev. standard abbreviations and pt. V of this documentation to identify the correct format to use in entering chronology data. For months and seasons in foreign languages, use English.

Example:

866_0|81|a1960:Jan.-Nov.

G. Punctuation

Use only the following punctuation symbols in the manner described (extracted from ANSI Standard Z39.44-1986)

1. Use a hyphen "-" to indicate an unbroken range of holdings data between a beginning and ending unit.

Examples:

866_0|81|av.1-4

866_0|81|at.1-10

866_0|81|av.1-21 (1969-1990)

866_0|81|ano.300-308 (1980:Jan.-Sept.)

866_0|81|a1984-1986

Record example:

AAJ5525 The English academy review

2. Use a comma ',' to designate a gap in a range of holdings. A 'gap' is defined as an issue or groups of issues which were published, but which are not held by the library location for any reason. For issues that were not published, compress holdings and add a note about the missing issue. Ex: v.7|zissue no. 8 not published

Examples:

866_0|81|av.2-4,6-7,9

866_0|81|av.1-6,9-10 (1961-1966,1969-1970)

866_0|81|a1969-1978,1980-1986

866_0|81|a1960-1962,1978-1983

Record example:

ISSN: 0031-7985 Philologus

ISSN: 0002-7375 American artists

3. Use a colon ':' to separate between multiple levels of data. Enter the highest level of data (the largest unit) first, followed by each lower level in decreasing order.

Examples:

Monographs:

866_0|81|av.1:no.1:pt.A-B

866_0|81|aser.2:v.1:pt.1-3

866_0|81|apt.A:v.1:no.1-2

866_0|81|aser.1:v.1-ser.6:v.10

Serials:

866_0|81|av.2:no1:pt.A-B (1989)

866_0|81|aser.3:v.1:pt.1-3 (1990)

866_0|81|av.7:no.1-2,5-12 (1990:Jan.-Feb.,Apr,-Dec.)

866_0|81|apt.A:v.1:no.1-2 (1991:Jan.-Feb.)

866_0|81|aser.1:v.1-ser.6:v.10 (1980-1990)

Record examples:

ISSN: 0002-7375 American artists

ISSN: 0360-5302 Communications in partial differential equations

When using series and a new series has begun: Each new line of the run of the new series must begin with 'n.s.'

Examples:

866_0|81|av.1-10 (1968-1970)

866_0|81|an.s.:v.1-8 (1971-1979)

866_0|81|an.s.:v.11-20 (1981-1990)

4. Use parentheses '( )' to enclose chronology information when it follows enumeration information. If holdings are expressed by chronological information alone (newspapers, etc.), do not use parentheses. Do not use for monographs.

Examples:

866_0|81|av.1-5,7-8 (1976-1981,1983-1984)

866_0|81|av.1:no.1-2 (1979:Jan.-Feb.)

866_0|81|a1987:Mar.1-Apr.22

866_0|81|a1960-1986

Record examples:

ISSN: 0038-4941 Social science quarterly

ISSN: 1069-0727 Journal of career assessment

5. Use the slash '/' to indicate combined volumes, issues, etc., when one or more volumes or years are issued by the publisher in a single physical piece.

Examples:

866_0|81|av.1/2

866_0|81|av.1-7 (1965/1966-1972/1972)

866_0|81|ano.9/10 (1960:Sept./Oct.)

866_0|81|a1960/1965

Record example:

ISSN: 1091-4706 Reaching today's youth
Always use a slash when a single volume covers combined years.

Examples:

for:

v.1 Oct. 1979-Sept.1981

use:

866_0|81|av.1 (1979/1981)

not:

866_0|81|av.1 (1979:Oct.-1981:Sept.)

*Do not create a MARC holdings record for one single piece that is 2 volumes in 1.

6. For enumeration data, use the equals sign '=' to indicate that the data that follows is an alternative numbering scheme.

Example:

866_0|81|av.1:no.5=no.11

Record example:

ISSN: 0038-6952 The Spectator

ABR4745 The new beacon

7. Use square brackets '[ ]' to enclose translated Gregorian dates.

Example:

866_0|81|aShowa 56-nendo [1981/1982]

8. Use two spaces to separate enumeration and chronology information within a statement line. Do not use spaces to separate elements within an enumerations or chronology data area.

Example:

866_0|81|av.7:no.6 (1986:June)

866_0|81|a1984-1985

866_0|81|a1986:Mar.13-Apr.12,May1-Dec.31

9 . Volume designators that do not end in periods (e.g. disk, fiche, etc.) have a space before the holdings enumeration.

Examples:

866_0|81|afiche 1-34

866_0|81|adisk 1-2

All abbreviated designators DO NOT have a space.

Examples:

866_0|81|av.1-3

866_0|81|apt.1-2

866_0|81|aBd.1

H. Use of statement lines.

1. A sequence of completed units at the highest level of enumeration and/or chronology will be entered on a single statement line.

Examples:

866_0|81|av.1-21 (1940-1960)

866_0|81|a1912-1967

2. Incomplete units will be entered in correct sequence on separate statement lines.

866_0|81|v.1-2,4-7 (1985-1990),

866_0|81|av.8:no.2-3 (1986:Spring-Summer),

866_0|81|av.9 (1987)

Note the use of commas in the example above. Commas are used to denote gaps between statement lines as well as gaps within a statement line. Assuming this is a quarterly publication, the comma at the end of the first statement line indicates that v.8:no.1 is not held by the library, and the comma at the end of the second statement line indicates that library holdings lack v.8:no.4. The holdings for v.8 are listed on a separate line since it is an incomplete volume.

I. Supplements:

For supplements with independent numbering schemes, use that numbering to record the holdings.

Example:

If we receive numbers 1-3 of the supplements to a title, we should record the holdings as:

866_0|81|av.1-10 (1990-2000)

867_0|89|ano.1-3

|8* link and sequence number should be a high number such as |88 or

|89. This will cause the supplements to display after the main holdings.

Do not use for unnumbered monographic supplements.

Unnumbered monographic supplements are entered in a separate 866 line in the MARC holdings record.

Example:

866_0|81|av.1-5

866_0|81|asuppl.

J. Indexes:

Do not use for unnumbered monographic indexes, use the 866 field.

1. When adding subject/author/title indexes:

If each is separately bound, list each one separately, preceding the holdings with:

SUBJ. (in all caps)

AUTHOR (in all caps)

TITLE (in all caps)

Examples:

868_0|89|aSUBJ. v.1-5 (1985-1990)

868_0|89|aAUTHOR v.1-5 (1985-1990)

868_0|89|aTITLE v.1-5 (1985-1990)

|8* link and sequence number should be a high number such as |88 or |89. This will cause the indexes to display after the main holdings.

2. When adding key indexes that are separately bound: Precede the indexes holdings with KEY: (in all caps)

Example:

868_0|89|aKEY:1991-1990,1992

3. If the index covers more than one year and is bound in with a regular volume or issue, then do NOT add the index to the volume holdings. Instead, add the index to the bibliographic record in a 555 field in the following format:

555::dates & years of index, in vol. # it is included in.

Examples:

1. 555::Vols. 1 (1927)-23 (1951), in v.26, no.1

This will print to the public as:

INDEXES:

Vol. 1 (1927)-25 (1951), in v.26, no.1

2. 555::Author index, v.1 1915-6 (1921), with v.6; subject index, v.1 (1915)-6 (1921), with v.6.

This will print to the public as:

INDEXES:

Author index, v.1 (1915)-6 (1921), with v.6;
Subject index, v.1 (1915)-6 (1921), with v.6.

Source: Princeton University Cataloging Documentation
http://infoshare1.princeton.edu/katmandu/reference/formsubdiv.htm

UNIFORM TITLES: CATALOGING PROCEDURES

INTRODUCTION

All uniform title headings found in LC copy are retained. Consult an original cataloguer if in doubt.

Original cataloguers create headings as required according to AACR2, chapter 25, and create authority records if needed, for certain categories of material.

For a list of the main categories, see Situations Where Uniform Titles Are Used.

See MARC Tags Used with Uniform Titles for information about coding uniform titles in general. More details about specific cases are in this document.
A vertical bar 'I' is used here for subfirld delimiter

SERIAL TITLES

Authority records are sometimes made for serial titles. This is done in at least three cases.

- More than one serial has **the same title**. This often happens with a short or common title (and especially with newspapers). A **qualifier** with the place of publication is added to the title in the 130 field, and in any 630 or 730 entries or any linking fields that may be needed. It also sometimes happens that a serial changes its title and later changes back again; in this case the qualifier would include the beginning date.

- A serial exists in **multiple formats**, for instance print and electronic. In this case a 130 with the qualifier (Online) at the end of the title is added to distinguish the electronic format, and used in any 630 or 730 fields *that refer to that format only*, or any linking fields, including the 776 field. A 130 with the qualifier (Print) is not yet common but may become so.

- The serial title is used as an **added entry** and Queen's does not have a bibliographic record for the serial. An authority record is created to provide access from variant titles, and to record publication data and other information that can help distinguish the title in hand from other, similar titles. (If the library has catalogued the serial, then this information is contained in the serial record itself.) A qualifier would not *necessarily* be added in this case.

COMPUTER PROGRAMS

The Library of Congress originally treated the names of computer programs as subject headings. LC is gradually converting these names to uniform title format. Since this format is now being used in the subject file, the uniform title is also being used as an access point in the bibliographic records for consistency.

Authority records are made for these uniform titles to provide subject information as well.

100　　1 |a Binder, Kate.

245　　10|a Easy Adobe Photoshop 6 : |b see it done, do it yourself/ |c Kate Binder.

630　　00|a Adobe Photoshop.

245　　00|aOffice97 simplified / |c MaranGraphics.

630　　00|a Microsoft Office.

CLASSICS AND TRANSLATIONS

When a work (literary, historical, philosophical, scientific, etc.)

- is so well-known that other works are written about it,
- is translated, or
- is known by more than one title even in the original language,

a uniform title can be used to bring together all the variants.
If the work is anonymous or has a title main entry for any reason, use tags 130 / 630 / 730. If the work has a personal or corporate author use 100 / 240, 600 |t, 700 |t, or 110 / 240 610 |t, 710 |t, tags as appropriate.

130 0 |a Gawain and the Grene Knight. |l English & English (Middle English)

245 10 |a Sir Gawain and the Green Knight : |b a dual-language version

100 1 |a Tolstoy, Leo, |c graf, |d 1828-1910.

240 10 |a Voina i mir. |l English

245 10 |a War and peace.

600 10 |a Tolstoy, Leo, |c graf, |d 1828-1910. |t Voina i mir.

Note that a 600 |t or 630 would include any |p subfields but would *not* include subfields for language, version, or date. It might of course include |v or |x subfields.
Practice has varied (both at LC and at Queen's) as to whether one authority is established for the work, with references from forms in different languages, or an authority for each language with references from titles appearing on different translations. The latter would be preferable if there are multiple translations into any one language.

COLLECTIVE TITLES

A publication that consists of an author's complete or selected works presents a special case, since the title is assigned by the publisher and may be different from another publication with the same contents.

If the publication contains more than three works, a collective uniform title may be assigned. Choose if possible from the following list (except for music):

- Works
- Selections
- Correspondence
- Essays
- Novels
- Plays
- Poems
- Prose works
- Short stories
- Speeches

All but the first two of these may have |k **Selections** added if the works in the specified form are not complete.

Add a |l subfield for language if the work in hand is a translation. (If the original language and a translation are combined, add the original language last, after an ampersand). A |s subfield can be used to specify a translator or version. A |f subfield for the publication date may be added at the end.

100   00 |a Voltaire, |d 1694-1778.

240   10 |a Works. |l English & French. |f 1968

245   14 |a The complete works of Voltaire.

100   10 |a Shakespeare, William, |d 1564-1616

240   10 |a Plays. |f 1904

245   10 |a Mr. William Shakespear's comedies, histories, and tragedies.

SACRED SCRIPTURES, ETC.

A uniform title (main/added entry) is used for religious scriptures such as the Bible, the Talmud, and the Koran. Because these works, especially the Bible, exist in many languages and multiple translations into many of them, and also because their constituent parts are often published separately, their uniform titles can be quite long.

130   0 |a Bible. |l German (Middle Low German)|f 1961.

130   0 |a Bible. |p O.T. |p Ezekiel XXI-XXXVII. |l English. |s Greenberg. |f 1997.

630   00 |a Talmud. |p Minor tractates.|p Avot de-Rabbi Nathan.

130 or 730 headings of this type could also include a subfield |k **Selections**, immediately before the date subfield. 630 headings would normally have only |p and |v or |x subfields.

MANUSCRIPTS

Entries are made for manuscripts which are in libraries or archives when works are published based on their contents. When there is no popular title for the manuscript, these entries are set up in tags 110 / 240, 610 |k and 710 |k in the form: corporate name + form heading + specific designation. Note the use of the |k and |n subfields.

710   2 |a British Library. |k Manuscript. |n Arundel 384

Some old manuscripts (codexes), etc.h are better known by popular names. The authority record should have a reference from the formal name if known.

130   0 |a Book of Kells

LAWS, TREATIES, LITURGIES, ETC.

Laws, treaties, liturgical works, etc. are usually set up as corporate name-title entries in 110 / 240, 610 |t and 710 |t tags.

710   1 |a Ontario. |t Laws, etc. (Ontario acts)

610   20 |a Catholic Church. |t Codex Juris canonici

610   1 |a Canada. |t Charter of Rights and Freedoms

710   1 |a Canada. |t Treaties, etc. |g United States, |d 1988 Jan. 2

710   1 |a Canada. |t Treaties, etc. |d 1992 Oct. 7

110   2 |a Church of England.

240   10 |a Book of common prayer. |f 1716

There are exceptions to this as well. For example, a treaty involving up to three parties is entered under the one that comes first in alphabetical order, like the hard-to-recognize headings above for the FTA and NAFTA, but a treaty involving four or more parties is entered under title. A legal document not connected with any particular country may also be entered under title.

630   00 |a Treaty of Utrecht |d (1713)

130   00 |a Universal Declaration of Human Rights

Collective Artistic Works

Collective artistic works include motion pictures, television programs, etc. A uniform title is *not* created or used to avoid conflict with an identical 245 title already in the database (where the |h GMD and other information should make the situation clear). However, uniform titles *should* be created and used for these types of works whenever a 630 or 730 heading is called for, whether there is a conflict or not.

245   00 |a Hamlet, Prince of Denmark |h [videorecording]

630   00 |a Casablanca (Motion picture)

Uniform title qualifiers for works of this type should include a term identifying the type of work, followed if necessary by a date, personal name, etc. For detailed examples, see LC Rule Interpretations for Chapter 25.

For artistic works with personal authors, such as paintings, uniform titles with qualifiers are unlikely to be needed unless there is a conflict, but any 600 |t or 700 |t heading will still be a uniform title.

MUSIC

Uniform titles are established for virtually all music scores. Generally, the same principles that apply to classic works are applicable to music.

See Music Scores: Uniform Titles for fuller information.

Note regarding **librettos**: Retain the 240 tag in the bibliographical record.

- These are the texts/literary works which are set to music (operas). Although there is usually no music in these publications and they are classed in ML49 or ML50 (with books, not scores), they are catalogued with composer as main entry and therefore require Uniform Titles.

Due to rule changes and old cataloguing practices, there is considerable cleanup of music headings to be done. The OPAC index displays are further confused by the fact that the records for many scores are in book format. Only those catalogued since 1988 are in the proper music format display.

FORM SUBDIVISIONS

FREE-FLOATING

While items in this list normally function as form subdivisions, most of them may also function as topical subdivisions depending on whether the item itself is in that format, or whether it discusses that format. (*Current with 14th ed. of 'Free-floating subdivisions : an alphabetical index'*)

2-harpsichord scores
2-piano scores
3-piano scores

A

Abbreviations
Abbreviations of titles
Abridgments
Abstracts
Acronyms
Adaptations
Aerial photographs
Aerial views
Almanacs
Amateurs' manuals
Anecdotes
Apologetic works

Archives
Art
Art and the war, [revolution, etc.]
Atlases
Audio adaptations
Audiotape catalogs
Autographs

B

Bathymetric maps
Bibliography
Bibiliography |v Catalogs
Bibliography |v Early

Bibliography |v Exhibitions
Bibliography |v Graded lists
Bibliography |v Microform
catalogs
Bibliography |v Union lists
Bibliography of bibliographies
Bio-bibliography
Biography
Biography |v Anecdotes
Biography |v Caricatures and
cartoons
Biography |v Dictionaries
** |x Biography |x History and
criticism
Biography |v Humor
Biography |v Pictorial works
Biography |v Portraits
Biography |v Sermons
Book reviews
By-laws

C

Cadenzas
Calendars
Caricatures and cartoons
Case studies
Cases
Catalogs
Catalogs, Manufacturers'
Catalogs and collections (may
sub geog)
Catalogues raisonnes
Catechisms
Catechisms |x English,
[French, German, etc.]
CD-ROM catalogs
Census
Census, [date]
Chapel exercises
Charters
Charters, grants, privileges
Charts, diagrams, etc.
Children's sermons

Chord diagrams
Chorus scores with organ
Chorus scores with piano
Chorus scores without
accompaniment
Chronology
Classification
Code numbers
Code words
Comic books, strips, etc.
Commentaries
Commercial treaties
Compact disc catalogs
Comparative studies
Computer games
Concordances
Concordances, English
[French, German, etc.]
Concordances, English |x
Authorized, [Living Bible,
Revised Standard, etc.]
Congresses
Constitution
Controversial literature
Conversation and phrase
books
Conversation and phrase
books |x English [French,
German, etc.]
Conversation and phrase
books (for ...)
Correspondence
Creeds
Cross-cultural studies
Cross references
Curricula

D

Data tape catalogs
Databases
Designs and plans
Devotional literature
Diaries

Dictionaries
Dictionaries |v Early works to
1700
Dictionaries |x French,
[Italian, etc.]
Dictionaries, Juvenile
** |x Diet therapy |v Recipes
Digests
Directories
Discography
Drama
Drawings

E

Early works to 1800
Electronic discussion groups
Encyclopedias
Encyclopedias, Juvenile
Examinations, questions, etc.
Excerpts
Excerpts, Arranged
Exercises for dictation
Exhibitions

F

Facsimiles
Fake books
Fiction
Film and video adaptations
Film catalogs
Films for foreign speakers
Films for French, [Spanish,
etc.] speakers
Firing regulations
Folklore
** |x Foreign relations |v
Executive agreements
Forms

G

Gazetteers
Genealogy
Gift books

Glossaries, vocabularies, etc.
Glossaries, vocabularies, etc.
|x Polyglot
Guidebooks

H

Handbooks, manuals, etc.
Harmonies
Harmonies, English [French,
German, etc.]
Humor
Hymns

I

Identification
Illustrations
Imprints
In art
Index maps
Indexes
Instructive editions
Instrumental settings
Interactive multimedia
Interlinear translations
Interlinear translations,
French [German, etc.]
Interviews
Introductions
Inventories

J

Job descriptions
Job descriptions (may subd
geog)
Juvenile
Juvenile drama
Juvenile fiction
Juvenile films
Juvenile humor
Juvenile literature
Juvenile poetry
Juvenile software
Juvenile sound recordings

K L

Laboratory manuals
Lead sheets
Legends
** |x Library |v Marginal
    notes
Librettos
Life skills guides
Lists of vessels
Literary collections
Literatures
Liturgical lessons, English
[Dutch, etc.]
** |x Liturgy |v Calendar
** |x Liturgy |x Texts |v
Rubrics
Longitudinal studies

M

Maps
Maps, Comparative
Maps, Manuscript
Maps, Mental
Maps, Outline and base
Maps, Physical
Maps, Pictorial
Maps, Topographic
Maps, Tourist
Maps for ....
Marginal readings
Meditations
Methods
Methods |v Group instruction
Methods |v Self-instruction
Methods (Jazz, etc.)
Microform catalogs
Miscellanea
Music
Misc |v Discography
Musical settings

N

Necrology

Newspapers
Nomenclature
Nomenclature (Popular)
Nomenclature (Popular) |x
English, [French, etc.]
Nomograms
Non-commissioned officers'
handbooks
Notation
Notebooks, sketchbooks, etc.

O

Obituaries
Observations
Observers' manuals
Officers' handbooks
Orchestra studies
Order-books
Outlines, syllabi, etc.

P

Pamphlets
Papal documents
Parallel versions, English
[French, etc.]
Paraphrases
Paraphrases, English [French,
German, etc.]
Parodies, imitations, etc.
Parts
Parts (solo)
Pastoral letters and charges
Patents
Pedigrees
Performance records
Periodicals
** |x Periodicals |v
    Abbreviations of titles
** |x Periodicals |v
    Bibliography
** |x Periodicals |v
    Bibliography |v Catalogs
** |x Periodicals |v

Bibliography |v Union lists
** |x Periodicals |v Indexes
Personal narratives
Personal narratives, ...
Petty officers' handbooks
Phonetic transcriptions
Photographs
Photographs from space
Piano scores
Piano scores (4 hands)
Pictorial works
Picture Bibles
Platforms
Poetry
Popular works
Portraits
Posters
Prayer-books and devotions
Prayer-books and devotions
|x English [French, German,
etc.]
Prayers
Prefaces
Private bills
Problems, exercises, etc.
Programmed instruction

Q

Quotations
Quotations, maxims, etc.

R

Readers
Readers |v [form]
Readers |x [topic]
Readers for new literates
Records and correspondence
Reference editions
Registers
Registers of dead
Registers of dead (may subd
geog)
Regulations

Relief models
Remote-sensing images
Remote-sensing maps
Resolutions
Reverse indexes
Reviews
Romances
Rules
Rules and practice

S

Sacred books
Sailors' handbooks
Scenarios
Scholia
Scores
Scores and parts
Scores and parts (solo)
Self-instruction
Self-portraits
Sermons
Simplified editions
Slides
Software
Solo with ...
Solos with ...
Songs and music
Sound recordings for foreign
speakers
Sound recordings for French,
[Spanish, etc.] speakers
Sources
Specifications (may subd
geog)
Specimens
Speeches in Congress
Spurious and doubtful works
Stage guides
Statistics
Statistics, Medical
Statistics, Vital
Stories, plots, etc.
Studies and exercises

Studies and exercises (Jazz, [Rock, etc.])
Study guides
Surveys

T

Tables
Tables of contents
Teaching pieces
Telephone directories
Telephone directories |v Yellow pages
Terminology
Terms and phrases
Textbooks
Textbooks for English [French, etc.] speakers
Textbooks for foreign speakers
Textbooks for foreign speakers |x English, [French, etc.]
Texts

Thematic catalogs
Tours
Trademarks
Translations
Translations into French [German, etc.]
** |x Translations into French [German, etc.] |x History and criticism
Treaties
Trials, litigation, etc.

U

Union lists

V

Video catalogs
Video recordings for ...
Vocal scores with ....
Vocal scores without accompaniment

W X Y Z

Source: Library of Congress
Cataloging Policy and Support Office http://www.loc.gov/catdir/cpso/

ROMANIZATION TABLES FOR INDIC LANGUAGES

ALA-LC ROMANIZATION TABLES

The following alphabetically arranged romanization tables are nearly identical to the **National Library (India) transliteration tables** most widely used in dictionaries and grammars of Indic languages:

- Bengali
- Gujarati
- Hindi
- Kannada
- Malayalam
- Marathi
- Oriya
- Panjabi
- Sanskrit
- Tamil
- Telugu
- Urdu

Bengali

Vowels and Diphthongs (see Note 1)

অ	a		ৠ	r̥̄
আ	ā		৯	l̥
ই, ঈ	i		এ	e
ঈ, ৠ	ī		ঐ	ai
উ, ঊ	u		ও	o
ঊ, ঊ	ū		ঔ	au
ঋ	r̥			

Consonants (see Note 2)

Gutturals		Palatals		Cerebrals		Dentals	
ক	ka	চ	ca	ট	ṭa	ত	ta
খ	kha	ছ	cha	ঠ	ṭha	ৎ	ṭa
গ	ga	জ	ja	ড	ḍa	থ	tha
ঘ	gha	ঝ	jha	ড়	ṛa	দ	da
ঙ	ṅa	ঞ	ña	ঢ	ḍha	ধ	dha
				ঢ়	ṛha	ন	na
				ণ	ṇa		

Labials		Semivowels		Sibilants		Aspirate	
প	pa	য	ya	শ	śa	হ	ha
ফ	pha	য়	ẏa	ষ	sha		
ব	ba (See Note 3)	র	ra	স	sa		
ভ	bha	ল	la				
ম	ma	ব	ba (see Note 3)				

Anusvāra		*Bisarga*		*Candrabindu* *(anunāsika)* (see Note 4)		*Abagraha* (see Note 5)	
ং	ṃ	ঃ	ḥ	ঁ	n̐, m̐	ঽ	' (apostrophe)

Notes

1. Only the vowel forms that appear at the beginning of a syllable are listed; the forms used for vowels following a consonant can be found in grammars; no distinction between the two is made in transliteration.

2. The vowel *a* is implicit after all consonants and consonant clusters and is supplied in transliteration, with the following exceptions:

   (a) when another vowel is indicated by its appropriate sign; and

   (b) when the absence of any vowel is indicated by the subscript symbol (◌) called *hasanta* or *birāma*.

3. ব is used both as a labial and as a semivowel. When it occurs as the second consonant of a consonant cluster, it is transliterated *va*. When ব is doubled, it is transliterated *bba*.

4. *Candrabindu* before guttural, palatal, cerebral, and dental occlusives is transliterated ñ̇. Before labials, sibilants, semivowels, the aspirate, vowels, and in final position it is transliterated m̐.

5. When doubled, *abagraha* is transliterated by two apostrophes (").

SPECIAL CHARACTERS AND CHARACTER MODIFIERS IN ROMANIZATION

Special character	*Name*	*USMARC hexadecimal code*
'	apostrophe	27

Character modifiers	*Name*	*USMARC hexadecimal code*
́	acute	E2
̃	tilde	E4
̄	macron	E5
̆	breve	E6
̇	dot above	E7
̐	candrabindu	EF
̣	dot below	F2
̲	underscore	F6

Gujarati

Vowels and Diphthongs (see Note 1)

અ	a		ઋ	r̥
આ	ā		એ	e
ઇ	i		ઍ	ê
ઈ	ī		ઐ	ai
ઉ	u		ઓ	o
ઊ	ū		ઑ	ô
			ઔ	au

Consonants (see Note 2)

Gutturals		**Palatals**		**Cerebrals**		**Dentals**	
ક	ka	ચ	ca	ટ	ṭa	ત	ta
ખ	kha	છ	cha	ઠ	ṭha	થ	tha
ગ	ga	જ	ja	ડ	ḍa	દ	da
ઘ	gha	ઝ	jha	ઢ	ḍha	ધ	dha
ઙ	ṅa	ઞ	ña	ણ	ṇa	ન	na

Labials		**Semivowels**		**Sibilants**		**Aspirate**	
પ	pa	ય	ya	શ	śa	હ	ha
ફ	pha	ર	ra	ષ	sha		
બ	ba	લ	la	સ	sa		
ભ	bha	ળ	ḷa				
મ	ma	વ	va				

Anusvāra (see Note 3)		*Visarga*		*Avagraha* (see Note 4)	
ં	ṃ	ઃ	ḥ	ઽ	' (apostrophe)

1. Only the vowel forms that appear at the beginning of a syllable are listed; the forms used for vowels following a consonant can be found in grammars; no distinction between the two is made in transliteration.

2. The vowel *a* is implicit after all consonants and consonant clusters and is supplied in transliteration, with the following exceptions:

   (a) when another vowel is indicated by its appropriate sign; and

   (b) when the absence of any vowel is indicated by the subscript sign (ˎ) called *halanta* or *virāma*.

3. Exception: *anusvāra* is transliterated by:

   ṅ before gutturals,

   ñ before palatals,

   ṇ before cerebrals,

   n before dentals, and

   m before labials.

4. When doubled, *avagraha* is transliterated by two apostrophes (ʺ).

SPECIAL CHARACTERS AND CHARACTER MODIFIERS IN ROMANIZATION

Special character	Name	USMARC hexadecimal code
ʼ	apostrophe	27

Character modifiers	Name	USMARC hexadecimal code
ó	acute	E2
ô	circumflex	E3
õ	tilde	E4
ō	macron	E5
ȯ	dot above	E7
ọ	dot below	F2
o̥	circle below	F4

Hindi

Vowels and Diphthongs (see Note 1)

Traditional Style	New Style	Romanization
अ	अ	a
आ	आ	ā
इ	बि	i
ई	बी	ī
उ	बु	u
ऊ	बू	ū
ऋ	बृ	r̥
ॠ	बॄ	r̥̄
ऌ बॢ ऍ	ऍ	ḷ ĕ
ए बे	ए बे	e
ऐ	बॅ	ê
ऐ	बे	ăi
ऐ	बै	ai
ओ	ऑ	ŏ
ओ	ओ	o
आं	आं	ô
औ	औ	ău
औ	औ	au

Consonants (see Notes 2 and 3)

Gutturals		Palatals		Cerebrals		Dentals	
क	ka	च	ca	ट	ṭa	त	ta
[क़	qa]	छ	cha	[ड़	ṭa]	थ	tha
ख	kha	ज	ja	ठ	ṭha	द	da
[ख़	k͟ha]	[ज़	za]	ड	ḍa	ध	dha
ग	ga	झ	jha	ड़	ṛa	न	na
[ग़	g͟ha]	ञ	ña	ढ	ḍha		
घ	gha			ढ़	ṛha		
[घ़	g͟ha]			ण	ṇa		
ङ	ṅa						

Labials		Semivowels		Sibilants		Aspirate	
प	pa	य	ya	श	śa	ह	ha
फ	pha	र	ra	व	sha	[ह़]	ḥa]
[फ़]	fa]	ल	la	स	sa		
ब	ba	व	va	[स़]	ṣa]		
भ	bha						
म	ma						

| *Anusvāra* | | *Anunāsika* | | *Visarga* | | *Avagraha* | |
(see Note 4)		(see Note 5)				(see Note 6)	
ं	ṃ	ँ	n̐, m̐	:	ḥ	ऽ	'
							(apostrophe)

Notes

1. Only the vowel forms that appear at the beginning of a syllable are listed; the forms used for vowels following a consonant can be found in grammars; no distinction between the two is made in transliteration.

2. The vowel *a* is implicit after all consonants and consonant clusters and is supplied in transliteration, with the following exceptions:

    (a) when another vowel is indicated by its appropriate sign; and

    (b) when the absence of any vowel is indicated by the subscript sign (‿) called *halanta* or *virāma*.

3. The dotted letters, shown in brackets in the table, are used in Urdu words.

4. Exception: *Anusvāra* is transliterated by:

    ṅ before gutturals,

    ñ before palatals,

    ṇ before cerebrals,

    n before dentals, and

    m before labials.

5. *Anunāsika* before guttural, palatal, cerebral, and dental occlusives is transliterated n̐. Before labials, sibilants, semivowels, aspirates, vowels, and in final position it is transliterated m̐.

6. When doubled, *avagraha* is transliterated by two apostrophes (").

Kannada

Vowels and Diphthongs (see Note 1)

ಅ	a		ೠ	ḷ̥
ಆ	ā		ಎ	e
ಇ	i		ಏ	ē
ಈ	ī		ಐ	ai
ಉ	u		ಒ	o
ಊ	ū		ಓ	ō
ಋ	r̥		ಔ	au
ೠ	r̥̄			

Consonants (see Note 2)

Gutturals		**Palatals**		**Cerebrals**		**Dentals**	
ಕ	ka	ಚ	ca	ಟ	ṭa	ತ	ta
ಖ	kha	ಛ	cha	ಠ	ṭha	ಥ	tha
ಗ	ga	ಜ	ja	ಡ	ḍa	ದ	da
ಘ	gha	ಝ	jha	ಢ	ḍha	ಧ	dha
ಙ	ṅa	ಞ	ña	ಣ	ṇa	ನ	na

Labials		**Semivowels**		**Sibilants**		**Aspirate**	
ಪ	pa	ಯ	ya	ಶ	śa	ಹ	ha
ಫ	pha	ರ	ra	ಷ	ṣa		
ಬ	ba	ಱ	ṟa	ಸ	sa		
ಭ	bha	ಲ	la				
ಮ	ma	ಳ	ḷa				
		ೞ	ḻa				
		ವ	va				

Anusvāra (Bindu
or *Sonne)*
(see Note 3)

Visarga

೦	ṃ	ಃ	ḥ

1. Only the vowel forms that appear at the beginning of a syllable are listed; the forms used for vowels following a consonant can be found in grammars; no distinction between the two is made in transliteration.

2. The vowel *a* is implicit after all consonants and consonant clusters and is supplied in transliteration, with the following exceptions:

   (a) when another vowel is indicated by its appropriate sign; and

   (b) when the absence of any vowel is indicated by the superscript sign (ˊ)

3. Exception: *Anusvāra* is transliterated by:

   ṅ before gutturals,

   ñ before palatals,

   ṇ before cerebrals,

   n before dentals, and

   m before labials.

CHARACTER MODIFIERS IN ROMANIZATION

Character modifiers	Name	USMARC hexadecimal code
́	acute	E2
̃	tilde	E4
̄	macron	E5
̇	dot above	E7
̣	dot below	F2
̤	double dot below	F3
̥	circle below	F4
̲	underscore	F6

Malayalam

Vowels and Diphthongs (see Note 1)

അ	a			ൠ	r̥̄
ആ	ā			ൢ	l̥
ഄ	ã (see Note 2)			എ	e
ഇ	i			ഏ	ē
ഈ	ī			ഐ	ai
ഉ	u			ഒ	o
ഊ	ū			ഓ	ō
ഋ	r̥			ഔ	au

Consonants (see Note 3)

Gutturals		Palatals		Cerebrals		Dentals	
ക	ka	ച	ca	s	ṭa	ത	ta
ഖ	kha	ഛ	cha	o	ṭha	ഥ	tha
ഗ	ga	ജ	ja	ഡ	ḍa	ദ	da
ഘ	gha	ഝ	jha	ഢ	ḍha	ധ	dha
ങ	ṅa	ഞ	ña	ണ	ṇa	ന	na

Labials		Semivowels		Sibilants		Aspirate	
പ	pa	യ	ya	ശ	śa	ഹ	ha
ഫ	pha	ര	ra	ഷ	ṣa		
ബ	ba	ഺ	ṟa	സ	sa		
ഭ	bha	൦൦	ṯṯa (see Note 4)				
മ	ma	ല	la				
		ള	ḷa				
		ഴ	ḻa				
		വ	va				

Anusvāra (see Note 5)		*Visarga*		*Avagraha*	
ം	ṃ	ഃ	ḥ	ഽ	’ (apostrophe)

1. Only the vowel forms that appear at the beginning of a syllable are listed; the forms used for vowels following a consonant can be found in grammars; no distinction between the two is made in transliteration.

2. When ꭥ is used in combination with the vowel *u* (ꭲ), the combination is also transliterated by *à*.

3. The vowel *a* is implicit after all consonants and consonant clusters and is supplied in transliteration, with the following exceptions:
   (a) when another vowel is indicated by its appropriate sign;
   (b) when the absence of any vowel is indicated by the superscript sign ˅ (also used for the vowel *à*); and
   (c) when the following modified consonantal forms are used:

᭐	k	᭐	n	᭐	l	᭐	r
᭐	ṇ	᭐	t	∞	ḷ		

4. When ᠬᠬ appears as a subscript in a cluster, it is transliterated *ṭa*.

5. Exception: *Anusvāra* is transliterated by:
   ṅ before gutturals,
   ñ before palatals,
   ṇ before cerebrals,
   n before dentals, and
   m before labials.

CHARACTER MODIFIERS IN ROMANIZATION

Character modifiers	Name	USMARC hexadecimal code
ú	acute	E2
ũ	tilde	E4
ū	macron	E5
ů	dot above	E7
ụ	dot below	F2
ụ	underscore	F6

Marathi

Vowels and Diphthongs (see Note 1)

Traditional Style	New Style	Romanization
अ	अ	a
आ	आ	ā
इ	बि	i
ई	बी	ī
उ	बु	u
ऊ	बू	ū
ऋ	बृ	ṛ
ॠ	बॄ	ṝ
ऌ		ḷ
ए	बे	e
बॅ	बॅ	ê
ऐ	बै	ai
ओ	ओ	o
बॉ	बॉ	ô
औ	औ	au

Consonants (see Note 2)

Gutturals		**Palatals**		**Cerebrals**		**Dentals**	
क	ka	च	ca	ट	ṭa	त	ta
ख	kha	छ	cha	ठ	ṭha	थ	tha
ग	ga	ज	ja	ड	ḍa	द	da
घ	gha	झ	jha	ढ	ḍha	ध	dha
ङ	ṅa	ञ	ña	ण	ṇa	न	na

Labials		**Semivowels**		**Sibilants**		**Aspirate**	
प	pa	य	ya	श	śa	ह	ha
फ	pha	र	ra	ष	sha		
ब	ba	ल	la	स	sa		
भ	bha	ळ	ḷa				
म	ma	व	va				

	Anusvāra (see Note 3)	Visarga	Avagraha (see Note 4)
ṅ	ṁ	: ḥ	' ' (apostrophe)

Notes

1. Only the vowel forms that appear at the beginning of a syllable are listed; the forms used for vowels following a consonant can be found in grammars; no distinction between the two is made in transliteration.

2. The vowel *a* is implicit after all consonants and consonant clusters and is supplied in transliteration, with the following exceptions:
   (a) when another vowel is indicated by its appropriate sign;
   (b) when the absence of any vowel is indicated by the subscript sign (ˌ) called *halanta* or *virāma*.

3. Exception: *Anusvāra* is transliterated by:
   ṅ before gutturals,
   ñ before palatals,
   ṇ before cerebrals,
   n before dentals, and
   m before labials.

   In other circumstances it is transliterated by a tilde (m̃) over the vowel.

4. When doubled, *avagraha* is transliterated by two apostrophes (").

SPECIAL CHARACTERS AND CHARACTER MODIFIERS IN ROMANIZATION

Special character	Name	USMARC hexadecimal code
'	apostrophe	27

Character modifiers	Name	USMARC hexadecimal code
ó	acute	E2
ô	circumflex	E3
õ	tilde	E4
ō	macron	E5
ȯ	dot above	E7
ọ	dot below	F2
o̥	circle below	F4

Oriya

Vowels and Diphthongs (see Note 1)

ଅ	a	ଋ	ṝ
ଆ	ā	ଌ	ḷ
ଇ	i	ଏ	e
ଈ	ī	ଐ	ai
ଉ	u	ଓ	o
ଊ	ū	ଔ	au
ଋ	ṛ		

Consonants (see Note 2)

Gutturals		**Palatals**		**Cerebrals**		**Dentals**	
କ	ka	ଚ	ca	ଟ	ṭa	ତ	ta
ଖ	kha	ଛ	cha	ଠ	ṭha	ଥ	tha
ଗ	ga	ଜ	ja	ଡ	ḍa	ଦ	da
ଘ	gha	ଝ	jha	ଢ	ḍha	ଧ	dha
ଙ	ṅa	ଞ	ña	ଣ	ṇa	ନ	na

Labials		**Semivowels**		**Sibilants**		**Aspirate**	
ପ	pa	ଯ	ya	ଶ	śa	ହ	ha
ଫ	pha	ୟ	ẏa	ଷ	sha		
ବ	ba	ର	ra	ସ	sa		
ଭ	bha	ଲ	la				
ମ	ma	ଳ	ḷa				
		ଵ	ba (see Note 3)				

Anusvāra (see Note 4)		*Bisarga*		*Candrabindu* *(anunāsika)* (see Note 5)		*Abagraha* (see Note 6)	
ଂ	ṃ	ଃ	ḥ	ଁ	n̐, m̐	ଽ	,
							(apostrophe)

1. Only the vowel forms that appear at the beginning of a syllable are listed; the forms used for vowels following a consonant can be found in grammars; no distinction between the two is made in transliteration.

2. The vowel *a* is implicit after all consonants and consonant clusters and is supplied in transliteration, with the following exceptions:

    (a) when another vowel is indicated by its appropriate sign; and

    (b) when the absence of any vowel is indicated by the subscript sign (ֻ) called *hasanta*.

3. ব is used both as a labial and as a semivowel. When it occurs as the second consonant of a consonant cluster, it is transliterated *va*. When ব is doubled, it is transliterated *bba*.

4. Exception: *Anusvāra* is transliterated by:

    ṅ before gutturals,

    ñ before palatals,

    ṇ before cerebrals,

    n before dentals, and

    m before labials.

5. *Candrabindu* before gutteral, palatal, cerebral, and dental occlusives is transliterated n̆. Before labials, sibilants, semivowels, the aspirate, vowels, and in final position it is transliterated m̆.

6. When doubled, *abagraha* is transliterated by two apostrophes (").

SPECIAL CHARACTERS AND CHARACTER MODIFIERS IN ROMANIZATION

Special character	Name	USMARC hexadecimal code
'	apostrophe	27

Character modifiers	Name	USMARC hexadecimal code
́	acute	E2
̃	tilde	E4
̄	macron	E5
̇	dot above	E7
̆	candrabindu	EF
̣	dot below	F2
̥	circle below	F4

Panjabi
(in Gurmukhi Script)

Vowels and Diphthongs (see Note 1)

ਅ	a		ਏ ਐ	e
ਆ	ā		ਐ ਐ	ai
ਇ	i		ਓ	o
ਈ	ī		ਔ	au
ਉ	u			
ਊ	ū			

Consonants (see Notes 2 and 3)

Sibilants		Aspirate		Gutturals		Palatals	
ਸ	sa	ਹ	ha	ਕ	ka	ਚ	ca
ਸ਼	sha			ਖ	kha	ਛ	cha
				ਖ਼	k͟ha	ਜ	ja
				ਗ	ga	ਜ਼	za
				ਗ਼	g͟ha	ਝ	jha
				ਘ	gha	ਞ	ña
				ਙ	ṅa		

Cerebrals		Dentals		Labials		Semivowels	
ਟ	ṭa	ਤ	ta	ਪ	pa	ਯ	ya
ਠ	ṭha	ਥ	tha	ਫ	pha	ਰ	ra
ਡ	ḍa	ਦ	da	ਫ਼	fa	ਲ	la
ਢ	ḍha	ਧ	dha	ਬ	ba	ਲ਼	l̤a
ਣ	ṇa	ਨ	na	ਭ	bha	ਵ	wa
				ਮ	ma	ੜ	ṛa

Bindī		*Ṭippī*		*Adhik*	
(see Note 4)		(see Note 5)		(see Note 6)	
ਂ	ṃ	ੰ	m̐	ੱ	[doubles the following consonant]

1. Only the vowel forms that appear at the beginning of a syllable are listed; the forms used for vowels following a consonant can be found in grammars; no distinction between the two is made in transliteration.
2. The vowel *a* is implicit after consonant clusters and may be implicit after consonants except when they are final or when another vowel is indicated by its appropriate sign. The cases in which the vowel *a* is implicit, however, can be determined only from a knowledge of the language or from suitable reference sources. In such cases the *a* is supplied in transliteration.
3. The dotted letters are used in Urdu words.
4. Exception: *Bindī* is transliterated by:
   - *ṅ* before gutturals,
   - *ñ* before palatals,
   - *ṇ* before cerebrals,
   - *n* before dentals, and
   - *m* before labials.
5. Exception: *Ṭippī* is transliterated by:
   - *ṅ* before gutturals,
   - *ñ* before palatals,
   - *ṇ* before cerebrals,
   - *n* before dentals, and
   - *m* before labials.
6. Exception: When *adhik* implies the combination of a non-aspirated and an aspirated consonant, the combination is transliterated as a non-aspirated, followed by an aspirated consonant.

CHARACTER MODIFIERS IN ROMANIZATION

Character modifiers	Name	USMARC hexadecimal code
̃	tilde	E4
̄	macron	E5
̆	breve	E6
̇	dot above	E7
̣	dot below	F2
̲	underscore	F6

Sanskrit and Prakrit
(in Devanagari Script)

When Sanskrit is written in another script, the corresponding letters in that script are transliterated according to this table.

Vowels and Diphthongs (see Note 1)

अ	a	ऋ	$\bar{r}$
आ	ā	ॡ	$\bar{l}$
इ	i	ए	e
ई	ī	ऐ	ai
उ	u	ओ	o
ऊ	ū	औ	au
ऋ	ṛ		

Consonants (see Note 2)

Gutturals		**Palatals**		**Cerebrals**		**Dentals**	
क	ka	च	ca	ट	ṭa	त	ta
ख	kha	छ	cha	ठ	ṭha	थ	tha
ग	ga	ज	ja	ड	ḍa	द	da
घ	gha	झ	jha	ढ	ḍha	ध	dha
ङ	ṅa	ञ	ña	ण	ṇa	न	na

Labials		**Semivowels**		**Sibilants**		**Aspirate**	
प	pa	य	ya	श	śa	ह	ha
फ	pha	र	ra	ष	ṣa		
ब	ba	ल	la	स	sa		
भ	bha	ळ	ḷa				
म	ma	व	va				

Anusvāra (see Note 3)		*Anunāsika*		*Visarga*		*Jihvāmūlīya*	
ं	ṃ	ঁ	m̐	:	ḥ	)(	ẖ

Upadhmānīya		*Avagraha* (see Note 4)		
ᴗ	ḫ	ऽ	' (apostrophe)	

Notes

1. Only the vowel forms that appear at the beginning of a syllable are listed; the forms used for vowels following a consonant can be found in grammars; no distinction between the two is made in transliteration.

2. The vowel *a* is implicit after all consonants and consonant clusters and is supplied in transliteration, with the following exceptions:
   (a) when another vowel is indicated by its appropriate sign; and
   (b) when the absence of any vowel is indicated by the subscript sign (˸) called *halanta* or *virāma*.

3. Exception: *Anusvāra* is transliterated by:
   ṅ before gutturals,
   ñ before palatals,
   ṇ before cerebrals,
   n before dentals, and
   m before labials.

4. When doubled, *avagraha* is transliterated by two apostrophes (").

SPECIAL CHARACTERS AND CHARACTER MODIFIERS IN ROMANIZATION

Special character	Name	USMARC hexadecimal code
'	apostrophe	27

Character modifiers	Name	USMARC hexadecimal code
á	acute	E2
ã	tilde	E4
ā	macron	E5
ȧ	dot above	E7
ă	candrabindu	EF
ạ	dot below	F2
ḁ	circle below	F4
a̲	underscore	F6
a̠	upadhmaniya	F9

Tamil

Vowels and Diphthongs (see Note 1)

அ	a	எ	e
ஆ	ā	ஏ	ē
இ	i	ஐ	ai
ஈ	ī	ஒ	o
உ	u	ஓ	ō
ஊ	ū	ஔ	au

Consonants (see Note 2)

∴	ḳa	ம	ma
க	ka	ய	ya
ங	ṅa	ர	ra (see Note 3)
ச	ca	ல	la
ஞ	ña	வ	va
ட	ṭa	ழ	ḻa
ண	ṇa	ள	ḷa
த	ta	ற	ṟa
ந	na	ன	ṉa
ப	pa		

Sanskrit Sounds

ஜ	ja	ஸ	sa
ஶ	śa	ஹ	ha
ஷ	ṣa		

Notes

1. Only the vowel forms that appear at the beginning of a syllable are listed; the forms used for vowels following a consonant can be found in grammars; no distinction between the two is made in transliteration.
2. The vowel *a* is implicit after all consonants and consonant clusters and is supplied in romanization, with the following exceptions:
   (a) when another vowel is indicated by its appropriate sign; and
   (b) when the absence of any vowel is indicated by the superscript dot (்) called *puḷḷi*.
3. This letter has the same form as the vowel sign for *ā* appearing after a consonant. Where ambiguity arises, it is written ற .

CHARACTER MODIFIERS IN ROMANIZATION

Character modifiers	Name	USMARC hexadecimal code
ó	acute	E2
õ	tilde	E4
ō	macron	E5
ȯ	dot above	E7
ọ	dot below	F2
o̱	underscore	F6

Telugu

Vowels and Diphthongs (see Note 1)

అ	a	ఌ	l̥
ఆ	ā	ఎ	e
ఇ	i	ఏ	ē
ఈ	ī	ఐ	ai
ఉ	u	ఒ	o
ఊ	ū	ఓ	ō
ఋ	r̥	ఔ	au
ౠ	r̥̄		

Consonants (see Note 2)

Gutturals		**Palatals**		**Cerebrals**		**Dentals**	
క	ka	చ	ca	ట	ṭa	త	ta
ఖ	kha	ౘ	ĉa	ఠ	ṭha	థ	tha
గ	ga	ఛ	cha	డ	ḍa	ద	da
ఘ	gha	జ	ja	ఢ	ḍha	ధ	dha
ఙ	ṅa	ౙ	ĵa	ణ	ṇa	న	na
		ఝ	jha				
		ఞ	ña				

Labials		**Semivowels**		**Sibilants**		**Aspirate**	
ప	pa	య	ya	శ	śa	హ	ha
ఫ	pha	ర	ra	ష	ṣa		
బ	ba	ఱ	r̲a	స	sa		
భ	bha	ల	la				
మ	ma	ళ	ḷa				
		వ	va				

Sunna (see Note 3)		*Visarga*		*Ardhasunna* (see Note 4)	
ం	ṃ	ః	ḥ	‘, ఁ	m̐

1. Only the vowel forms that appear at the beginning of a syllable are listed; the forms used for vowels following a consonant can be found in grammars; no distinction between the two is made in transliteration.

2. The vowel *a* is implicit after all consonants and consonant clusters and is supplied in transliteration, with the following exceptions:

   (a) when another vowel is indicated by its appropriate sign; and

   (b) when the absence of any vowel is indicated by the superscript sign (ॆ) called *valapalagilaka*.

3. Exception: *Sunna* is transliterated by:

   ṅ before gutturals,

   ñ before palatals,

   ṇ before cerebrals,

   n before dentals, and

   m before labials.

4. *Ardhasunna* before gutturals, palatal, cerebral, and dental occlusives is transliterated ñ̇. Before labials, sibilants, semivowels, the aspirate, vowels, and in final position it is transliterated m̐.

CHARACTER MODIFIERS IN ROMANIZATION

Character Modifiers	Name	USMARC hexadecimal code
ó	acute	E2
ô	circumflex	E3
õ	tilde	E4
ō	macron	E5
ȯ	dot above	E7
ŏ	candrabindu	EF
ọ	cedilla	F0
ọ	dot below	F2
ọ	circle below	F4
ọ	underscore	F6

Urdu
(in Arabic Script)

Letters of the Alphabet

Initial	Medial	Final	Alone	Romanization
ا	ل	ل	ا	omit (see Note 1)
ب	ب	ب	ب	b
پ	پ	پ	پ	p
ت	ت	ت	ت	t
ٹ	ٹ	ٹ	ٹ	ṭ
ٹ	ٹ	ٹ	ٹ	ṭ
ث	ث	ث	ث	s̱
ج	ج	ج	ج	j
چ	چ	چ	چ	c
ح	ح	ح	ح	ḥ
خ	خ	خ	خ	kh
د	د	د	د	d
ڈ	ڈ	ڈ	ڈ	ḍ
ڈ	ڈ	ڈ	ڈ	ḍ
ذ	ذ	ذ	ذ	ẕ
ر	ر	ر	ر	r
ڑ	ڑ	ڑ	ڑ	ṛ
ڑ	ڑ	ڑ	ڑ	ṛ
ز	ز	ز	ز	z
ژ	ژ	ژ	ژ	zh
س	س	س	س	s
ش	ش	ش	ش	sh
ص	ص	ص	ص	ṣ
ض	ض	ض	ض	ẓ
ط	ط	ط	ط	ṭ
ظ	ظ	ظ	ظ	ẓ
ع	ع	ع	ع	ʻ (ayn)
غ	غ	غ	غ	gh
ف	ف	ف	ف	f
ق	ق	ق	ق	q
ك	ك	ك	ك	k
گ	گ	گ	گ	g
ل	ل	ل	ل	l
م	م	م	م	m

				Value
ﻦ	ﻨ	ﻧ	ن	n
ـ	ـ	ﮟ	ں	ṉ (see Note 2)
و	ﻮ	ﻭ	و	v
ﻪ	ﻬ	ﻫ	ه	h
-	-	ة	ة	t (see Rule 10)
ﻰ	ﻴ (ﻲ، ﻳ)	ﻰ (ﻲ، ﻳ)	ى (ي)	y (see Note 3)

Digraphs Representing Urdu Aspirates (see Note 4) Value

bh	بﮭ
ph	پﮭ
th	تﮭ
ṭh	ٹﮭ
jh	جﮭ
ch	چﮭ
dh	دﮪ
ḍh	ڈﮪ
ṛh	ڑﮪ
kh	کﮭ
gh	گﮭ

Urdu Vowels and Diphthongs (see Note 5) Value

a	◌َ
u	◌ُ
i	◌ِ
ā	◌ٰ، ﺍ
á	◌َﻯ ، ◌َﻯٰ
ū	◌ُﻭ
ī	◌ِﻯ
o	◌ﻭ
e	◌ِﻯ ، ◌ﮮ
au	◌َﻭْ
ai	◌َﻯْ ، ◌ﮮ

Notes to the Tables

1. For the use of ﺍ (*alif*) to support ٴ (*hamzah*) and آ (*maddah*) see rules 1 and 2, respectively. For the romanization of ٴ by ' (*alif*) see rule 12. For other orthographic uses of ﺍ see rules 3-4.
2. For the distinction between ن and ں see rule 6.
3. For the distinction between ﻯ and ﮮ see rule 11(c) and (e).
4. For the form of the letter ﻫ in these digraphs, see rule 9.
5. Vowel points are used sparingly, and for romanization must be supplied from a dictionary.

RULES OF APPLICATION

Letters Which May Be Romanized in Different Ways Depending on Their Conte

1. ‏ا‎ (*alif*), ‏و‎ and ‏ى‎ are used to support ‏ء‎ (*hamzah*); see rule 12. When so use represented in romanization.

2. ‏ا‎ (*alif*) is used to support ‏آ‎ (*maddah*); see rule 13. When so used, it romanization.

3. ‏ا‎ (*alif*) is used after a consonant to indicate the long vowel romanized $\bar{a}$.

rāj	راج
karnā	كرنا

In some words of Arabic origin this *alif* appears as a superscript letter over *maqṣūrah*.

da'vá	دعوىٰ

The *alif* is sometimes omitted in writing. It is always represented in roma

'Abdurrahmān   عبد الرحمن ، عبد الرحمان

When the long vowel $\bar{a}$ is initial, it is written ‏آ‎. See rule 13(a).

4. ‏ا‎ (*alif*) may be used as an orthographic sign without phonetic significance. represented in romanization. See rule 16.

'ilman	علما

5. ‏ط‎ appears as a superscript letter over ‏ت‎, ‏د‎, and ‏ر‎ when the latter represe romanized *ṭ*, *ḍ*, and *ṛ*, respectively.

6. Regardless of pronuncitation, undotted forms of the letter ‏ن‎ are romanized romanized *n*.

jahān̲	جهاں

7. ‏و‎ is used:

   (a) To represent the consonant sound romanized *v*.

dev	ديو
vujūd	وجود

     In some words of Persian origin this consonant, though written, has cea It is retained in romanization.

khvīsh	خويش

(b) To represent the long vowel romanized *ū*.

ūkh	اوخ
Urdū	اردو

(c) To represent the long vowel romanized *o*.

os	اوس
dost	دوست

For the romanization of the conjunction و as *o* see rule 19.

(d) To represent the diphthong romanized *au*.

aur	اور
qaumī	قومی

(e) To support ء (*hamzah*). See rule 12.
For the use of ّ (*shaddah*) with و see rule 14.

8.   ه is used to represent the consonantal sound romanized *h*.

ham	هم
gāh	گاه

Final ه , though often not pronounced, is normally retained in romanization.

kih	که
guldastah	گلدسته

Exception is made in the case of words whose final syllable ends in an aspirated consonant. When final ه is added to the letter ھ in this position, it is not represented in romanization.

mukh	مکهه

9.   ه (usually written in the form ھ) is used to represent the aspirated element of the sounds romanized *bh, ph, th, ṭh, jh, ch, dh, ḍh, ṛh, kh, gh*.

phūl	پهول
acchā	اچها

For the writing and romanization of words ending in an aspirated consonant, see rule 8.

10. ة and ت, which are sometimes used interchangeably, are both romanized *t*.

ḥikmat	حکمة ، حکمت

11. ی (often written ي) is used:

(a) To represent the consonant romanized *y*.

siyāsat	سیاست
dayā	دیا

(b) To represent the long vowel romanized ī.

taṣvīr	تصویر
īshvār	ایشوار

(c) To represent the long vowel romanized e.

sher	شیر
nevā	نیوا

When ی with this value is final, the form ے generally replaces ی.

se	سے
laṛke	لڑکے

(d) To represent the long vowel romanized á. See rule 3.

da‘vá	دعوی
‘uqbá	عقبی

(e) To represent the diphthong romanized ai.

maidān	میدان
bail	بیل

When ی with this value is final, it is sometimes written ے .

hai	ہے

(f) To support ء (hamzah). In this position ی is usually undotted. See rule 12.

For the use of ّ (shaddah) with ی see rule 14.

For the use of ی in a muẓāf see rule 17.

Romanization of Orthographic Symbols Other Than Letters and Vowel Signs

Although vowel signs are frequently omitted in printed texts, they are always taken into consideration in romanization. The rules for other symbols vary.

12.   ء (hamzah)

(a) In initial position ء is not represented in romanization.

(b) In medial and final position, when ء represents a consonant, it is romanized ’ (alif).

mu’min	مؤمن
li’e	لئے
bhā’ī	بهائی

PART

4

References
&
Glossary

Contents

PART 4

Source: Library of Congress.
Network Development and MARC Standards Office
www.loc.gov/marc/readings.html

A BRIEF BIBLIOGRAPHY OF WRITINGS ON MARC

Avram, Henriette D.
MARC, its history and implications / by Henriette D. Avram.
- Washington : Library of Congress, 1975. — iii, 49 p. ; 23cm.
— ISBN 0-8444-0176-5.

Byrne, Deborah J.
MARC Manual : understanding and using MARC records/
Deborah J. Byrne. — 2nd ed. — Englewood, Colo. : Libraries
Unlimited, 1998. — xxiii, 263 p. ; 28 cm. — ISBN 1-5630
8176-8.

Coyle, Karen.
Format integration and its effect on cataloging, training,
and systems / edited by Karen Coyle. — Chicago : American
Library Association, 1993. — x, 110 p. : ill. ; 23 cm. — ISBN
0-8389-3432-3.

Crawford, Walt.
MARC for library use / Walt Crawford. — Boston, MA : G.K.
Hall, 1989. — xvi, 359 p. ; 24 cm. — ISBN 0-8161-1887-6.

Ferguson, Anna.
MARC/AACR2/authority control tagging : blitz cataloging
workbook / Bobby Ferguson. — Englewood, CO : Libraries
Unlimited, c1998. — xi, 175 p. ; 28 cm. — ISBN 1-5630-
8644-1.

Fritz, Deborah A.

Cataloging with AACR2R and USMARC : for books, computer files, serials, sound recordings, video recordings / Deborah A. Fritz. – Chicago : American Library Association, 1998. – 580 p. ; 28 cm. – ISBN 0-8389-0728-8.

Fritz, Deborah A.

MARC 21 for everyone : a practical guide / Deborah A. Fritz and Richard J. Fritz. – Chicago : American Library Association, 2003. – 240 p. – ISBN 0-8389-0842-X.

Furrie, Betty.

Understanding MARC bibliographic : machine readable cataloging / [written by Betty Furrie, in conjunction with the Data Base Development Department of the Follett Software Company ; reviewed and edited by the Network Development and MARC Standards Office, Library of Congress]. – 6th ed. – Washington, DC : Library of Congress, Cataloging Distribution Service, 2000. – 29 p. ; 28 cm. – ISBN 0-8444-1033-0.

Gildea, Matthew E.

MARC content designation / prepared by Matthew E. Gildea (Technical Processing and Automation Instruction Office, Library Services). – 2nd ed. – Washington, DC : Library of Congress, Cataloging Distribution Service, 2002. – 2v. ; 29 cm. – ISBN 0-8444-1063-2 (instructor's manual) – ISBN 0-8444-1066-7 (trainee manual).

Gredley, Ellen.

Exchanging bibliographic data : MARC and other international formats / Ellen Gredley, Alan Hopkinson – Chicago : American Library Association, 1990. – xxi, 329 p. ; 23 cm. – ISBN 0-8389-2151-5

Hensen, Steven L.

Archives, personal papers, and manuscripts : a cataloging manual for archival repositories, historical societies, and manuscript libraries / compiled by Steven L. Hensen. – 2nd ed. – Chicago : Society of American Archivists, 1989. – ix, 196 p. – ISBN 0-9318-2873-2

Matters, Marion E.

Introduction to the USMARC format for archival and manuscripts control / by Marion Matters. – Chicago : Society of American Archivists, 1990. – 24 p.– ISBN 0-6140-1638-X.

Matters, Marion E.

Oral history cataloging manual / compiled by Marion Matters. — Chicago : Society of American Archivists, c1995. — viii, 109 p. ; 28 cm. — ISBN 0-9318-2897-X.

McRae, Linda.

ArtMARC sourcebook : cataloging art, architecture, and their visual images / Linda McRae and Lynda S. White, editors. — Chicago : American Library Association, 1998. — xii, 287 p. : ill. ; 28 cm. — ISBN 0-9398-0723-7.

Millsap, Larry.

Descriptive cataloging for the AACR2R and the integrated MARC format : a how-to-do-it workbook / Larry Millsap & Terry Ellen Ferl. — Rev. ed. — New York : Neal-Schuman, c1997. — ix, 266 p. : ill. ; 28 cm. — ISBN 1-5557-0099-3.

Not entered under main entry.

Cataloging sheet music : guidelines for use with AACR2 and the MARC format / prepared by the Working Group on Sheet Music Cataloging Guidelines, Bibliographic Control Committee, Music Library Association ; complied and edited by Lois Schultz, Sarah Shaw.

Lanham, Md. : Scarecrow Press ; [United States] : Music Library Association, 2003. — ISBN 0-8108-4750-7.

Olson, Nancy B.

A cataloger's guide to MARC coding and tagging for audiovisual material / Nancy B. Olson. — DeKalb, Ill. : Minnesota Scholarly Press, c1993. — iv, 112 p. ; 28 cm. — ISBN 0-9334-7449-0.

Piepenburg, Scott.

Easy MARC : incorporating format integration / Scott Piepenburg. — 3rd ed. — San Jose, Calif. : F&W Associates, 1999. — ISBN 0-9652-1260-2.

Piepenburg, Scott.

MARC authority records made easy : a simplified guide to creating authority records for library automation systems/ Scott Piepenburg. — San Jose, Calif. : F&W Associates, 2000. — ISBN 0-9652-1263-7.

Smiraglia, Richard P.

Describing archival materials : the use of the MARC AMC format / Richard P. Smiraglia, editor. — New York :

Haworth Press, c1990. — 228 p. : ill. ; 23 cm. — ISBN 0-8665-6916-2.

Weitz, Jay.

Music coding and tagging : MARC 21 content designation for scores and sound recordings / by Jay Weitz ; foreword by Richard P. Smiraglia. — 2nd ed. — Belle Plaine, Minn. : Soldier Creek Press, 2001. — ISBN 0-9369-9677-3.

Web Literature on Cataloging Resources

Brugger, Judith M. **Cataloging the Internet.**
URL: http://ublib.buffalo.edu/libraries/units/cts/Internet/brugger.html

Caplan, Priscilla. **You Call It Corn, We Call It Syntax-Independent Metadata for Document-Like Objects.**
Public-Access Computer Systems Review 6, no. 4 (1995): 19-23.
URL: http://www.ifla.org/documents/libraries/cataloging/caplan3.txt

Caplan, Priscilla. **Cataloging Internet Resources.**
The Public-Access Computer Systems Review 4, no. 2 (1993): 61-66.
URL: http://www.ifla.org/documents/libraries/cataloging/caplan.txt

Caplan, Priscilla. **Providing Access to Online Information Resources: A Paper for Discussion.**
Harvard University Library. February 14, 1992. Response to MARBI Discussion Paper No. 54 (Providing Access to Online Information Resources).
URL: http://www.ifla.org/documents/libraries/cataloging/caplan2.txt

Chang, Kevin, et. al. **STARTS. Stanford Protocol Proposal for Internet Search and Retrieval.** Stanford University.
URL:http://www-db.stanford.edu/~gravanostarts_home.html

Cooper, Ian. **Indexing the World.**
>Computing Laboratory, University of Kent. England.
>URL: http://www.cs.ukc.ac.uk/pubs/1994/82/

Graham, Peter. **The Mid-Decade Catalog and its Environment.**
>Pre-print draft: as submitted to ALCTSE Newsletter, January, 1994.
>URL: http://www.ifla.org/documents/libraries/cataloging/cffc.htm

Guedon, Jean-Claude. **Why are Electronic Publications Difficult to Classify?: The Orthogonality of Print and Digital Media.**
>This article originally appeared in the 4th Edition of the *Directory of Electronic Journals, Newsletters and Academic Discussion Lists*, published by the Association of Research Libraries in May 1994. 1994.
>URL: http://www.ifla.org/documents/libraries/cataloging/guej1.txt

Koch, Traugott. **The role of classification schemes in Internet resource description and discovery.**
>DESIRE project deliverable.
>URL: http://www.lub.lu.se/desire/radar/reports/D3.2.3/class_v10.html
>PDF: http://www.ifla.org/documents/libraries/cataloging/classv10.pdf

Levy, David. **Cataloging in the Digital Order.**
>Digital Libraries '95. The Second Annual Conference on the Theory and Practice of Digital Libraries. June 11-13, 1995 Austin, Texas, USA.
>URL: http://csdl.tamu.edu/DL95/contents.html

Library of Congress.
>URL: http://lcweb.loc.gov/homepage/lchp.html
>**Machine-Readable Cataloging (MARC).**
>Network Development and MARC Standards Office (Library of Congress).
>URL: http://lcweb.loc.gov/marc/
>**Cataloging at the Library of Congress: Programs and Services.**
>URL: gopher://marvel.loc.gov/11/services/cataloging
>**Interlibrary Loan at the Library of Congress.**
>URL: http://lcweb.loc.gov/rr/loan/
>**Library of Congress Cataloging Newsline.**
>URL: gopher://marvel.loc.gov/11/services/cataloging/lccn
>**USMARC documents.**
>URL: http://lcweb.loc.gov/marc/

The USMARC Formats: Background and Principles.
URL: http://www.ifla.org/documents/libraries/cataloging/usmarc.txt

Field 856 (Electronic Location and Access) Guidelines.
URL: http://lcweb.loc.gov/marc/856guide.html
URL: http://www.ifla.org/documents/libraries/cataloging/marc856.txt

File Label Specification for USMARC records transferred by FTP.
URL: http://www.ifla.org/documents/libraries/cataloging/ftplabel.txt

CONSER Cataloging Manual, Module 31: Remote Access Computer File Serials.
URL: http://lcweb.loc.gov/acq/conser/module31.html

Lim, Jong-Gyun. **Using Coollists to Index HTML Documents in the Web.**
URL: http://www.ncsa.uiuc.edu/SDG/IT94/Proceedings/Searching/lim/coollist.html

MARBI. **MARBI Proposals and Discussion Papers.**
URL: gopher://marvel.loc.gov/11/services/usmarc/marbipro

Dictionary of Data Elements for Online Information Resources. Marbi Discussion Paper No. 49
URL: http://www.ifla.org/documents/libraries/cataloging/marbi49.txt

Providing Access to Online Information Resources.
Marbi Discussion Paper No. 54.
URL: http://www.ifla.org/documents/libraries/cataloging/marbi54.txt

Morgan, Eric Lease. **Mr. Serials, an electronic serials acquisitions librarian.**
URL: http://www.lib.ncsu.edu/staff/morgan/mr-serials-at-NASIG.html

Northwestern University. **Interactive Electronic Serials Cataloging Aid.**
This tool primarily provides ready access to cataloging rules, interpretations, examples of MARC bibliographic records in serial and computer file formats linked to instructional annotations, and a glossary of cataloging and computer terminology.
URL: http://www.library.nwu.edu/iesca/

OCLC. **OCLC Collections and Technical Services.**
URL: http://www.oclc.org/oclc/menu/col.htm

OCLC/NCSA Metadata Workshop Report.
URL: http://www.ifla.org/documents/libraries/cataloging/
oclcmeta.htm
Mapping the Dublin Core Metadata Elements to USMARC.
Discussion Paper No. 86. May, 1995.
URL: http://www.ifla.org/documents/libraries/cataloging
dublin1.txt
The Future Is Now: The Changing Face of Technical Services.
Proceedings of the OCLC Symposium, ALA Midwinter Conference, February 4, 1994.
URL: ftp://ftp.rsch.oclc.org/pub/documentation
ala_symposia/cataloging1994/
Cataloging and Database Services Strategy.
URL: ftp://ftp.rsch.oclc.org/pub/documentation/
whitepapers/cataloging_strategy
CORC—Cooperative Online Resource Catalog.
URL: http://www.oclc.org/oclc/research/projects/corc/
Intercat - Internet Cataloguing Project Home Page.
URL: http://www.oclc.org/oclc/man/catproj/catcall.htm
Cataloguing Internet Resources: A Manual and Practical Guide. Nancy Olson, editor.
URL: http://www.oclc.org/oclc/man/9256cat/toc.htm
URL: http://www.ifla.org/documents/libraries/cataloging
manual.txt
.**Proceedings of the Seminar on Cataloging Digital Documents.**
University of Virginia Library, Charlottesville and the Library of Congress - October 12-14, 1994.
URL: http://lcweb.loc.gov/catdir/semdigdocsseminar.html
Riddle, Prentiss. **Library culture, computer culture, and the Internet haystack.**
Rice University.
URL: http://is.rice.edu/~riddle/dl94.html
URL: http://www.ifla.org/documents/libraries cataloging/
dl94.htm
Schwartz, Michael, ed. **Report of the Distributed Indexing/ Searching Workshop.**
May 28-19, 1996. Cambridge, Massachusetts. Sponsored by the World Wide Web Consortium.

URL: http://www.w3.org/Search/9605-Indexing Workshop/

Sha, Vianne Tang. **Guidelines for cataloging Internet resources.** URL: http://www.ifla.org/documents/libraries cataloging/ sha1.txt

Tillett, Barbara B. **Cataloguing Rules and Conceptual Models.** OCLC Distinguished Seminar Series. January 9, 1996. URL: http://www.ifla.org/documents/libraries cataloging/ tilb1.htm

Stewart, Barbara. **Top 200 Technical Services Benefits of Home Page Development.** URL: http://tpot.ucsd.edu/Cataloging/Misc/top200.html

VIVA Cataloging and Intellectual Access Task Force. **Guidelines for Cataloging VIVA Electronic Collections** June 24, 1997 URL: http://www.lib.virginia.edu/~ejs7y/vivacat guidelines.html

Vizine-Goetz, Diane . **Online Classification: Implications for Classifying and Document[-like Object] Retrieval.** Electronic version of a paper published in Knowledge organization and change: proceedings of the 4th international ISKO conference, 15-18 July 1996, Washington, D.C. URL: http://orc.rsch.oclc.org:6109/dvgisko.htm

Vizine-Goetz, Diane. **Using Library Classification Schemes for Internet Resources.** OCLC Internet Cataloging Project Colloquium. URL: http://www.oclc.org/oclc/man/colloq/v-g.htm

Source: INTERNET LIBRARY FOR LIBRARIANS
http://www.itcompany.com/inforetriever/cat_marc.htm

CATALOGING: MARC FORMATS

A Portal Designed for Librarians to Locate Internet Resources Related to Their Profession.

TITLE:	**Brief Guide to LC Policy and Practice for Format Integration — Books**
DESCRIPTION:	Summarizes Library of Congress policy and practice for fields 246; 505; 525; 538; 546 after format integration.
E-MAIL:	cpso@mail.loc.gov
KEYWORDS:	usmarc format, format integration

TITLE:	**Cataloging Calculator**
CREATOR:	Banerjee, Kyle.
DESCRIPTION:	Provides quick assistance to those who want to locate information about a USMARC tag for bibliographic record and its examples. But it contains information about the variable data fields only.
KEYWORDS:	usmarc format, marc tag

TITLE:	**Cataloging Cheat Sheet**
DESCRIPTION:	A concise description of the fixed and variable fields in USMARC. Created by: J. McRee Elrod, Updated/ Corrected by: Anna Kroll, HTML version by: Charlene Hu.
KEYWORDS:	usmarc format
TITLE:	**Catalogers' Reference Shelf**
DESCRIPTION:	"The Cataloger's Reference Shelf, a component of the help systems in ITS for Windows and the Library.Solution

integrated online library system, has recently been published in web format and is available for free use by any cataloger with a web browser. The CRS is a collection of 21 MARC manuals and other reference works frequently accessed by technical services staff."

E-MAIL: info@TLCdelivers.com

KEYWORDS: cataloging, classification, subject headings

TITLE: **Format Integration Test Records**

DESCRIPTION: Intended for use by system developers who are in the process of planning for the last phase of Format Integration which will be implemented by the Library of Congress in March 1996. The test file consists of approximately 175 records containing examples of the new fixed field 006, as well as the new leader and field 008 values. Some of the records contain an atypical number of fields and are longer than 9050 characters. Because this is a Library of Congress working file, it does not contain records representing all record types at this time. Records for books, music, visual materials, and computer files are included in this test file.

E-MAIL: LC's MARC Distribution Services, cdsinfo@mail.loc.gov

KEYWORDS: usmarc format, format integration

TITLE: **Guidelines for Coding Electronic Resources in Leader/ 06**

CREATOR: Library of Congress. Network Development and MARC Standards Office.

DESCRIPTION: "This document is intended to assist MARC users in deciding how to code records for electronic resources in Leader/06 (Type of record) and Computer Files 008/ 26 and 006/09 (Type of computer file)."—Title screen.

E-MAIL: lcweb@loc.gov

KEYWORDS: cataloging electronic resources, type of record

TITLE: **Guidelines for the Use of Field 856**

CREATOR: Library of Congress. Network Development and MARC Standards Office.

DESCRIPTION: A guideline prepared by Library of Congress for applying the 856 field to electronic resources.

E-MAIL: lcweb@loc.gov

KEYWORDS: cataloging internet resources, url, 856 field

TITLE: **Initial Definite and Indefinite Articles**

DESCRIPTION: From USMARC Format for Bibliographic Data and USMARC

Format for Authority Data, Appendix E, this is a list of definite and indefinite articles and the languages in which they are used alphabetically by the article.

E-MAIL: lcweb@loc.gov
KEYWORDS: usmarc format, initial articles, foreign languages

TITLE: **Understanding MARC Bibliographic: Machine-Readable Cataloging**
DESCRIPTION: Another high quality publication offered by Library of Congress, the Web version of this book covers the basic concepts of the MARC format, summary of USMARC fields and sample records.
E-MAIL: lcweb@loc.gov
KEYWORDS: usmarc format, marc

TITLE: **USMARC**
DESCRIPTION: Stores USMARC proposals, discussion papers, formats documents, discussion list messages archives, etc. USMARC Concise Format for Authority DataUSMARC Concise Format for Bibliographic DataUSMARC Concise Format for Classification DataUSMARC Concise Format for Community informationUSMARC Concise Format for Holdings DataUSMARC Code List for CountriesUSMARC Code List for LanguagesUSMARC Code List for Relators, Sources, Description ConventionsUSMARC Code List for Geographic Areas
E-MAIL: lcweb@loc.gov
KEYWORDS: usmarc format

TITLE: **USMARC Advisory Group Forum**
DESCRIPTION: Is a moderated e-conference open to members of the group and anyone interesting in discussing the implementation, maintenance, and development of the USMARC formats. Sponsored by LC Network Development and MARC Standards Office.
INSTRUCTION: subscribe USMARC
E-MAIL: lcweb@loc.gov
NOTE: Monthly archives
KEYWORDS: usmarc format

TITLE: **USMARC Format for Authority Data: Field List**
DESCRIPTION: This document notes the changes contained in the updates of the USMARC Format for Authority Data.
KEYWORDS: usmarc format

TITLE:	**USMARC Format for Bibliographic Data: Field List**
DESCRIPTION:	This document notes the changes contained in the updates of the USMARC Format for Bibliographic Data.
KEYWORDS:	usmarc format

TITLE:	**Winship, Douglas. A Guide to Looking at Marc Records Online.**
DESCRIPTION:	Shows how MARC records look online.
INSTRUCTION:	GET MARC OPACS
E-MAIL:	Douglas Winship, winship@tenet.edu
KEYWORDS:	usmarc format

Available from: Library of Congress, Cataloging Distribution Service
http://www.loc.gov/cds/desktop/contacts.html

CATALOGER'S DESKTOP

The most widely used cataloging documentation resources in an integrated, online system; includes the current version of AACR2.

Available now on the Web and on CD-ROM

Resource List

- Anglo-American Cataloguing Rules (AACR2)
- Library of Congress Rule Interpretations
- MARC 21 Formats for Bibliographic Data, Authority Data, Holdings Data, Classification Data, Community Information
- Latest editions of all MARC Code Lists
- Subject Cataloging Manual: Classification, Shelflisting, Subject Headings
- Archival Moving Image Materials: A Cataloging Manual
- BIBCO, NACO, SACO Participants' Manuals
- Link to Classification Web (a separate subscription service)
- CONSER Cataloging Manual
- CONSER Editing Guide
- Descriptive Cataloging Manual
- Descriptive Cataloging of Rare Books

- Graphic Materials: Rules for Describing Original Items and Historical Collections
- Library of Congress Filing Rules
- Map Cataloging Manual
- Link to the National Library of Medicine's *Medical Subject Headings*
- Links to metadata resources
- Music Cataloging Decisions
- Standard Citation Forms for Published Bibliographies used in Rare Book Cataloging
- Thesaurus for Graphic Materials
- AACR2 Rule Interpretations of Library and Archives Canada
- Canadian Subject Headings (Library and Archives Canada)
- Library of Congress Classification Outline
- Subject Cataloging Manual: Web Resources for SACO Proposals

CATALOGING CALCULATOR

		Search Options	
	Find it!		
Enter Query Above		○ LC Cutter	○ Language Codes
Enter Fixed Field Below		○ Geog. Cutter	○ AACR2 Abbrevs.
Books ▾		○ Geog. Area Codes	● MARC Var. Fields
		○ Country Codes	

TechKNOW
Volume 7, Issue 3 - August 2001
A Quarterly Newsletter of Bright Ideas for the Technical Services Division

Cataloging Calculator

http://ucs.orst.edu/~banerjek/cutter.html

Kyle Banerjee got tired of looking up information in various table one day, decided there had to be a better way, and the Cataloging Calculator was born.

This is a website for the cataloger in all of us. Decide what kind of information you need, type in a search term and out pops the correct coding. You can search for LC main entry cutters, geographic cutters, geographic area codes, country codes, language codes, and AACR2 abbreviations. For example, click on "geographic area codes", type Greece and the correct geographic code for Greece is displayed. You can keyword search for MARC variable field numbers and coding. You can even click on OCLC Fixed Field elements and access lists of codes—all from the same compact screen. Designed primarily to aid kyle's worl flow, it is updated regularly.

MARC RECORD SERVICES

Introduction

This category includes any service that distributes MARC 21 records, such as records for copy cataloging, records supplied with materials, records used for recon purposes, updated records, conversion services, etc. Free services are indicated in the title of each listing.

Brodart Retrospective Conversion

www.brodart.com/automation/proacacus.htm

Cassidy Cataloguing Services, Inc.

Cassidy Cataloguing Services, Inc. provides MARC 21 bibliographic records for print, electronic, audiovisual, rare books, foreign language, union lists, cataloging-in-publication for authors and publishing houses plus onsite processing services. Specializing in original cataloging, CCSs records load into any MARC 21-compliant software and adhere to the national bibliographic standards set forth in the AACR2 Rev. 2002 and include Library of Congress subject headings, LC classification numbers and DDC numbers where requested. Subject strengths are LAW, BUSINESS, SCIENCE AND TECHNOLOGY supporting corporate research. Products available include Web-Hosted OPAC—now with interactive serials check-in, labels, cards, paper shelflist and book cataloges.

www.cassidycataloguing.com/

Internet e-mail address: mailto:%20info@cassidycat.com

Telephone: +1-973-481-0900

Fax: +1-973-481-9110

Follett Alliance Plus

www.fsc.follett.com/products/allianceplus/

Follett Authority Record Program

www.fsc.follett.com/products/authority_record/index.cfm

Impact/ONLINE MARCit

Impact/ONLINE MARCit is a cataloging support system that provides access to over 50 million MARC 21 bibliographic and authority records via the Web. Features include authority control, full screen interactive editor, FTP record delivery and Z39.50 access. Minimum hardware requirements: Windows 95 or 98 or NT 4.0 operating system, 166 MMX MHz Pentium processor, 32MB RAM memory, 28.8K BPS modem, 15MB free hard disk space, Web browser, either Netscape Navigator 4 or higher or Microsoft Internet Explorer 4 or higher. http://www.ag-canada.com/

Internet e-mail address: mailto:bam@ag-canada.com

Telephone: +1-800-225-8534 extension 307

Fax: +1-416-236-7489

ITS.MARC

The Library Corporation's ITS.MARC™ provides Z39.50 or Web access to over 16 million MARC records, with Z39.50 access to the 84 million record RLIN database. ITS.MARC is updated daily with records from the Library of Congress. Other databases are updated as new cataloging is received. Users may search ITS.MARC by title, author, subject, keyword, or any of eleven standard numbers. ITS.MARC includes full Boolean support for more powerful searching. Once a user finds a desired record, he can click on 'Save' to open an editor window or save to a queue for later retrieval. Users may edit records using the ease and sophistication of the industry's only third generation technical services workstation, ITS.forWindows™, which is part of ITS.MARC.

www.tlcdelivers.com/

Internet e-mail address: info@tlcdelivers.com

Telephone: +1-800-325-7759

Fax: +1-304-229-0295

LaserQuest ® CD-ROM Cataloging System

LaserQuest ®, the world's largest CD-ROM cataloging database, has more than 10 million MARC records from the Library of Congress, National Library of Canada and clients that provide high hit rates for retrospective and new cataloging. Numeric and title searching results in match lists that provide title, author, publication information, pagination and source record symbols. Enjoy effortless networking and monthly or bimonthly updates. LaserQuest® supports the MARC 21 bibliographic format.

http://www.att.com/gov/library/

Internet e-mail address: vblades@att.com

Telephone: +1-800-933-5383 (U.S. or Canada) or +1-805-879-4278

Fax: +1-805-967-7094

LibraryCom

http://www.librarycom.com/cgi-bin/lc.exe/lc_services.html

Library of Congress Cataloging MARC Distribution Service

The Library of Congress Cataloging MARC Distribution Service offers MARC 21 bibliographic, authority and classification records via Internet FTP. It provides cataloging for materials in hundreds of languages—some as diverse as Swahili and Arabic, with some non-roman alphabet languages like Chinese, Hebrew, Japanese, Korean, Arabic and Yiddish available in vernacular scripts. It adheres to the national level cataloging for almost all English-language imprints and includes cataloging from CONSER and NACO participants.

www.loc.gov/cds/mds.html

Internet e-mail address: cdsinfo@loc.gov

Telephone: Toll-free in U.S.: 1-800-255-3666 (CDS Products and Services Only) *or* +1-202-707-6100

Fax: +1-202-707-1334

For bills, credits, and payment information, call (202) 707-6104

Library Technologies, Inc.

Since 1989, Library Technologies, Inc. has authorized 200+ million bibliographic records for over one thousand domestic and international libraries. A client list is found on its web site and includes all types and sizes of libraries, using every ILS vendor. In addition to LC name (personal, corporate, conference, uniform titles and series) headings and LCSH topical and geographic headings, libraries may authorize LC Children's subjects, Sears subjects, and NLM MeSH subjects. Both 'limited review' and full manual review authority control options are offered. For limited review processing, databases under one-half million catalog records usually take about three weeks to process. Following batch authority control, libraries may opt to receive FTP- and/or web-based continuing services for authorizing new cataloging and for keeping current with Library of Congress revisions. LTI also delivers a broad range of ancillary library database preparation services, including: duplicate record resolution; union catalog creation; item field builds specific to each local system vendor's requirements; smart and dumb photocomposed barcode labels; item field remaps preliminary to migration from one ILS to another; and custom bibliographic data projects.

http://www.authoritycontrol.com/

Internet e-mail address: lti@librarytech.com

Telephone: +1-800-795-9504

FAX: +1-215-830-9422

MarciveWeb SELECT

MarciveWeb SELECT enables librarians to search 10 million records from LC, NLM, NLC, GPO, A/V Access(R), and other sources, and obtain customized MARC 21 bibliographic records, catalog cards, smart barcode labels, book labels, and MARC 21 authorities records. Bibliographic records can be automatically enriched with Table of Contents (TOC) data, additional Fiction/Biography access points, and summaries. Other database quality improvement services include retrospective conversion from shelflists; upgrade from brief records to full MARC 21 format; deduplication; reclassification; and authority control. Requirements: MARCIVE profile and a browser such as Navigator or Explorer.

http://www.marcive.com/

Internet e-mail address: info@marcive.com

Telephone: +1-800-531-7678

FAX: +1-210-646-0167

MARC Link Retrospective Conversion

MARC Link Retrospective Conversion provides full MARC 21 records (for bibliographic, authority, holdings and community information formats), authority control, LC reclass, non-roman languages, barcode and custom labels, union database creation, etc. Through excellent communication practices, MARC Link Retrospective Conversion customizes libraries' retrospective conversion projects based on libraries' unique needs and specifications, while producing high quality services. All services come with lifetime quality guarantees.

http://www.marclink.com/

Internet e-mail address: mailto:info@marclink.com

Telephone: +1-800-288-1265 extension 27

Fax: +1-801-356-8220

NOTEbookS MARC Import

NOTEbookS MARC Import brings MARC bibliographic, authority, holdings, classification and community information records into a Lotus Notes database.

http://www.rasco.com/

Internet e-mail address: bschless@rasco.com

Telephone: +1-978-443-2996

Fax: +1-978-443-7602

OPUS Retrospective Conversion/Custom Cataloguing & Processing

Duncan Systems Specialists Inc. (DSS) provides customized cataloging, processing services and cataloging products for all types of libraries including: retrospective conversion, recataloging, reclassification, derived and original cataloging (book, non-book and non-English language materials, including many non-Roman alphabet languages), database upgrades/migrations, data format conversions (non-MARC to MARC and vice versa), shelf-ready and CIRC-ready item processing, print products such as label sets, card kits, smart barcodes, edit lists, etc. and full or partial outsourcing solutions. DSS's OPUS database and cataloging utility contains in excess of 12,000,000 unique, full MARC 21 records and currently consists of the complete Library of Congress (LC) database, the National Library of Canada (NLC) database, DSS's own UNIQ file, as well as DSS customer union databases, which are housed and maintained by DSS.

http://www.duncansystems.com/

Internet e-mail address: dss@duncansystems.com

Telephone: +1-800-836-5049

Fax: +1-905-338-1847

Sagebrush Corporation

Sagebrush offers original cataloging and conversion services for all types of libraries—school, corporate, public and for libraries with any automation system. Sagebrush offers impressive options designed to provide products that match libraires' exact specifications. The full MARC 21 records produced contain call numbers and subject headings that conform to AACR2 and MARC 21 bibliographic standards and meet the ISBD punctuation standard.

www.sagebrushcorp.com/dataservices

Internet e-mail address: mailto:info@sagebrushcorp.com

Telephone: +1-800-642-4648

Fax: +1-512-342-2827

SLC Library Cataloguing Services

Special Libraries Cataloguing (SLC) provides MARC 21 bibliographic records via disk, tape, or FTP for library acquisitions. The records are created based on photocopies of title pages (recto and verso) with collation written on and may be loaded into any MARC 21 compliant OPAC. AACR2 1988 and LCSH are used. The library's choice of LCC, DDC, NLM, Moys and CanKF classifications is available. Print products, including spine and circulation labels, book catalogues, and catalogue cards are also available.

www.slc.bc.ca/

Internet e-mail address: mailto:mac@slc.bc.ca

Telephone: +1-250-474-3361

Fax: +1-250-474-3362

Validator ™ Subjects and Names Authority Database

Validator ™ Subjects and Names Authority database includes 270,000 subject headings and over 5 million names records specifying personal and corporate names, series and uniform titles.

See description under MARC Tools at Validator

MARC SPECIALIZED TOOLS

The directory list includes names of application software, official websites along with brief notes indicating how the software utilities serve MARC cataloguing activities.

Aurora ZMarc Collector

A 'hands-free' search tool that uses a text file of ISBN numbers and searches multiple library databases around the world in order to find and save MARC bibliographic records associated with the ISBN numbers. www.ait.com.au/; ftp://www.ait.com.au/ZMarc/

Contact: Internet e-mail address: sales@ait.com.au

BIBLIObase

BIBLIObase is a cataloging system that allows one to generate appropriate and complete MARC 21 bibliographic records. The search facilities allowed are: Quick, Oriented, Advanced and Free Search. www.bibliosoft.pt

Contact: Internet e-mail address: bibliosoft@esoterica.pt

BookWhere

WebClarity Software Inc.'s BookWhere product allows users to simultaneously search and retrieve metadata from over 1900 pre-defined databases located around the globe. Bibliographic and media records can be found in seconds and exported in a wide variety of formats including MARC 21, FINMARC and UNIMARC. www.webclarity.info

Contact: Internet e-mail address: sales@webclarity.info

Cataloging Calculator - Free

The Cataloging Calculator finds variable and fixed MARC fields (bibliographic and authority data), language codes, geographic area codes, publication country codes, AACR2 abbreviations, LC main entry and geographic Cutter numbers. http://home.earthlink.net/~banerjek/calculate/

Contact: Internet e-mail address: banerjek@earthlink.net

eZcat/eZcat Pro

Book Systems' eZcat and eZcat Pro products offer librarians a complete suite of Z39.50 compliant utilities for managing MARC 21 records. eZcat includes tools for simultaneous searching, downloading, uploading, filtering and cleaning of www.booksys.com

Contact: Internet e-mail address: sales@booksys.com

FRBR Display Tool - Free

The FRBR Display Tool sorts the bibliographic data found in a set of MARC records into hierarchical displays by grouping the bibliographic data using the 'Works,' 'Expressions,' and 'Manifestations' FRBR concepts. Possible uses for the FRBR Display Tool include experimenting with the collocation and sorting of search result sets into the FRBR categories to test concepts; and applying FRBR to local data to evaluate its consistency for FRBR-type development. www.loc.gov/marc/frbr/tool.html

Contact: Internet e-mail address: ndmso@loc.gov

Impact/ONLINE CAT

Impact/ONLINE CAT is a Windows-based cataloging system, which provides users with the ability to search multiple databases of MARC 21 bibliographic, authority and community information records. Features include a MARC Editor with built-in MARC validation, and the ability to download records to the local hard drive. www.auto-graphics.com

Contact: Internet e-mail address: abf@auto-graphics.com

InfoWorks Link Checker

InfoWorks Link Checker is designed for librarians to quickly check URL links in MARC 21 records and works with flat MARC files containing URLs. InfoWorks Link Checker can also check multiple links simultaneously by applying multiple threading technology. www.itcompany.com/linkcheck.htm

Contact: Internet e-mail address: jsong@itcompany.com

InfoWorks Spelling Checker for Database Maintenance

Locates spelling errors and cleans up bibliographic databases. It works with flat MARC files in any integrated library systems. InfoWorks Spelling Checker for Database Maintenance allows users to define which languages and fields to check and provides both batch and interactive checking. It includes a special dictionary for library use and allows users to build custom dictionaries. www.itcompany.com/checkerd.htm

Contact: Internet e-mail address: jsong@itcompany.com

MARCBreaker - Free

The current version (2.5) does not run under Windows NT or UNIX. The program converts structurally sound MARC records and reformats the information into an ASCII text file format. MARCBreaker Program (www.loc.gov/marc/makrbrkr.h tml # download)

Contact: Internet e-mail address: ndmso@loc.gov

MarcEdit - Free

MarcEdit 4.5 is a Marc Editor, a Script Maker to help users generate simply scripting solutions, and a Delimited Text Translator, which allows users to import delimited text files and convert the data into MARC. It also includes Unicode support and all Global Editing functions. http://oregonstate.edu/~reeset/marcedit/html/

Contact: Internet e-mail address: terry.reese@oregonstate.edu

MarciveWeb SELECT

Enables librarians to search 10 million records from LC, NLM, NLC, GPO, A/V Access(R), and other sources, and obtain customized MARC 21 bibliographic records, catalog cards, smart barcode labels, book labels, and MARC 21 authorities records. www.marcive.com

Contact: Internet e-mail address: info@marcive.com

MARConvert™

MARConvert™ handles special problems or unusual requirements in converting records into or out of MARC 21, USMARC, CanMARC, UNIMARC, or MARCXML. It will also convert MARC records to another character set, such as ANSEL, Latin-1, Unicode, or UTF-8. Operates in both interactive mode, and batch mode for converting multiple files without intervention. For Windows 95/98/NT/2000/XP. www.systemsplanning.com/marc/mvd.asp

Contact: Internet e-mail address: toney@systemsplanning.com

MARC Magician

Mitinet/MARC Software's MARC Magician program cleans up and maintains MARC collection, automatically corrects dozens of MARC errors, provides global editing commands, and checks spelling errors. It complements all MARC-based automation systems. www.mitinet.com

Contact: Internet e-mail address: sales@mitinet.com

MARCMaker - Free

MARCMaker is developed by the Library of Congress (LC) that generates the MARC record structure from preformatted text. It runs under DOS or Windows 95/98/ME/2000. (www.loc.gov/marc/makrbrkr.h tml#download)
(www.loc.gov/marc/makrbrkr.html)

Contact: Internet e-mail address: ndmso@loc.gov

MARC Perl Modules - Free

The MARC Perl modules are a simple set of modules designed to convert MARC 21 bibliographic records into various formats. www.library.adelaide.edu.au /~sthomas/scripts/

Contact: Internet e-mail address: stephen.thomas@adelaide. edu.au

marc.pl - Free

marc.pl is a utility for extracting records from a file of MARC 21 records, and converting records between standard MARC format and a text representation. Records may be converted from text format to raw MARC, or vice-versa. www.library.adelaide.edu.au /~sthomas/scripts/

Contact: Internet e-mail address: stephen.thomas@adelaide.edu.au

MARC Report

MARC Report validates MARC records according to the latest LC and OCLC standards. The validation that is applied is customizable by the user. The program runs either in interactive mode (record-by-record) or in batch mode (producing a report of all problems found). Unique to MARC Report are hundreds of cataloging cross-checks which check the internal logic of each record, making sure that data elements present in one field do not conflict with those present in another. www.marcofquality.com

Contact: Internet e-mail address: tmq@marcofquality.com

MARC RTP - Free

MARC RTP will read files of bibliographic records in MARC format, and convert them to a format that the user designs. The program can also produce a human readable listing or summarize the structure of a file of records. www.loungebythelake.com/marcrtp/

Contact: Internet e-mail address: rpj@callisto.canberra.edu.au

MARC Template Library - Free

The MARC Template Library is a C++ library for MARC 21 bibliographic records using C++ templates and the Standard

Template Library. Open Source released under a BSD License.
http://mtl.sourceforge.net

Contact: Internet e-mail address: markbasedow@bigpond.com

MARCView™

MARCView™ is an easy-to-use program to view, search, and print any MARC 21, USMARC, CanMARC, UNIMARC, or MARCXML bibliographic or authority file. Records are formatted for easy viewing and printing. Navigation to any record in the file is instantaneous. Searches can specify field, subfield, both, or neither.
www.systemsplanning.com/marc

Contact: Internet e-mail address: toney@systemsplanning.com

Surpass Copycat

Surpass Copycat is a Windows-based Z39.50 copy cataloging tool that allows users to find and download free MARC records from the Internet. Search multiple libraries simultaneously, such as the Library of Congress, public libraries, medical libraries, state-wide union catalogs and more. Over 100 libraries come pre-configured. Copycat also features 'scan and search' that allows the user to simply scan the EAN/ISBN barcode from the back of the book they wish to catalog to instantly launch a search for that book.
www.surpasssoftware.com/copycat.htm

Contact: Internet e-mail address: www.SurpassSoftware.com/contact.htm

USEMARCON Plus - The Universal MARC Record Convertor - Free

Like the original UseMARCON program, the USEMARCON Plus program enables libraries to create rules-based systems to convert records between national MARC formats. It also allows users to create and modify rules files, used to achieve MARC conversions, in order to meet specific local requirements.
www.bl.uk/services/bibliographic/usemarcon.html

Contact: The British Library
Internet e-mail address: usemarcon@bl.uk

Validator™ Subjects and Names Authority Database

Validator ™ Subjects and Names Authority database includes the complete Library of Congress Subjects and Names Authority Files on CD-ROM. Included are 248,000 subject headings and 4.7 million names records specifying personal and corporate names, series and uniform titles. Validator is versatile and useful to both catalogers and reference staff. www.att.com/gov/library/

Contact: Internet e-mail address: vblades@att.com

Visual MARC Editor

The Visual MARC Editor is an interactive, visual, Windows GUI-based MARC records viewer and editor for all five MARC 21 formats: Bibliographic, Authority, Classification, Holdings and Community Information.

Contact: Internet e-mail address: slim@vsnl.com

Web & XML Tools please see the LC webpage from where the above directory entries have been selectively extracted and tailored.

Source: Library of Congress
http://www.loc.gov/z3950/lcserver.html

Z39.50 IMPLEMENTATIONS

The Library of Congress Z39.50 Server provides free access to the MARC records of bibliographic holdings of the institutions named here. Where applicable, the software vendor for the target Z39.50 implementation is given in parentheses after the name of the institution.

A

Academica Sinica — Taiwan (INNOPAC)
Academy of Natural Sciences — Philadelphia, PA (INNOPAC)
Acadia University — Nova Scotia, Canada (SIRSI)
ACCESS Pennsylvania Database (INNOPAC)
Adelphi University — Garden City, NY (INNOPAC)
American Museum of Natural History — New York, NY (INNOPAC)
Angelo State University — San Angelo, TX (Endeavor)
Arizona Health Sciences Library (SIRSI)
Arizona Historical Society — Tucson, AZ (Endeavor)
Arkansas Technical University (Endeavor)
Assumption College — Worcester, MA (Endeavor)
Astrophysics Data System — Smithsonian Astrophysical Observatory, Cambridge, MA
Auburn University (Endeavor)
Auckland University of Technology — Auckland, NZ (Endeavor)
Aurora Public Library — Aurora, CO (INNOPAC)

Australian Defence Force Academy (Endeavor)
Australian National University (INNOPAC)

B

Baton Rouge Community College (SIRSI)
Bedford Public Library — Bedford, TX (INNOPAC)
Berry College — Mount Berry, GA (Endeavor)
Biblioteca de Castilla y León—Valladolid, Spain (Baratz)
Biblioteca Virtual Miguel de Cervantes — Alicante, Spain
Bibliothèque nationale du Québec (Best-Seller)
Bibliothèques de l'Université de Moncton (GEAC)
BIBSYS—Norway
Bossier Parish Community College — North Bossier City, LA (SIRSI)
Boston Athenaeum Library (Endeavor)
Boston College (ALEPH)
Boston University (INNOPAC)
Boulder Public Library — Boulder, CO (INNOPAC)
Brandeis University (ALEPH)
Brescia University — Owensboro, KY (Endeavor)
British Columbia Institute of Technology (INNOPAC)
British Library Integrated Catalogue (ALEPH)
Brock University — Ontario, Canada (INNOPAC)
Brown University (INNOPAC)
Brunel University — UK (SIRSI)
Bucknell University — Lewisburg, Pa. (SIRSI)

C

California Institute of Technology (INNOPAC)
California Institute of the Arts (Endeavor)
California State Library (DRA)
California State University, Bakersfield (Endeavor)
California State University, Fresno (GEAC)
California State University, Fullerton (INNOPAC)
California State University, Hayward (INNOPAC)
California State University, Humboldt (Endeavor)
California State University, Long Beach — COAST (INNOPAC)
California State University, Monterey Bay (Endeavor)
California State University, Sacramento (INNOPAC)
California State University, San Diego (INNOPAC)
California State University, San Francisco (INNOPAC)
California State University, San Luis Obispo (INNOPAC)

California State University, San Marcos (INNOPAC)
California State University, Sonoma (INNOPAC)
Camosun College — Victoria, BC (SIRSI)
Canada. Dept. of Foreign Affairs and International Trade (INNOPAC)
Canada Institute for Scientific and Technical Information — CISTI (INNOPAC)
Cape Library Cooperative (CALICO) — Cape Town, South Africa (ALEPH)
Cardiff University — Cardiff, Wales (Endeavor)
Carleton College — Northfield, MN (INNOPAC)
Carnegie Mellon University (SIRSI)
Center for Research Libraries (INNOPAC)
Central College — Pella, Iowa (INNOPAC)
Chinese University of Hong Kong (INNOPAC)
Chisholm Institute — Melbourne, Australia (DRA)
Christchurch City Libraries — Christchurch, NZ (SIRSI)
Christchurch Polytechnic Library — Christchurch, NZ (Endeavor)
Clive Public Library — Clive, Iowa (INNOPAC)
Colgate University — Hamilton, NY (INNOPAC)
College of the Rockies — Cranbrook, BC (SIRSI)
College of William and Mary (SIRSI)
Colorado School of Mines — Golden, CO (Endeavor)
Colorado State University — Fort Collins, CO (INNOPAC)
Colorado Unified Catalog — Prospector (INNOPAC)
Columbia University — New York, NY (Endeavor)
Columbia University. Law School Library (INNOPAC)
Commonwealth Scientific and Industrial Research Organization (CSIRO) — Clayton South, VIC, Australia (Endeavor)
Concordia University—Montreal, Canada (INNOPAC)
Concordia University Wisconsin (INNOPAC)
Congreso de los Diputados — Spain (Baratz)
Cornell University (Endeavor)
COPAC (CURL OPAC Project) Database — Manchester, England

D

Dallas Theological Seminary (SIRSI)
Danish Technical Knowledge Center & Library (ALEPH)
Deakin University — Geelong, Vic., Australia (INNOPAC)
Delgado Community College — New Orleans, LA (SIRSI)
Des Moines University Osteopathic Medical Center (INNOPAC)

Drexel University — Philadelphia, PA (INNOPAC)
Duke University (ALEPH)

E

Earth Sciences Information Centre—Ottawa, Canada (INNOPAC)
Eastern University — St. Davids, PA (SIRSI)
Eastern Michigan University — Ypsilanti, MI (Endeavor)
École Polytechnique de Montréal — Quebec, Canada (GEAC)
Ector County Library — Odessa, TX (SIRSI)
Edgewood College — Madison, Wisconsin (INNOPAC)
Edith Cowan University — Western Australia (INNOPAC)
Emory University (SIRSI)
Encyclopaedia Britannica Online

F

Fletcher Technical Community College — Houma, LA (SIRSI)
Flinders University — Adelaide, Australia (Endeavor)
Florida Center for Library Automation
Florida Northwest Regional Library System (The Library Corporation)
Fort Stockton Public Library — Fort Stockton, TX (Dynix)
Four Colleges Database (INNOPAC)
FRESCO — Frick Art Reference Library Catalog Online — New York City (INNOPAC)

G

George Mason University — Fairfax, VA (Endeavor)
George Washington University Medical Center (SIRSI)
Getty Center for the History of Art and the Humanities (Endeavor)
Glasgow University — Glasgow, Scotland (INNOPAC)
Göteborg University — Göteborg, Sweden (VTLS)
Grambling State University — Grambling, LA (SIRSI)
Griffith University—Nathan, Australia (GEAC)
Grinnell College — Grinnell, Iowa (INNOPAC)
Grosse Pointe Public Library — Grosse Pointe Farms, MI (INNOPAC)

H

Hamilton College — Clinton, NY (Endeavor)
Hawaii Medical Library — Honolulu, Hawaii (Endeavor)
Hawaii Voyager Consortium (Endeavor)
Hong Kong Academy of Performing Arts (INNOPAC)
Hong Kong Institute of Education (INNOPAC)

Hong Kong University of Science and Technology (INNOPAC)
Hull University — UK (INNOPAC)
Hurst Public Library — Hurst, Texas (SIRSI)

I

Idaho State University (Endeavor)
Indiana State University Consortium (Endeavor)
Indiana University (SIRSI)
Instituto Tecnológico y de Estudios Superiores de Monterrey—
Monterrey, Mexico (INNOPAC)
Iowa State Library (Dynix)
Iowa State University (Dynix)
Italian National Library Service - SBN Servizio Bibliotecario
Nazionale (ICCU)

J

James Cook University — North Queensland, Australia
Jeffersonville Township Public Library — Jeffersonville, Indiana
(GEAC)
Johns Hopkins University — Baltimore, MD (Dynix)

K

Kansas City Public Library (DRA)
Keene State College — Keene, NH (INNOPAC)
Kentucky Historical Society (Endeavor)
King's College London (ALEPH)
Kwantlen University College — Vancouver, BC (SIRSI)

L

La Trobe University — Melbourne, Australia (INNOPAC)
Leeds University — Leeds, England (INNOPAC)
Lehigh University — Bethlehem, Pennsylvania (SIRSI)
LIBIS-Net—Belgium (DOBIS/LIBIS)
Library Consortium of Health Institutions in Buffalo (SIRSI)
LIBRIS — Swedish Union Catalog
LINCS (Literacy Information and Communication System) of the
National Institute for Literacy via Kentucky Virtual Library —
Frankfort, KY (SiteSearch)
London School of Economics — London, England (Endeavor)
Louisiana State University (SIRSI)
Louisiana State University—Alexandria (SIRSI)

Louisiana State University Center for Energy Studies (SIRSI)
Louisiana State University—Eunice (SIRSI)
Louisiana State University Law Center (SIRSI)
Louisiana State University Medical Center Libraries (INNOPAC)
Louisiana State University—Shreveport (SIRSI)
Louisiana Tech University — Ruston, LA (SIRSI)
Louisiana Universities Marine Consortium (SIRSI)
Loyola University, New Orleans (SIRSI)
Lubbock City-County Library — Lubbock, Texas (SIRSI)
Luther College — Decorah, Iowa (INNOPAC)

M

McGill University — Montreal, Canada (ALEPH)
McNeese State University — Lake Charles, LA (SIRSI)
Malaspina University-College — Nanaimo, BC (SIRSI)
Manitoba (Canada) Union Catalog — MAPLIN (GEAC)
Marin County (Calif.) Public Library — Marinet (INNOPAC)
Marine Biological Laboratory/Woods Hole Oceanographic Institution Library—MBL/WHOI—Woods Hole, MA (Endeavor)
Marquette University — Milwaukee, WI (INNOPAC)
Marshall University — Huntington, WV (VTLS)
Massachusetts Institute of Technology (ALEPH)
Mehran University of Engineering and Technology, Pakistan
Memorial University of Newfoundland (SIRSI)
Metro Boston Library Network (Dynix)
Metropolitan Library System — Oklahoma County, Okla.
Middlebury College — Middlebury, VT (DRA)
Michigan State University (INNOPAC)
Milwaukee Public Library (INNOPAC)
Minneapolis Public Library (INNOPAC)
Minnesota State Colleges and Universities/Project for Automated Library Services (MnSCU/PALS)
Mississippi State University (DRA)
Missouri Bibliographic Information User System (MOBIUS) — LANCE Cluster (INNOPAC)
Missouri Bibliographic Information User System (MOBIUS) — MERLIN Cluster (INNOPAC)
Monash University — Clayton, VIC, Australia (Endeavor)
Morehead State University — Morehead, KY (Endeavor)
Murdoch University — Western Australia (INNOPAC)

N

Nashville Public Library (INNOPAC)
National Art Library — UK (Dynix)
National Library for the Blind — UK (GEAC)
National Agricultural Library Catalog (Endeavor)
National Library of Australia (Endeavor)
National Library of Canada (CGI)
National Library of Medicine (Endeavor)
National Library of Poland (INNOPAC)
National Library of Scotland (Endeavor)
National Library of Wales (GEAC)
National Sea Grant Library — University of Rhode Island)
National Széchényi Library — Budapest, Hungary (LibriCore)
Natural History Museum — London, England (SIRSI)
NCompasS Consortium — Nova Scotia Provincial Library (DRA)
NEBIS — Network of Libraries and Information Centers in Switzerland (ALEPH)
NEOS Consortium — University of Alberta (SIRSI)
New Haven Free Public Library — New Haven, CT (INNOPAC)
New York State Department of Health (INNOPAC)
New York State Library (SIRSI)
New York University (GEAC)
Newton Public Library — Newton, Iowa (SIRSI)
Nicholls State University — Thibodaux, LA (SIRSI)
NOAA/Coastal Services Center Library (SIRSI)
North Carolina Central Database (INNOPAC)
North Carolina Central University (DRA)
North Carolina Coastal Database (INNOPAC)
North Carolina Western Database (INNOPAC)
North Carolina State University (DRA)
North of Boston Library Exchange—NOBLE (INNOPAC)
North Richland Hills Public Library — North Richland Hills, Texas (INNOPAC)
Northwestern State University of Louisiana — Natchitoches, LA (SIRSA)
Northwestern University (Endeavor)
Novanet, Inc. — Nova Scotia, Canada (GEAC)
Nunez Community College — Chalmette, LA (SIRSI)

O

OhioLINK Central Catalog (INNOPAC)
Ohio State University (INNOPAC)
Oklahoma State University (Endeavor)
Oklahoma State University—Tulsa (Endeavor)
Old Dominion University — Norfolk, VA (INNOPAC)
Ontario (Canada) Legislative Library (Endeavor)
Open University — Milton Keynes, UK (Endeavor)
Oregon State University (INNOPAC)
Our Lady of the Lake College — Baton Rouge, LA (SIRSI)
Our Lady of the Lake University — San Antonio, TX (SIRSI)
Oxford University (GEAC)

P

Pennsylvania State University
Princeton Public Library — Princeton, NJ (INNOPAC)
Princeton University (Endeavor)
Purdue University (Endeavor)
Purdue University Calumet (Endeavor)
Purdue University North Central (Endeavor)

Q

Queen Margaret University College — Edinburgh, Scotland (SIRSI)
Queensland University of Technology — Australia (INNOPAC)

R

Radford University (INNOPAC)
Rensselaer Polytechnic Institute — Troy, NY (INNOPAC)
REVEAL Database — UK (GEAC)
River Bend Library System — Eastern Iowa/Western Illinois (GEAC)
River Parishes Community College — Sorrento, LA (SIRSI)
Rochester Institute of Technology (INNOPAC)
Royal Library of Denmark (ALEPH)
RMIT University—Melbourne, VIC, Australia (GEAC)

S

Sacramento Public Library (INNOPAC)
St. Catharine College — St. Catharine, KY (Endeavor)
St. Paul Public Library (INNOPAC)
Salt Lake City Public Library (INNOPAC)

San Francisco State University (INNOPAC)
Selkirk College — Castlegar, BC (SIRSI)
Sheffield Hallam University — Sheffield, UK (INNOPAC)
Shinawatra University — Pathumthani, Thailand (Dynix)
Simon Fraser University — British Columbia, Canada (INNOPAC)
South Bank University — UK (Dynix)
South Dakota Library Network (PALS)
South Louisiana Community College — Lafayette, LA (SIRSI)
Southeastern Louisiana University (SIRSI)
Southern University — Baton Rouge, LA (SIRSI)
Southern University Law Center — Baton Rouge, LA (SIRSI)
Southern University—New Orleans (SIRSI)
Southern University—Shreveport/Bossier (SIRSI)
Sowela Technical Community College—Lake Charles, LA (SIRSI)
Spokane Public Library (DRA)
Spring Arbor College—Spring Arbor, Mich. (SIRSI)
Spring Hill College—Mobile, Alabama (SIRSI)
State of Iowa Libraries Online—SILO (Dynix)
State Library of Florida (SIRSI)
State Library of Louisiana (Dynix)
State Library of South Australia (INNOPAC)
State Library of Victoria — Melbourne, Australia (Endeavor)
State Library of Western Australia—LISWA (INNOPAC)
State University of New York at Albany (GEAC)
State University of New York at Binghamton (ALEPH)
State University of New York at Stony Brook (NOTIS)
Stavanger bibliotek — Stavanger, Norway (ALEPH)
Stockholm University (Endeavor)
Stonehill College — North Easton, Massachusetts (INNOPAC)
Strathclyde University — Scotland (Dynix)
Sul Ross State University — Alpine, TX (SIRSI)
Supreme Court of Canada (Best-Seller)
Swinburne University of Technology — Australia (Dynix)
Syracuse University — Syracuse, NY (Endeavor)

T

Tamkang University — Tan-shui chen, Taiwan (VTLS)
Technological Educational Institute of Thessaloniki — Greece (VTLS)
Temple University — Philadelphia, PA (INNOPAC)
Texas A & M University—Corpus Christi (INNOPAC)
Texas A & M University (Endeavor)

Texas State Library (SIRSI)
Texas Wesleyan University (SIRSI)
Theological Consortium of Greater Columbus (Endeavor)
Tom Green County Library — Texas (GEAC)
Tri-Institutional Library Catalog (Tri-Cat)—New York (INNOPAC)
TriUniversity Group of Libraries—Ontario, Canada (Endeavor)
Truman State University—Kirksville, Mo. (INNOPAC)
Tufts University — Medford, MA (INNOPAC)
Tulane University — New Orleans, LA (Endeavor)
Tulsa-City County Library (NOTIS)

U

UNILINC—Sydney, Australia (DRA)
United States Naval Academy, Annapolis (INNOPAC)
Universidad Complutense de Madrid (INNOPAC)
Universidad de Alcalá de Henares — Madrid, Spain (SIRSI)
Universidad de Chile — Santiago, Chile (DRA)
Universidad de Granada — Spain (INNOPAC)
Universidad de Jaén—Jaén, Spain (Baratz)
Universidad Nacional de Educación a Distancia — Madrid, Spain (SIRSI)
Universidad Politécnica de Madrid (SIRSI)
Universitat de les Illes Balears — Spain (INNOPAC)
Université catholique de Louvain — Belgium (VTLS)
Université de Montréal (GEAC)
Université de Sherbrooke (DRA)
Université Laval (SIRSI)
University College—Cork, Ireland (INNOPAC)
University College, Galway—Ireland (Dynix)
University College of North Wales—Bangor, Wales (INNOPAC)
University College of the Cariboo — Kamloops, BC (SIRSI)
University College of the Fraser Valley — Abbotsford, BC (SIRSI)
University of Adelaide — Australia (Endeavor)
University of Alabama, Birmingham (Endeavor)
University of Alabama, Huntsville (SIRSI)
University of Arizona (INNOPAC)
University of Arkansas, Fayetteville (INNOPAC)
University of Arkansas, Little Rock (INNOPAC)
University of Auckland — Auckland, NZ (Endeavor)
University of Ballarat — Victoria, Australia (INNOPAC)
University of British Columbia (DRA)

University of Calgary (SIRSI)
University of California — MELVYL System (ALEPH)
University of California, Irvine (INNOPAC)
University of California, Riverside (INNOPAC)
University of California, San Francisco (INNOPAC)
University of Colorado, Boulder (INNOPAC)
University of Colorado, Colorado Springs (INNOPAC)
University of Colorado Health Sciences Center (INNOPAC)
University of Connecticut (Endeavor)
University of Denver (INNOPAC)
University of Dubuque — Dubuque, Iowa (Dynix)
University of Edinburgh — Scotland (Endeavor)
University of Georgia (Endeavor)
University of Hertfordshire — Hatfield, UK (Endeavor)
University of Hong Kong (INNOPAC)
University of Houston (INNOPAC)
University of Iowa (ALEPH)
University of Illinois, Chicago (NOTIS)
University of Kentucky (Endeavor)
University of Lethbridge (INNOPAC)
University of London (INNOPAC)
University of Louisiana at Lafayette (SIRSI)
University of Louisiana at Monroe (SIRSI)
University of Manitoba (DRA)
University of Massachusetts at Amherst (INNOPAC)
University of Massachusetts Boston (Endeavor)
University of Massachusetts Dartmouth (Endeavor)
University of Massachusetts Medical School (Endeavor)
University of Medicine and Dentistry of New Jersey (Endeavor)
University of Michigan (NOTIS)
University of Michigan, Dearborn (INNOPAC)
University of Michigan, Flint (NOTIS)
University of Minnesota — Twin Cities (ALEPH)
University of Minnesota, Morris (GEAC)
University of Missouri (INNOPAC)
University of Nebraska—Lincoln (INNOPAC)
University of New Brunswick (SIRSI)
University of Newcastle — Australia (INNOPAC)
University of New Orleans (SIRSI)
University of North Carolina at Chapel Hill (DRA)
University of North Carolina at Greensboro (DRA)

University of North Texas (INNOPAC)
University of Northern Colorado (INNOPAC)
University of Northern Iowa (INNOPAC)
University of Notre Dame (ALEPH)
University of Notre Dame. Kresge Law Library (INNOPAC)
University of Oklahoma (NOTIS)
University of Oregon (INNOPAC)
University of Otago — Dunedin, NZ (Endeavor)
University of Pennsylvania (Endeavor)
University of Pennsylvania Law Library (INNOPAC)
University of Pittsburgh (Endeavor)
University of Queensland (INNOPAC)
University of Reading — Reading, UK (SIRSI)
University of Rochester (Endeavor)
University of Saskatchewan (INNOPAC)
University of Scranton (INNOPAC)
University of South Australia (Dynix)
University of South Carolina (NOTIS)
University of South Alabama (NOTIS)
University of Southern California (SIRSI)
University of Southern Queensland — Australia (VTLS)
University of Stockholm (Endeavor)
University of Sydney (INNOPAC)
University of Tampa — Tampa, Florida (Endeavor)
University of Technology, Sydney (INNOPAC)
University of Texas at Austin. Tarlton Law Library (INNOPAC)
University of Texas Southwestern Medical Center (SIRSI)
University of the Sunshine Coast — Queensland, Australia (VTLS)
University of Toronto (SIRSI)
University of Victoria — Victoria, BC (Endeavor)
University of Virginia (SIRSI)
University of Waikato — Hamilton, NZ (Endeavor)
University of Wales — Aberystwyth, UK (Endeavor)
University of Washington (INNOPAC)
University of Western Australia (INNOPAC)
University of Western Ontario (INNOPAC)
University of Western Sydney — Australia (Endeavor)
University of Wisconsin, Colleges (Endeavor)
University of Wisconsin—Eau Claire (Endeavor)
University of Wisconsin—Green Bay (Endeavor)
University of Wisconsin—La Crosse (Endeavor)

University of Wisconsin—Madison (Endeavor)
University of Wisconsin—Milwaukee (Endeavor)
University of Wisconsin—Oshkosh (Endeavor)
University of Wisconsin—Parkside (Endeavor)
University of Wisconsin—Platteville (Endeavor)
University of Wisconsin—River Falls (Endeavor)
University of Wisconsin—Stevens Point (Endeavor)
University of Wisconsin—Stout (Endeavor)
University of Wisconsin—Superior (Endeavor)
University of Wisconsin—Whitewater (Endeavor)
University of Wollongong — New South Wales, Australia (INNOPAC)

V

Vanderbilt University (SIRSI)
Victoria University — Melbourne, Australia (INNOPAC)
Victoria University of Wellington New Zealand (Endeavor)
Vigo County Public Library — Terre Haute, Indiana (SIRSI)
Villanova University — Villanova, PA (Endeavor)
Virginia Commonwealth University (ALEPH)
Viterbo University — La Crosse, Wis. (INNOPAC)

W

Washington (D.C.) Research Library Consortium (Endeavor)
Washington State University (INNOPAC)
Washington University — St. Louis, MO (INNOPAC)
Waterloo Public Library — Waterloo, Iowa (INNOPAC)
Wayne State University — Detroit, MI (INNOPAC)
Wellesley College (INNOPAC)
West Virginia State College — Institute, WV (VTLS)
Western Washington University (INNOPAC)
Wheeling Jesuit University — Wheeling, WV (SIRSI)
Worcester Polytechnic Institute — Worcester, MA (Endeavor)
Wright State University (INNOPAC)

Y

Yale University (Endeavor)

About the Z39.50 Gateway

Z39.50 is a national and international (ISO 23950) standard defining a protocol for computer-to-computer information retrieval. Z39.50 makes it possible for a user in one system to search and retrieve information from other computer systems (that have also implemented Z39.50) without knowing the search syntax that is used by those other systems. Z39.50 was originally approved by the National Information Standards Organization (NISO) in 1988.

The Z39.50 Maintenance Agency Page, includes documentation and information related to the development and ongoing maintenance of the Z39.50 standard.

Z39.50 Resources, maintained by Dan Brickley, Institute for Learning and Research Technology, and Z39.50 Resource Page, maintained by NISO, will provide hyperlinks to many Z39.50-related resources.

Using a Z39.50 client, it is currently possible to search the Library of Congress bibliographic file. Information that will be required to configure your Z39.50 client to search the LC server directly is provided in LC Z39.50 Server Configuration Guidelines. It is also possible to access the LC server by using the appropriate search forms listed under "Search Library of Congress Catalog" above.

This gateway makes use of an earlier version of the ISearch-CGI public domain software that is available from CNIDR. It should be noted that many search and retrieval capabilities that are available in the Z39.50 protocol are not implemented in this gateway. The Initialization, Search, and Retrieval facilities have been implemented.

GLOSSARY

Sources of definitions are indicated in parenthesis at the end of each entry.

A

16-BIT
Software for MS-DOS or Microsoft Windows originally ran on the 16-bit Intel 8088 and 80286 microprocessors. (LIBHQ)

32-BIT
32-bit programs are written for the Intel 80386 and more recent processors, and allow greater speed of execution. (LIBHQ)

AACR2
Anglo-American Cataloguing Rules, Second Edition. The national/international standard for cataloging library materials. The rules are designed for use in the construction of catalogues and other lists in general libraries of all sizes. (OCLC)

ACCESS POINT
A name, term, code or other indexed characteristic of an authority or bibliographic record that helps make the record

searchable and identifiable. For example, titles, names, and subjects are access points. (OCLC)

ADDED ENTRY
An entry, additional to the main entry, by which an item is represented in a catalog; a secondary entry. See also Main entry. (MARC)

ALA CHARACTER SET
American Library Association defined characters used in MARC records, including standard alphabetic characters, diacritics, special characters, 14 superscript characters, 14 subscript characters, and 3 Greek characters. These characters are valid in MARC records (ALA)

APPENDIX
Follows the text of a book and contains notes, charts, tables, lists, or other detailed information discussed in the text. (MARC)

AREA
A major section of the bibliographic description, comprising data of a particular category or set of categories. See also Element. (MARC)

AUTHORITY RECORD
A collection of information about one name, uniform title, or topical term heading. (OCLC)

AUTOMATION
Automatic, as opposed to human, operation or control of a process, equipment or a system; or the techniques and equipment used to achieve this. In libraries, automation refers to the process of automating functions such as circulation, cataloging, or acquisitions. (LIBHQ)

B

BARCODE
A printed horizontal strip of vertical bars used for identifying specific items or users. The codes, which represent numerical

data, are read by a bar code reader and interpreted via software or hardware decoders. In libraries, barcodes are affixed to both books and library cards to assist in circulation and collection control. (LIBHQ)

BIBLIOGRAPHIC RECORD
The description of a discrete item, such as a book, a videorecording, or a serial. Machine-readable forms of bibliographic records are stored in and retrieved from automated online catalogs, either locally or nationally via the Internet, or magnetic tape provided by a vendor (MARC). Catalogrs create records by encoding this information using tags, indicators, and subfield codes. (OCLC)

BIBLIOGRAPHIC RESOURCE
Forms the basis for a bibliographic description; may be tangible (a book) or intangible (a website). (AACR2)

BIBLIOGRAPHY
Lists sources used by the author in creating a work such as a book. Also lists additional sources on important subjects covered in the text. (MARC)

BOOLEAN OPERATORS
Words such as AND, OR, and NOT used to broaden or narrow a search. For example, cats AND dogs narrows the search to titles about both cats and dogs, while cats OR dogs broadens the search. (LIBHQ)

BROWSE SEARCHING
A feature of a catalog, which allows the user to search by the first word in a field, not a word appearing anywhere in the field. Compare to Keyword Searching. (LIBHQ)

BROWSER
See Web Browser. (LIBHQ)

C

CALL NUMBER
A set of letters, numerals or other symbols (in combination

or alone) used by a library to identify a specific copy of a work. A call number consists of the class number and book number (or Cutter number). (OCLC)

CATALOG

1. A list of library materials contained in a collection, a library, or a group of libraries, arranged according to some definite plan. Access to the list may be provided in a catalog book, a traditional card file, on microform, or online, electronically.
2. In a wider sense, a list of materials (prepared for a particular purpose (e.g. an exhibition catalog, a sales catalog). (MARC)

CATALOGING AGENT MODE

An authorization mode that allows the Cataloging Agent of a resource-sharing group to process cataloging records on a member's behalf. Agents process unresolved records from the group's batchloading activity. (OCLC)

CATALOGING IN PUBLICATION

A Library of Congress program that provides bibliographic data for new books in advance of publication. Records are created from information supplied by publishers. (OCLC)

CATALOGING SOURCE

The agency that created the bibliographic record. Four elements of OCLC-MARC records have cataloging source information – (1) Srce in the bibliographic fixed field; (2) Source in the authority fixed field; (3) Field 040 (Cataloging Source) in bibliogr. (OCLC)

CATALOGUE

see CATALOG

CATALOGUING

see CATALOGING

CHARACTER SET

A standard collection of characters. A character set may include letters, digits, punctuation, control codes, graphics, mathematical symbols, and other signs. Each character in the set is represented by a unique character code, which is a binary number used for storage and transmission. (LIBHQ)

CHIEF SOURCE OF INFORMATION
The source of bibliographic data to be given preference as the source from which a bibliographic description (or portion thereof) is prepared. Example of the chief source are the title page of a book, the title screen of a video, or the title screen from a computer software product. (MARC)

CIP
See Cataloging In Publication. (OCLC)

CLIENT/SERVER
A common type of distributed system in which software is split between server tasks and client tasks. A client sends requests to a server asking for information or action, and the server responds. There may be either one centralized server or many distributed ones. (LIBHQ)

CODEN
The Chemical Abstracts Service assigns six-character codes to serials. The first five characters have a mnemonic relationship to the serial. The last character is an alphabetic or numeric check character. For example, AISJB6, CADIDW. (OCLC)

COLLECTIVE TITLE
A title proper that is an inclusive title for an item containing several individual works, such as essays or poems. 'The collected works...' is a good example of a collective title. (MARC)

COMMAND
Designated words and abbreviations of words that signal the sevice what to do. Send commands and the system carries out the request. (OCLC)

COMMUNICATIONS FORMAT
In machine-readable cataloging (MARC), the standards for representation and exchange of data in machine-readable form. In the USA, this is an implementation of an ANSI standard. MARC 21 Format for Bibliographic Data (formerly called USMARC) is an implementation. (OCLC)

COMPILER
1. One who creates or produces a collection by selecting and putting together matter from the works of various persons or bodies.
2. One who selects and puts together in one publication matter from the works of one person or body. See also Editor. (MARC)

CONSTANT DATA RECORD
A partial record that contains standardized content for reuse in creating or editing a record so you can add text without retyping. Constant data records are created by and shared among librarians at a given institution. (OCLC)

CONTENT DESIGNATION
In machine-readable cataloging (MARC), the codes and conventions established to identify and characterize the data elements within a record and to support manipulation of that data.

CONTENT DESIGNATOR
A code (such as a tag, indicator, or subfield) that identifies the nature of a particular data element in a record. (MARC)

CONTENT OF THE RECORD
The data in the MARC records. The content is defined by standards outside the format, such as Anglo-American Cataloguing Rules, Library of Congress Subject Headings, ANSI/NISO Standards for Serials Holdings Statements or other rules and codes used by the organization that creates the record. (OCLC)

CONTINUING RESOURCE
A bibliographic resource that is issued over time with no predetermined conclusion. Continuing resources include serials and ongoing integrating resources. (AACR2)

CONTROL NUMBER
A unique sequential number supplied by the system to each new bibliographic record when it is entered into the online catalog. (MARC)

COPY DISPLAY
A secondary work area in which you can place a record. Use with the Main Display to work with two records. (OCLC)

COPYRIGHT
Usually appears on the verso of the title page of a book and states that the book's contents are the property of the author or publisher. (MARC)

CORPORATE BODY
An organization or group of persons that is identified by a particular name and that acts, or may act, as an entity. Typical examples of corporate bodies are associations, institutions, business firms, nonprofit enterprises, governments, government agencies, religious bodies, local churches, and conferences. (MARC)

CORPORATE NAME
The names of associations, institutions, businesses, firms, nonprofit enterprises, governments, agencies, performing groups used as entries in records. (OCLC)

D

DATABASE
A structured set of data, generally accessed via a software program. A simple database might be a single file containing many records, each of which contains the same set of fields, such as a series of companies with name, address, phone, and contact fields for each one. (LIBHQ)

DATABASE MANAGEMENT SYSTEM (DBMS)
Complex set of programs that control the organization, storage and retrieval of data for many users. Data is organized in fields, records and files. Examples include Oracle, Sybase, and Datacom. (LIBHQ)

DEDICATED LINE
A permanent connection between computers using telephone, ISDN, or other types of lines. (LIBHQ)

DEFAULT

The selection made by the computer in the absence of specific instructions by the user. (OCLC)

DEFAULT HOLDING LIBRARY CODE

The holding library code that appears automatically in bibliographic field 049 (Local Holdings) when a user displays a bibliographic record. Each authorization number/password combination has a default holding library code. (OCLC)

DELIMITER

A Special character used in conjuction with a subfield code to introduce each subfield in a variable field where each element, or unit of data, is not necessarily limited to a prescribed size, content and position in the record. (MARC)

DERIVE NEW RECORD

Using a pre-existing record to create and add a new record to system. (OCLC)

DIACRITIC

A mark that modifies the phonetic value of another character or characters. It does not occur alone but is used in conjuction with another character. In records each diacritic occupies its own position, directly preceding the modified character. (MARC)

DIALUP

A temporary, as opposed to dedicated, connection between machines established over a telephone line using modems. A patron might use a dialup connection from home (using a personal computer, modem, and telephone line) to dial into and use the library catalog. (LIBHQ)

DIGITAL DOCUMENT

Books, articles, papers, etc. that can be accessed via a computer. (LIBHQ)

DIGITAL MEDIA

Media in various digital forms, including scanned images, audio, video, multimedia, drawings and intelligent documents. (LIBHQ)

DIRECTORY
In a file of records, the series of entries that contain the tag, length and starting location of each variable field in a record. (OCLC)

DOMAIN NAME SYSTEM (DNS)
The unique name of a collection of computers connected to a network such as the Internet. A replicated, distributed data query service for looking up host IP addresses based on host names. The DNS is hierarchical, consisting of domains, subdomains, sites, and hosts. Unique names are formed from smallest to largest, and are of the form: user@host.site. subdomain.domain, where host and site are often optional. (LIBHQ)

DOWNLOAD
To copy a file from an external computer to a local one. You may download software updates from a vendor to your library system via the Internet. (LIBHQ)

DUBLIN CORE
A minimal set of metadata elements used to describe networked information resources which aids users in locating specific items. (LIBHQ)

DUMB TERMINAL
An output device (not a computer) that contains no internal microprocessor; a display monitor with no processing capabilities. (LIBHQ)

E

EAD
Encoded Archival Description is the emerging standard for archival finding aids and is used by Library of Congress and other research institutions. Finding aids are inventories, registers, indexes, or guides that provide detailed information about specific collections. Standardizing the format of these tools makes it easier to display them on a network. (LIBHQ)

EDIFACT (ISO 9735)
Electronic data interchange (EDI) refers to any electronic commerce standard that defines a protocol for exchange of business data between software applications. EDIFACT (EDI for Administration, Commerce, and Transport) is the international standard for EDI. (LIBHQ)

EDITION
Books, pamphlets, fascicles, single sheets, etc. All copies produced from essentially the same type image (whether by direct contact or by photographic or other methods) and issued by the same entity. Intellectual content is unique and unchanged to the work. Significant variation of the content requires a new edition statement. (MARC)

EDITOR
One who prepares for publication for an item not his or her own. The editorial work may be limited to the preparation of the item for the manufacturer, or it may include supervision of the manufacturing, revision, (restitution), or elucidation of the content of the item, and the addition of introduction, notes, and other critical matter. (MARC)

ELEMENT
A word, phrase, or group of characters representing a distinct unit of bibliographic information and forming part of an area of the description.(MARC)

EMBEDDED HOLDINGS DATA
Holdings information added to an existing MARC 21 bibliographic record rather than being in a separate linked holding record. (OCLC)

ENCODING LEVEL (ENC LVL)
The level of completeness of the authority record. The level of specificity of the holdings statement. (OCLC)

ENCRYPTION
The process of scrambling a message so that a key, held only by authorized recipients, is needed to unscramble and read the message. (LIBHQ)

END-OF-FIELD MARKER
The same thing as a field terminator, ( ) which signals to the computer the information is complete for that field. (MARC)

ENTRY
A bibliographic record of an item in a catalog. See also Heading. (MARC)

ENTRY WORD
The word by which a bibliographic entry is arranged in the catalog, usually the first word (other than an article) of the heading. See also Heading. (MARC)

EXPORT
(1) A command or action that causes a displayed record to be converted MARC communications format and output to a file on a workstation or in a local system. (2) Downloading a record from WorldCat. (OCLC)

EXTENT OF ITEM
The first element of the physical description area. It gives the number and the specific material designation of the units of the item being described and, in some cases, other indications of the extent (e.g. duration). (MARC)

EXTRANET
An extended intranet connecting not only internal personnel, but also select customers, suppliers, and strategic partners. Compare to Internet and Intranet.(LIBHQ)

F

FACSIMILE REPRODUCTION
A reproduction simulating the physical appearance of the original in addition to reproducing its content exactly. See also Reprint. (MARC)

FAQ
Frequently Asked Questions. Web page or text file with common questions about various topics along with the answers.

Especially useful for first-time visitors to a site or new participants in a newsgroup or listserv. (LIBHQ)

FIELD
One or more data elements that form a logical unit. In a bibliographic record, for example, one field contains publication data, another physical description, etc. Typically, each field begins with a start of message (ç) and ends with a field terminator ( ). (MARC)

FIELD NUMBER
The same thing as a Line number, typically 3 characters, beginning with 001 and ending 999. (MARC)

FIELD TERMINATOR
A special character that indicates the end of a field. On most screens, it appears as the symbol. (MARC)

FILE STRUCTURE
See record structure. (OCLC)

FILE TRANSFER PROTOCOL (FTP)
File Transfer Protocol (FTP) is a TCP/IP-based protocol that is generally available for file transfers to and from a large variety of hosts including IBM mainframes, Tandem Guardian systems, and Unix hosts.

FILL CHARACTER
A marker, found in certain positions of fixed and variable fields, that indicates where a valid character must be entered before the system will accept that field. Fill characters appear on work forms. On most screens, it appears as a symbol _ . (MARC)

FILTERING SOFTWARE
A program to block access to certain web pages. Depending on the program, it may block certain specified sites, all sites with certain words, or it may use more sophisticated criteria to determine which pages to block. See the LibraryHQ's Internet Filtering and Blocking page. (LIBHQ)

FINITE RESOURCE
A bibliographic resource complete at the time of publication (a single part monograph) or having a predetermined conclusion (e.g. a multipart monograph). (AACR2)

FIREWALL
A gateway used to protect a server or a network from unauthorized access. A firewall generally consists of both hardware and software components. (LIBHQ)

FIXED FIELD
In OCLC-MARC, the field in which mnemonic labels identify elements that contain coded information for describing the item and the record. Each element has a fixed length. The fixed field is the OCLC-MARC format's combination of various MARC 21 control fields. (OCLC)

FORMAT
A standard for the representation and exchange of data in machine-readable form. Standard organization for MARC bibliographic records. The library community uses formats so that MARC records can be readily transferred among automated systems. (OCLC) In its widest sense, a particular physical presentation of an item. (e.g.monograph, serial, videorecording, map, etc.) (MARC)

FRONTISPIECE
An illustration preceding the title page of a book and usually on the verso of the half title page. (MARC)

FTP
See File Transfer Protocol (FTP). (OCLC)

FTU
First time use. The first time a library uses a record already in WorldCat that it did not input. (OCLC)

G

GENERAL MATERIAL DESIGNATION
A term indicating the broad class of material to which an

item belongs and indicated in field 245 subfield $h (e.g. microfilm, sound recording, computer file). See AACR2r98 for authorized list of terms. (MARC)

GRAPHICAL USER INTERFACE (GUI)
The use of pictures rather than just words to represent the input and output of a program. The program displays icons, buttons, dialogue boxes etc. in its windows on the screen; the user controls it by moving a mouse or pointer on the screen, selecting objects by pressing buttons on the mouse. Compare to Command Line Interface. (LIBHQ)

H

HALF TITLE
A title of a publication appearing on a leaf preceding the title page. (MARC)

HEADING
A name, word, or phrase placed at the head of a catalog entry to provide an access point. See also Access point. (MARC)

HITS
The number of times a record or word is found by the system. (OCLC)

I

IMPORTED/EXPORTED BIBLIOGRAPHY RECORDS
Because of the standards established for the creation and transferal of library bibliographic records, libraries can exchange records through import and export. (LIBHQ)

INDEX
A detailed alphabetical or numerical list. List entries represent an aspect of a bibliographic record and are organized into searchable files used to retrieve records in a database or set of records. (OCLC)

INDEX LABEL
A two- or three-character code that indicates to the system, which index to match a search against. (OCLC)

INDICATOR
A one-digit code that provides information to the computer about a variable field. The presence, meaning, and use of indicators will vary from field to field. Depending on the tag number of the field, either a numeric indicator value or a blank occupies each of the two reserved indicator positions in each field which always follows the tag number after one space. (MARC)

INTEGRATING RESOURCE
A bibliographic resource that is added to or changed by means of updates that do not remain discrete and are integrated into the whole. Integrating resources can be finite or continuing. Examples of integrating resources include updating loose-leafs and webpage. (AACR2)

INTERFACE
In hardware, an interface is a connector used to link devices. In software, it allows communication between two software systems or between people and systems. In the automation field, interface refers to the method by which users can access the automated library system. See Graphical User Interface. (LIBHQ)

INTERNATIONAL STANDARD BOOK NUMBER (ISBN)
A unique identification number assigned to a work by its publisher. Each ISBN has ten characters. The tenth character is a check character that may be a number or the letter x. In printed form, the ISBN has three hyphens. (OCLC)

INTERNATIONAL STANDARD SERIAL NUMBER (ISSN)
A unique identification number assigned to a serial through the ISSN Network. Each ISSN has eight characters. The eighth character is a check character that may be a number or the letter x. A hyphen follows the fourth character. (OCLC)

INTERNET
A network of networks; a group of networks interconnected via routers. The Internet is the world's largest network. (LIBHQ)

INTRANET

A network of computers and servers accessed via web browsers, but maintained within an organization or company, and not generally accessible to those outside the organization. (LIBHQ)

ISBN (ISO 2108)

see

International Standard Book Number

ISSN (ISO 3297)

see

International Standard Serial Number

ITEM

1. The physical embodiment of a work or representation that shares the same physical characteristics. For example, a book is an item; an audiocassette recording of the book is another item. An institution may have multiple copies of an item. (OCLC)

2. A document or set of documents in any physical form, published, issued, or treated as an entity, and as such forming the basis for a single bibliographic description. (MARC)

ITERATION

An instance of an integrating resource, either as first published or after it has been updated. (AACR2)

J

JOINT AUTHOR

A person who collaborates with one or more other persons to produce a work in relation to which the collaborators perform the same function. See also Shared responsibility. (MARC)

K

KEYWORD SEARCHING

A keyword search looks for specific words or terms that occur anywhere in a field (title, subject, heading, contents, etc.).

Keyword searching is useful when you have incomplete information. Compare to Browse Searching. (LIBHQ)

L

LOCAL AREA NETWORK
A geographically limited data communications network that connects several computers. Library automation systems require a LAN to enable all users to access the same database. (LIBHQ)

LEADER
Data elements that provide information for the processing of the record. The data elements contain numbers or coded values and are identified by relative character position. The leader is fixed in length at 24 character positions and is the first field. (OCLC)

LEAF
One of the units into which the original sheet or half sheet of paper, parchment, etc. is folded to form part of a book, pamphlet, journal, etc., Each leaf consists of two pages, one on each side, either or both may be blank. (MARC)

LEGACY SYSTEM
An older computer system or program that is still valuable to the user, but may not be compatible with newer systems. (LIBHQ)

LINE NUMBER
The sequential numeric identification assigned by the system to each variable field in a record, appearing directly to the left of the field's tag. Also, the sequential numeric identification assigned to each entry in the display of a multiple record search result. (MARC)

LISTSERV
A Listserv is a program that automatically redistributes e-mail to names on a mailing list. Users can subscribe, unsubscribe, and send messages to everyone on the list by sending notes to a specific email address. (LIBHQ)

LOCAL DATA
Data that is pertinent only to the institution cataloging the record. For example, local processing information and catalogr's notes are local data. Certain 9xx fields are reserved for local data. Local data is not preserved in the master record. (OCLC)

LOCAL SYSTEM
The institution's computer system that manages cataloging, acquisitions, circulation, serials and/or an online catalog. (OCLC)

LOG OFF
The process of disconnecting from a local or remote system. (OCLC)

LOG ON
The process of connecting to a local or remote system. (OCLC)

M

MACHINE-READABLE CATALOGING
MARC Bibliographic information, which is arranged in a prescribed format and on a medium, such as magnetic tape, that allows that information to be read by electronic data processing equipment, such as computers. (MARC)

MAIN DISPLAY
The primary work area in which records are viewed. Use with the Copy Display to work with two records. (OCLC)

MAIN ENTRY
The complete catalog record of an item, presented in the form by which the entity is to be uniformly identified and cited. The main entry may include the tracing(s). See also Added entry. (MARC)

MAIN HEADING
The first part of a heading that includes a subheading. (MARC)

MARC

MARC refers to (1) a computer record structure, (2) a set of tags and indicators to identify parts of the record, (3) the level of cataloging information contained in the Library of Congress's MARC records, and (4) the body of records distributed by the Library of Congress MARC Distribution Service. (LIBHQ). An internationally acceptable standard for the exchange of bibliographic data in machine-readable form. (OCLC)

MARC FORMAT

A format for communicating machine-readable cataloging records, originally developed by the Library of Congress and used by many online systems, such as OCLC. (MARC)

MARC RECORD

Machine-Readable Cataloging record. An internationally accepted standard for the exchange of bibliographic data in machine-readable form. See also communications format. (OCLC)

MASTER RECORD

A master record is the version of the WorldCat or Authority File record available to all users. It does not include local data for any library. Other users can retrieve the record or edit it locally while you have the master record locked for editing. (OCLC)

MASTHEAD

A statement of title, ownership, editors, etc. of a newspaper or periodical. In the case of newspapers, it is commonly found on the editorial page or at the top of page one, and, in the case of periodicals, on the contents page. (MARC)

MATCHES

The number of times the system identifies a search term. (OCLC)

MAXIMUM FIELD SIZE

The system capacity for a field in a record in WorldCat is 9,999 characters; however, this capacity is never reached because the total record size must be less than 4,096 characters. (OCLC)

MIXED RESPONSIBILITY
A work of mixed responsibility is one in which different persons or bodies contribute to its intellectual or artistic content by performing different kinds of activities (e.g. adapting or illustrating a work written by another person). See also Joint author, Shared responsibility. (MARC)

MNEMONIC
Relating to or assisting the memory. An aid used in remembering. (OCLC)

MODIFIED RECORD
A record that has been modified. (OCLC)

MODULE/APPLICATION MODULE
A module is a software segment that performs a specific function, such as acquisition or circulation. Automation system vendors may sell modules separately, though circulation and cataloging modules are often sold together, with add-on modules as possible extra purchases. (LIBHQ)

MONOGRAPH
A nonserial item (i.e., an item either complete in one part or complete, or intended to be completed, in a finite number of separate parts). (MARC)

MULTIPART ITEM
A monograph complete, or intended to be completed, in a finite number of separate parts. (MARC)

N

NAME-TITLE ADDED ENTRY
An added entry consisting of the name of a person or corporate body and the title of an item. (MARC)

NETWORK
A group of interconnected computers, including the hardware, software, and cabling used to connect them. (LIBHQ)

NEW RECORD
An authority record that does not previously exist. This record may be created.(OCLC)

NON-FILING CHARACTERS
Typically, articles at the beginning of a title, such as 'a,' 'an,' or 'the' including the space that follows, are counted as non-filing characters. 'The' would count as 4 non-filing characters (i.e. 3 letters, t h e plus the space). (MARC)

O

OCLC
Nonprofit membership organization serving libraries around the world to further access to the world's information and reduce library costs by offering services for libraries and their users. (OCLC)

OCLC AUTHORITY FILE
A database which establishes, for consistency, the authoritative forms of names (personal or corporate) or subject headings to be used in a catalog. (OCLC)

OCLC ONLINE UNION CATALOG
The former name of WorldCat. See WorldCat. (OCLC)

OCLC-MARC FORMAT
OCLC's implementation of the MARC bibliographic format. (OCLC)

OPAC
Online Public Access Catalog: Provides access to the library's holdings via a computer monitor, replacing the traditional card catalog. May also be called a PAC (Public Access Catalog). (LIBHQ)

OPERATING SYSTEMS (OS)
The low-level software on a computer that schedules tasks, allocates storage, handles the interface to peripheral hardware, and presents a default interface to the user when no application program is running. Examples: UNIX, Windows98, Windows NT. (LIBHQ)

OTHER TITLE INFORMATION

A title borne by an item other than the title proper, or parallel or series title(s); also any phrase appearing in conjunction with the title proper, etc. indicative of the character, contents, etc., of the item or the motives for, or occasion of, its production or publication. The term includes subtitles, avant-titles, etc. but does not include variations on the title proper (e.g. spine titles. sleeve titles). (MARC)

P

PART

1. One of the subordinate units into which an item has been divided by the author, publisher, or manufacturer. In the case of printed monographs, generally synonymous with volume; it is distinguished from a fascicle by being a component unit rather thana temporary division of a work.

2. As used in the physical description area, 'part' designates bibliographic units intended to be bound several to a volume. (MARC)

PERSONAL AUTHOR

The person chiefly responsible for the creation of the intellectual or artistic content of a work. (MARC)

PLATE

A leaf containing illustrative matter, with or without explanatory text, that does not form part of either the preliminary or the main sequence of pages or leaves. (MARC)

PREFACE

The author's discussion of the various aspects of the creation of the book. Follows the title page of the book. (MARC)

PRELIMINARIES

The title page(s) of an item, the verso of the title page(s), any pages preceding the title page(s), and the cover. (MARC)

PROTOCOLS

Sets of rules or standards that let computers communicate over the Internet. HTTP (Hypertext Transfer Protocol) allows transfer of web pages via a browser. FTP (File Transfer Protocol) allows transfer of files through the Internet from one computer to another. (LIBHQ)

PSEUDONYM
A name assumed by an author to conceal or obscure his or her identity. (MARC)

PUBLISHER
The persons or companies responsible for placing the book on the market. A publisher and printer may be the same person or entity, although in modern publishing this is not usually the case. (OCLC)

Q

QUERY
A user's request for information from a database or search engine. A query is a search string entered by a patron when searching for a particular library item or subject in the library's catalog, or OPAC. (LIBHQ)

R

RDBMS
Relational Database Management System. See Relational Database. (LIBHQ)

RECORD CONVERSION
Record conversion is an aspect of retrospective conversion, in which book records on a tape or disk are converted to MARC format for use in an automation system. Conversion is usually processed by the automation system or by an outside vendor specializing in retrospective conversion. (LIBHQ)

RECORD FORMAT
A standard for the representation and exchange of data in machine-readable form. See also record structure. (OCLC)

RECORD MATCHING
Computer system operation that compares one record to another to determine a match. (OCLC)

RECORD STRUCTURE

In MARC 21 formats, record structure is the order in which the content designators and content appear in the record and/or file. Record structure can include such specifications as tape media, header, blocking techniques, and characters sets used. (OCLC)

RECTO

1. The right-hand page of a book, usually bearing an odd page number.
2. The side of a printed sheet intended to be read first. Typically, the title page or leaf is a recto page or leaf. (MARC)

REFERENCE SOURCE

Any publication from which authoritative information may be obtained. Not limited to reference works. (MARC)

RELATIONAL DATABASE

A database in the form of tables having rows and columns to show the relationships between items. If data is changed in one table, it will be changed in all related tables. See Database. (LIBHQ)

REMOTE ACCESS

Service allowing users away from the server or network to access these resources from remote locations. (LIBHQ)

REPRINT

1. A new printing of an item made from the original type image, commonly by photographic methods. The reprint may reproduce the original exactly (an impression or it may contain minor but well-defined variations (an issue).
2. A new publication of an edition with substantially unchanged text. (MARC)

RETROSPECTIVE CONVERSION

Retrospective conversion is the process by which libraries convert a shelflist (such as a card catalog) to a searchable, computerized database. This database can then be used as the backbone of an automation system. (LIBHQ)

RETROSPECTIVE CONVERSION MODE
The authorization mode used by institutions for retrospective conversion projects. (OCLC)

RUNNING TITLE
A title, or abbreviated title, that is repeated at the head or foot of each page or leaf. (MARC)

S

SERIAL
A continuing resource issued in a succession of discrete parts, usually bearing numbering, that has no predetermined conclusion. Examples of serials include journals, magazines, electronic journals, continuing directories, annual reports, newspapers, and numbered monographic series. (AACR2)

SERIES
1. A group of separate items related to one another by the fact that each item bears, in addition to its own title proper, a collective title applying to the group as a whole. The individual items may or may not be numbered.

2. Each of two or more volumes of essays, lectures, articles, or other writings, similar in character and issued in sequence (e.g. Lowell's Among my books, second series).

3. A separately numbered sequence of volumes within a series or serial (e.g. Notes and queries, 1st series, 2nd series, etc.) (MARC)

SERVER
A computer that provides some service for other computers connected to it via a network. The library's database containing all book records is located on a server so that several client machines (OPACs) can access the files. See Client/Server. (LIBHQ)

SINE LOCO (S.L.)
Without place (i.e., the name of the place of publication, distribution, etc. is unknown). (MARC)

SINE NOMINE (S.N.)
Without name (i.e., the name of the publisher, distributor, etc. is unknown). (MARC)

SPECIAL CHARACTER
Alphabetic or phonetic character other than that used in modern English. In records, each special character occupies its own position, whether or not it is used in conjunction with another character. (OCLC)

STATEMENT OF RESPONSIBILITY
A statement, transcribed from the item being described, relating to persons responsible for the intellectual or artistic content of the item, to corporate bodies from which the content emanates, or to person or corporate bodies responsible for the performance of the content of the item. (MARC)

STOPWORDS
Words you omit from a search because they are so common that they have no informational value. Stopwords are not indexed and are therefore ignored by the system if you type them. See stopword lists for keyword searches and for derived corporate name searches. (OCLC)

SUBFIELD
The smallest logical unit of information in a variable field. Subfield codes (letters or numbers) identify subfields and are preceded by a delimiter. (OCLC) A subdivision of a variable field containing data logically identifiable as a discrete unit of that field. (MARC)

SUBFIELD CODE
A character, usually lowercase alphabetic or numeric, that identifies the data within a particular subfield. (MARC)

SUBFIELD DELIMITER
See delimiter. (OCLC)

SUBHEADING
Part of a corporate heading other than the main heading. (MARC)

SUPPLIED TITLE
A title provided by the catalogr for an item that has no title proper on the chief source of information or its substitute. It may be taken from elsewhere in the item itself or from a reference source, or it may be composed by the cataloger. (MARC)

T

TABLE OF CONTENTS
Usually comes at the end of the preliminary material in a book and lists in order the book's main topics or the headings of the individual units and their page numbers. (MARC)

TAG
Element of a MARC record that identifies variable fields. Tags are grouped numerically by function. For example, field 245 is a title field (OCLC). A three-digit identifier, usually numeric, of a variable field, beginning with 001 and ending with 999. (MARC)

TAG GROUP
A collection of tags, beginning with the same first digit, that store similar kinds of information and share a similar function within a record. When referring to a tag group, the second and third digits are generally replaced with XX. For example, all tags in the 6XX tag group are subjects. (MARC)

TCP/IP
Transmission Control Protocol/Internet Protocol, the suite of communications protocols used to connect computers on the Internet. (LIBHQ)

TITLE
A word, phrase, character, or group of characters, normally appearing in an item, that names the item or the work contained in it. (MARC)

TITLE PAGE
A page at the beginning of an item bearing the title proper and usually, though not necessarily, the statement of

responsibility and the data relating to publication. The leaf bearing the title page is commonly called the 'title page' although properly called the 'title leaf.' Use t.p. to abbreviate the term. (MARC)

TRACING
1. A record of the headings under which an item is represented in the catalog.
2. A record of the references that have been made to a name or to the title of a item that is represented in the catalog. See also Access points. (MARC)

TRUNCATION
In searching, truncation means that the system will allow wildcards to extend a search term. For example, a truncated term with a wildcard, such as app*, will retrieve all entries that begin with app, from apples to application. See Wildcard. (LIBHQ)

TYPE OF RECORD (TYPE)
The element in the fixed field that differentiates records created for various types of machine-readable information and specific types of material. Codes used in Type of Record are also used in field 006. (OCLC)

U

UNICODE
A 16-bit, language-independent character set that enables representation of all of the characters commonly used in information processing. (LIBHQ)

UNIFORM TITLE
Collects the publications of an author, composer, or corporate body into a unit. The unit may contain several expressions and manifestations of the work. For example, complete works, works in a particular literary or musical form, or translations into various languages for commonly known or classical works. (OCLC)

UNIMARC
An international MARC format that accepts records created in any of the more than 20 MARC formats, thus facilitating conversion of records among them. (LIBHQ)

V

VALIDATE A RECORD
Examine the data in certain fields for consistency and compliance with various rules via the Validate (val) command. The system also performs automatic validation on records when you Replace, Produce, Update, or Delete Holdings. (OCLC)

VARIABLE CONTROL FIELDS
In MARC 21, the 00x fields. They identify the field tag in the Directory but they contain neither indicator positions nor subfield codes. In contrast to variable data fields, control fields may contain either a single data element or a series of fixed-lenth. (OCLC)

VARIABLE DATA FIELDS
Any variable field other than the 00x fields. They are identified by the field tag in the directory. Variable fields contain 2 indicator positions at the beginning of each field and a 2-character subfield code preceding each data element in the field. (OCLC)

VARIABLE FIELD
Fields of variable length in a record that can contain coded data but usually contain textual information separated by subfields. See variable control fields, variable data fields. See also fixed field; subfield. (OCLC). A field in a machine-readable bibliographic record that is not limited to a prescribed size, content or position within the record. (MARC)

VERSO
1. The left-hand page of a book, usually bearing an even page number.
2. The side of a printed sheet intended to be read second. The verso of the title page shows the official date of publication and where the book was published. (MARC)

VOLUME

In the bibliographic sense, a major division of a work, regardless of its designation by the publisher, distinguished from other major divisions of the same work by having its own inclusive title page, half title, cover title, or portfolio title, and usually independent pagination, foliation, or signatures. This major bibliographic unit may include various title pages and/or pagination. The volume as a material unit may not coincide with the volume as a bibliographic unit. (MARC)

W

WEB BROWSER

Software program that allows you to access web pages on the Internet, an Intranet, or an Extranet. The two most popular browsers are Microsoft's Internet Explorer and Netscape Navigator. (LIBHQ)

WIDE AREA NETWORK (WAN)

A network, usually constructed with serial lines, extending over distances greater than one mile. A library system may use a WAN to connect branch libraries to the greater automation system. (LIBHQ)

WILDCARD

A special character such as *, $, or ? that can replace any character or characters in a string. Wildcards are used in catalog searches to extend a search term. See Truncation. (LIBHQ)

WORD

For searching purposes, any character or group of characters between two blank spaces, including initials or abbreviations. (OCLC)

WORKFORM

A template used to create an original record or local data record. The system automatically supplies some of the appropriate fields and data, depending on the format you select for the material you are cataloging. (OCLC)

WORKING COPY

A copy of the master record, displayed on the user's screen. When the user edits the working copy, the master record remains unchanged. (OCLC)

WORLDCAT

A database of more than 55 million records (as of mid-2004) for the bibliographic description of separately cataloged works from thousands of libraries (formerly called the OCLC Online Union Catalog or OLUC). (OCLC)

Z

Z39.50

A NISO (National Information Standards Organization) standard for information retrieval that allows any library using a Z39.50-compliant automated library system to access remote library collections. Z39.50 specifies a query/response protocol between a client and a server. See LibraryHQ's Z39.50 page. (LIBHQ)

PART

5

Appendix

CONTENTS

PART 5

Source: Library of Congress
Network Development and MARC standards office
www.loc.gov/marc/marcforum.html

MARC FORUM

The MARC Forum is a *moderated* electronic discussion forum open to anyone interested in discussing the implementation, maintenance, changes, and development of the MARC 21 formats. It is maintained by the Library of Congress Network Development and MARC Standards Office. The MARC Forum provides the opportunity for members of the information community to participate in discussions related to the formats.

Vendor, network, technical service, automation, and reference staff and researchers are encouraged to participate. While there is a close linkage between MARC 21 as a communications format and the cataloging of materials, the focus of the MARC Forum is on MARC 21 the communications format.
[*Click on the following option*:

- Join or leave the MARC Forum

and Access the registration form]

Join or Leave the MARC List

Top of Form

MARC	1

This screen allows you to join or leave the MARC list. To confirm your identity and prevent third parties from subscribing you to a list against your will, an e-mail message with a confirmation code will be sent to the address you specify in the form. Simply wait for this message to arrive, then follow the instructions to confirm the operation.

Alternatively, you can login with your LISTSERV password (if you have one) and update your subscription interactively, without e-mail confirmation.

Your E-Mail Address:		
Your Name:		

	Join MARC	Leave MARC	Leave all the Lists

Subscription Type:	⦿ Regular	[NODIGEST]
	○ Digest (traditional)	[NOMIME DIGEST]
	○ Digest (MIME format)	[NOHTML MIME DIGEST]
	○ Digest (HTML format)	[HTML DIGEST]
	○ Index (traditional)	[NOHTML INDEX]
	○ Index (HTML format)	[HTML INDEX]
Mail Header Style:	○ Normal LISTSERV-style header	[FULLHDR]
	⦿ LISTSERV-style, with list name in subject	[SUBJECTHDR]
	○ LISTSERV-style, short	[SHORTHDR]
	○ "Dual" (second header in mail body)	[DUALHDR]
	○ sendmail-style	[IETFHDR]
Acknowledgements:	○ No acknowledgements	[NOACK NOREPRO]
	○ Short message confirming receipt	[ACK NOREPRO]
	⦿ Receive copy of own postings	[NOACK REPRO]
Miscellaneous:	☐ Mail delivery disabled temporarily	[NOMAIL]
	☐ Address concealed from REVIEW listing	[CONCEAL]

	Join MARC	Leave MARC	Leave all the Lists

ONLINE DISCUSSION FORUMS

AUTOCAT

Subscribe: listserv@ubvm.cc.buffalo.edu

Send the message SUBSCRIBE AUTOCAT [Firstname Lastname]

Moderated e-conference which focuses on cataloguing and authorities issues.

COOPCAT

Subscribe: listserv@iubvm.indiana.edu

Send the message SUBSCRIBE COOPCAT [Firstname Lastname]

This list acts as a clearinghouse of information to aid in the formation of cooperative cataloging arrangements between libraries.

INTERCAT

Subscribe: listserv@oclc.org

Send the message SUBSCRIBE INTERCAT [Firstname Lastname]

Public list for information and discussion concerning the OCLC Internet Cataloging Project.

TSIG-L

Subscribe: listproc@acadiau.ca

Send the message SUBSCRIBE TSIG-L [Firstname Lastname]

Canadian Library Association's Technical Services Interest Group.

USMARC-L

Subscribe: listserv@loc.gov

Send the message SUBSCRIBE USMARC [Firstname Lastname]

This moderated e-conference which is open to anyone interested in discussing the implementation, maintenance, and development of the USMARC formats.

Web4Lib

Subscribe: listserv@library.berkeley.edu

Send the message SUBSCRIBE WEB4LIB [Firstname Lastname]

Web4Lib is a forum to foster the discussion of issues related to the creation and management of library-based WWW servers and clients. The list offers information about this list for librarians involved with web maintenance, as well as an archive of discussions.

URL: http://sunsite.berkeley.edu/Web4Lib/

Archive URL: http://sunsite.berkeley.edu/Web4Lib/archive.html

WebCat-L

Subscribe: LISTSERV@WUVMD.WUSTL.EDU

Send the message SUBSCRIBE WEBCAT-L [Firstname Lastname]

WebCat-L is a forum for discussion on the issues surrounding Web-based library catalogues.

MARC GROUP - YAHOO!

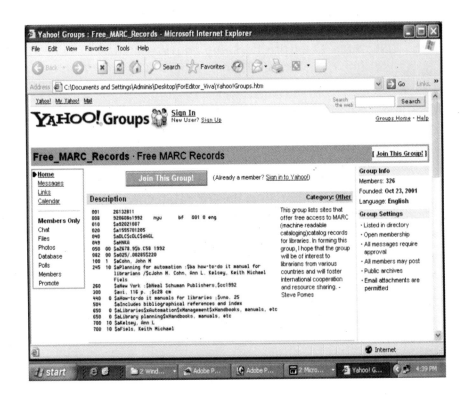

MARC 21 FORMATS
PROPOSED CHANGE FORM

File   Edit   View   Favorites   Tools   Help

Address   http://www.loc.gov/marc/chgform.html   Go

MARC 21 FORMATS PROPOSED CHANGE FORM

This form is to be used as the cover sheet on all proposals
for changes to the MARC 21 formats. The proposal itself should
consist of a detailed analysis of the problem, the proposed
solution, and the justification for the change. Include examples
of possible use where appropriate. All proposals are submitted to the
Network Development and MARC Standards Office at the address below.

As an attachment to the proposal, please respond to the
questions appended below.

Format Type: _____ Bibliographic   Date: _____
                    _____ Authorities
                    _____ Holdings
                    _____ Classification
                    _____ Community Information

Data Elements Affected by the Proposed Change (e.g., fields,
subfields, fixed-field character positions, etc.):

Brief Description of the Proposed Change:

*As an attachment to your proposal, please respond to the following questions.

1. In the view of the proposing body, is the proposal so minor as to require little or no cost consideration and no further response to these guildline questions?

2. What identifiable groups will be affected by the proposed change, e.g. public libraries, utilities, vendors of automated library systems, LC, archivists, music catalogers?

3. Will adoption of the proposal effectively be optional or mandatory by the groups affected?

4. Which groups will benefit from the proposal, and to what extent? Is the benefit demonstrable in fiscal terms?

5. Has any study of the cost impact of this proosal been done? If so, how are the results available to others?

6. If the proposing body sees the costs of the proposal as potentially significant, what body do you believe would be the most appropriate to carry out a study of those costs in order to gain further information and precision?

7. Which groups will incur costs as a result of the proposal?

8. What kinds of costs are associated with the proposal, e.g. labor, training, data processing, communications? Are they ontime or continuing costs?

9. Does the proposal have retrospective implications? Will existing records have to be changed, or materials reprocessed?

10. What proportion of materials processed, and of the records created for them, will be affected?

11. Are codes or standards affected other than those specifically addressed by the proposal?

12. Can the proposing body describe alternative ways of achieving the ends of the proposal?

LCSH Change Proposal Form

Refer to LC Subject Heading Change Guidelines for guidance in filling in this form. Write to:saco@loc.gov for questions, follow-up, etc.

Note: Use dollar sign to denote a delimiter before a subfield code (e.g., $x); copy diacritics from list and paste before letter (e.g., Kam(macron)anche)

---

010 LCCN of record to be changed: [＿＿＿＿＿] e.g.,sh200101234 (**do not** include hypens)

040 MARC 21 identification code: [＿＿＿＿＿] (not utility code

○ Change ○ Add ○ Delete **053:** [＿＿＿＿＿]

  1XX heading on existing record: [＿＿＿＿＿]

  Change **1XX to:**

○ Change ○ Add ○ Delete **4xx:** [＿＿＿＿＿＿＿＿＿]

○ Change ○ Add ○ Delete **4xx:** [＿＿＿＿＿＿＿＿＿]

○ Change ○ Add ○ Delete **4xx:** [＿＿＿＿＿＿＿＿＿]

○ Change ○ Add ○ Delete **5xx:** [＿＿＿＿＿＿＿＿＿]

○ Change ○ Add ○ Delete **5xx:** [＿＿＿＿＿＿＿＿＿]

○ Change ○ Add ○ Delete **5xx:** [＿＿＿＿＿＿＿＿＿]

Note: When adding 5XX RT, please note in comments box below. Add **670**; use dollar sign before subfield; copy diacritics from list and paste before letter (e.g., Kam [macron]anche)

Add **670**

Add **670**

○ Change ○ Add ○ Delete **680: Scope note:**

[text area]

○ Change ○ Add ○ Delete **781:**

[text area]

○ Change ○ Add ○ Delete **667:**

Comments; additional 053s, 4xxs; 670s, etc.:

Submitted by: [_____]

Institution: [_____] (if first time user please add otherwise, optional)

e-mail: [_____] Phone: [_____]
(if first time user please add otherwise, optional)

Wait! if you want a copy of your proposal please use your browser print button before clicking on SUBMIT button.

[SUBMIT] [Reset Form]

REQUEST FOR NEW OR REVISED
MARC 21 ORGANIZATION CODES

[ENGLISH] - - [ESPAÑOL] - - [PORTUGUÊS]

Organization (REQUIRED!)
(Full name of organization as it would be listed in a telephone directory. Use capital and small letter language of the name.)

Street (REQUIRED!)
(Give number and street and/or P.O.Box: Abbreviate the words "Street". "Road", "Lane", etc. to "St", "Rd", Ln".

City or Town (REQUIRED!)
(Give the city in the official language of the country. For example: "Den Haag", not "The Hague".)

State (for USA only)
(Type the first letter of the name: scroll to the correct state: press [TAB] to go to the next blank)

Choose a State ▾

Postal Code
(For U.S. organizations, provide the full ZIP+4postal code if known)

Country (REQUIRED!)
(Type the first letter of the English form of the name; scroll to the correct country; press [TAB] to go to the next blank

Choose a country ▾

Variant Name
(Such as the name of the organization in a different language)

Telephone (REQUIRED!)
(Provide country area (city) codes, separated by huphens; for the U.S., the country code is "1"; for example; 1-202-707-6237

Fax (If Available)
(Provide country and area (city) codes, separated by hyphens; for the U.S., the country code is "1"; example; 1-202-707-6237

Contact Person (REQUIRED!)
(Give the name of a person who can be contacted if questions arise)

Email (REQUIRED!)

(Provide an email address to which the MARC code assignment should be sent; this may be the contact person or the person requesting the code. You must provide an email address. Please type it carefully.)

[   ]

[SUBMIT REQUEST]   [Clear Form]

Source: MARC 21 Specifications for Record Structure,
Character Sets, and Exchange Media: Part 2
http://www.loc.gov/marc/specifications/speccharucs.html January 2000,
Updated June 2003

UCS/UNICODE ENVIRONMENT

INTRODUCTION

Use of the Universal Coded Character Set (UCS or ISO/IEC 10646) and its industry subset Unicode have been approved for standard interchange of MARC 21 records according to the following specifications. The restrictions in these specifications are intended to optimize the interchange of data encoded using the MARC-8 character sets and UCS/Unicode during the period of transition from a largely 8-bit environment to the 16-bit UCS/Unicode environment. The specifications are built around enabling round trip movement of MARC data between MARC-8 and UCS/Unicode with as little loss as possible. Since the characters permitted in MARC 21 records now include scripts which are only covered by UCS/Unicode, conversion back to the MARC-8 environment will not always be without loss. It is, however, without loss for all legacy data created prior to the establishment of UCS/Unicode as an accepted MARC 21 character encoding.

SPECIFICATION

MARC 21 Character Repertoire

MARC 21 has established a subset of the full repertoire of characters in UCS/Unicode that is permitted in MARC 21 records at this time. This subset is made up of the UCS characters that correspond to the over 16,000 characters defined in the separate MARC-8 character sets for MARC 21. The MARC 21 subset also includes a new group of 630 characters from the Unified Canadian Aboriginal Syllabic (CAS) script repertoire in UCS/Unicode. This is what is meant by the MARC 21 repertoire of characters. The correspond-ences between the legacy MARC-8 (8- and 24-bit) and UCS/Unicode (16-bit) character values are shown in character set lists that can be found at *Part 3: Code Tables.*

Encoding Rules

The encoding of UCS/Unicode characters follows the rules of UTF-8 (UCS Transformation Format-8) which uses designated bits to indicate whether a UCS/Unicode character is represented by 1 octet (8-bits) or multiple octets. This encoding has the advantage of allowing the Basic Latin (ASCII) subset of the MARC 21 repertoire to be encoded with the same 8-bit encodings as in MARC-8 (with only one octet per character), thus preserving the basic structural elements of the MARC 21 record, while enabling record content to be multiscript. A brief description of UTF-8 encoding follows, but a fuller description is carried in the UCS and Unicode standards.

UTF-8 is an encoding form for the UCS/Unicode 16-bit repertoire. It represents characters in a systematic way as 1, 2, or 3 octets, using the left-most bits of each octet to indicate how the octet is to be interpreted.

Left-most bits encoding	Meaning of left-most bits for character
0	character composed of 1 octet
110	first octet of 2 octet character
1110	first octet of 3 octet character
10	octet is not the first octet for a character, it is the 2nd, or 3rd octet of a multi-octet character

The following transformation is used when converting UCS/Unicode 16-bit characters to UTF-8.

UCS/Unicode values		UTF-8 values
Range	Form	
0000 to 007F hex	00000000 0xxxxxxx	0xxxxxxx
0080 to 07FF hex	00000xxx xxyyyyyy	110xxxxx 10yyyyyy
0800 to FFFF hex	xxxxyyyy yyzzzzzz	1110xxxx 10yyyyyy 10zzzzzz

Note: 'x' above represents the part of the UCS/Unicode character encoding that will be transferred to the first UTF-8 octet; 'y' represents the part that will be transferred to the second UTF-8 octet; and 'z' represents the part that will be transferred to the third UTF-8 octet.

Examples:

Character	MARC-8 encoding	UCS/Unicode encoding	UTF-8 encoding
Comma	00101100 (2C hex)	00000000 00101100 (002C hex)	00101100
Latin small letter h	01101000 (68 hex)	00000000 01101000 (0068 hex)	01101000
Macron	11100101 (E5 hex)	00000011 00000100 (0304 hex)	11001100 10000100
Hebrew letter tav	01111010 (7A hex)	00000101 11101010 (05EA hex)	11010111 10101010
Combining ligature left half	11101011 (EB hex)	11111110 00100000 (FE20 hex)	11101111 10111000 10100000

The transformation of surrogate pairs is not described above as they are not currently required for any of the MARC-8 repertoire. See the Unicode Standard 3.0 documentation for information on surrogate pairs.

UCS/Unicode Markers and the MARC 21 Record Leader

In MARC 21 records, Leader character position 9 contains value a if the data is encoded using UCS/Unicode characters. If any UCS/Unicode characters are to be included in the MARC 21 record, the entire MARC record must be encoded using UCS/Unicode characters. The record length contained in Leader positions 0-4 is a count of the number of octets in the record, not characters. The Leader position 9 value is not dependent on the character encoding used. This rule applies to MARC 21 records encoded using both the MARC-8 and UCS/Unicode character sets.

MARC Field 066 and subfield $6

Field 066 (Character Sets Present) is not needed in MARC 21 records encoded using UCS/Unicode characters since there is no need to identify specific character sets in the UCS/Unicode environment. During conversion of MARC 21 records from MARC-8 encodings to UCS/Unicode, field 066 is deleted. When converting from UCS/Unicode encodings to MARC-8, field 066 must be generated based on the presence of characters from repertoires of UCS/Unicode characters. Since MARC-8 and ISO 2022 (Character code structure and extension techniques) allow character sets to be designated as either G0 or G1 sets, the configuration of field 066 subfields and the script codes these subfields contain will depend on the desired assignment of MARC-8 sets to a particular graphic character value range.

Subfield $6 (Linkage) is used in MARC 21 records to link alternate graphic representations of the same data, to identify the presence of specific scripts in a field, and to flag fields in which the display/print directionality of data is right-to-left (e.g. for Arabic script). The script identification information in subfield $6 is superfluous in MARC 21 records encoded using UCS/Unicode since UCS/Unicode is by design a multiscript character set. This information can be dropped from subfield $6 when converting MARC-8 encodings to corresponding UCS/Unicode encodings. Linkage and directionality information may be useful regardless of encoding and can be retained when doing character conversion.

Standard UCS/Unicode

MARC 21 uses standard UCS/Unicode. The content of a MARC 21 record is consistent with UCS/Unicode conventions. For example, UCS/Unicode requires that characters in the combining class, this includes separately encoded diacritical marks used with base letters from the Latin and other scripts, be encoded *following* the base letter they modify. This is the opposite of the MARC-8 rule for encoding order. During conversion from MARC-8 to UCS/Unicode, care must be taken to handle the positioning of combining characters to meet the requirements of the target encoding. The encoding of bidirectional data is another area where UCS/Unicode rules must be followed. Data is recorded in logical order, from the first character to the last, regardless of field orientation, and with no exceptions.

Character values from the Private Use Area (PUA) have been used in mapping a small number of Chinese, Japanese and Korean characters in the MARC-8 East Asian Character Code (EACC) set to UCS/Unicode. This was done to allow a completely lossless EACC characters to UCS/Unicode. Work has been started to assign these characters non-PUA values in UCS/Unicode where possible, but for many, this is not possible (e.g., when the EACC character is already covered by a UCS/Unicode character in the Unified Han repertoire. The MARC-8 to UCS/Unicode mappings provide alternative non-PUA values for most EACC characters initially mapped to the PUA.

DISPLAYING AND SEARCHING
NON-ROMAN CHARACTERS (UNICODE)

LIBRARY OF CONGRESS ONLINE CATALOG
HELP PAGES

use the browser's [Back] button to resume searching

Displaying and Searching Non-Roman
Characters in the Online Catalog (Unicode)

Bibliographic records for items in most languages will display correctly without
changing any settings in your preferred Web browser. The instructions below
may be helpful if you want to view records containing non-Roman characters
(e.g., Unicode characters) in any of the JACKPHY languages (e.g., Japanese,
Arabic, Chinese, Korean, Persian, Hebrew, or Yiddish).

View Special Help Screens for the following languages:
Japanese - **Chinese** - **Korean** - Arabic - Persian - **Hebrew/Yiddish** new!

Special Note on Printing, Saving and Emailing: It is possible to successfully
Print or Save non-Roman characters using the "Save, Print or Email Records"
function of the Online Catalog (found at the bottom of search results and single
record displays). Best results occur if you have Unicode fonts and use Unicode
character encoding with automatic character encoding activated.

When printing or saving records, please make sure your brower's character
encoding (on the *View* pulldown menu) is set to:

- Text (Brief Information) **Unicode (UTF-8)**
- Text (Full Information) **Unicode (UTF-8)**
- MARC (non-Unicode/MARC-8) **Western or Western European**
- MARC (Unicode/UTF-8) **Unicode (UTF-8)**

At this time, it is not possible to Email records containing non-Roman characters
or words including any diacritic marks.

CJK Compatibility Database

Use the CJK Compatibility Database to quickly and conveniently replace non-
MARC21 characters with MARC21 equivalents, or a missing character symbol.
- Link to the CJK Compatibility database
- More about the CJK Compatibility database

MARC Tags

Headings List
Titles List
Titles List (Keyword)
References/Scope
Notes
Save, Print, Email

OTHER TOPICS:
Headings List Types
Material Types
Database Selection
Icons, Buttons & Tabs
Session Time-out Errors

Instructions for Windows

Installing the Unicode Font in Windows XP

If you are using *Microsoft Windows XP*, the "universal font" for Unicode should be automatically installed.

Arial Unicode MS font is a "full Unicode font" -- it contains all of the characters, ideographs, and symbols defined in the Unicode 2.1 standard.*

Unicode is a character encoding standard developed by the Unicode Consortium. By using more than one byte to represent each character, Unicode enables almost all of the written languages in the world to be represented by using a single character set.

If the "universal font" is not visible (i.e., you cannot see non-Roman characters), you will need to set the Latin-based font to **Arial Unicode MS** (if it is not available on your system, you may need to install it -- it will be called "Universal Font" on the installation disks.)

Installing the Unicode Font in Windows 2000

To display non-Roman characters:

1. Display the Windows *Start* menu
2. Select *Settings > Control Panel > Regional Options*
3. Within the *General* tab, check all of the languages you may want to display;
   * the more you set, the more you will be able to process multilingual data through all your applications, including your browser. This adds fonts as well as system support for these languages.
4. Select *OK* to accept your selections
5. You will have to reboot your system for the changes to take effect.

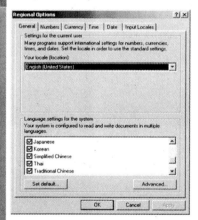

To install the "universal" font:

If you have *Microsoft Office 2000* and newer versions, you can install the **Arial Unicode MS** font, which supports display of most of the non-Roman characters. If you don't already have this font:

1. Insert the *Office CD*, and select "custom install."
2. Choose *Add or Remove Features*.
3. Click the (+) next to *Office Tools*, then *International Support*, then the *Universal Font* icon, and choose the installation option you want.

More Information for Windows 2000 Users:

http://office.microsoft.com/en-us/assistance/HP052558401033.aspx

Displaying Non-Roman Characters in Web Browsers

Setting up the browser to display non-Roman characters is a 2-step process.

Begin by setting the default font to **Arial Unicode MS**:

STEP 1:

To set the font in Internet Explorer, from the *Tools* pulldown menu:

1. Select *Internet Options --> Fonts*
2. Select "Latin based" from the *Language script:* menu
3. Select "Arial Unicode MS" from the *Web page font:* menu
4. Select "OK" to save the change.

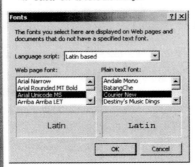

To set the font in Firefox, from the *Tools* pulldown menu

1. Select *Options --> General*
2. Select the button for *Fonts & Colors*
3. Select "Western" in the *Fonts for:* drop-down menu
4. Select "Arial Unicode MS" in the *Sans-serif:* drop-down menu.
5. Select "OK" to save the change.

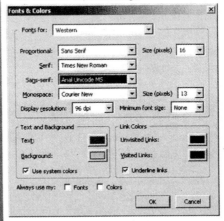

STEP 2:

When viewing catalog records, you will also need to make sure that the character encoding for the page you are looking at is set to **Unicode (UTF-8)**. Often, the browser sets the encoding automatically. You may also have to choose the setting yourself, and this setting doesn't always "stick" (so you may have to reset it).

To set UTF-8 encoding in Internet Explorer... from the *View* pulldown menu select *Encoding > Unicode (UTF-8)*

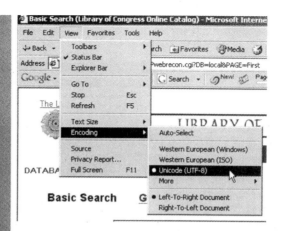

Also, make sure that *Auto-Select* is unmarked. Please note, if "Unicode (UTF-8)" is not currently displaying in your *Encoding* menu, select "More" to find it.

To set UTF-8 encoding in Firefox... from the *View* pulldown menu select *Character Encoding -->Unicode (UTF-8)*.

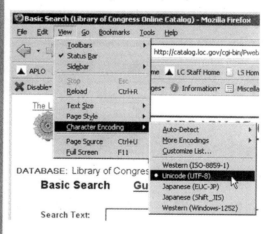

In this case, you can set the *Auto-Detect* option to "Universal." Please note, if

"Unicode (UTF-8)" is not currently displaying in your *Character Encoding* menu, select "More Encodings" to find it.

Installing IMEs for Entering Non-Roman Characters

If you want to search using non-Roman characters, you will need to install the appropriate input keyboard layouts for the languages you wish to search in. These keyboards layouts are called **Input Method Editors** (IMEs).

No rebooting or special privileges are needed to add them to your system. In order to install them, go to:

Start Menu > Settings > Control Panel > Regional Options (General)

Then put a check mark next to all of the languages you want to use.

The Library of Congress currently uses the following IMEs:

Arabic (Egypt) -- Arabic (101)
Chinese (PRC) -- Chinese (Simplified) - US Keyboard
Chinese (Taiwan) -- Chinese (Simplified) - US Keyboard
Hebrew -- Hebrew
Japanese -- Japanese Input System (MS-IME2000)
Korean -- Korean (Hangul) (MS-IME-98)
Russian*

* Note that there are no Cyrillic characters in the LC Online Catalog. All records in languages that use Cyrillic are romanized and can only be retrieved using Roman (Latin) characters in searches. The Library uses the Russian keyboard to search other electronic resources.

For more information on IMEs, please see:

- Microsoft Global Input Method Editors (IMEs)
- What is an IME (Input Method Editor) and how do I use it?

Instructions for Macintosh

Your operating system should be OS 10.3.x or higher. Additionally, the most current version of your browser should be used; check the Web to be sure there are no updates available. As of May 2005 this includes *Firefox 5*, *Safari 1.3*, and

Netscape 7.0. None will work perfectly for all purposes, but all three are adequate for most purposes.

Be sure the **Lucida Grande** font is installed (a default font within OS X).

When viewing catalog records, make sure that the character encoding for the page you are looking at is set to *Unicode (UTF-8)*. Often, the browser sets the encoding automatically. You may occasionally have to choose the setting yourself.

In Firefox - From the View pulldown menu
  Select *Character Encoding -->Unicode (UTF-8)*

In Safari - From the View pulldown menu
  Select *Text Encoding-->Unicode (UTF-8)*

In Netscape - From the View pulldown menu
  Select *Character Coding -->Unicode (UTF-8)*

Support for bidirectional scripts in Mac OS X browsers depends upon the functionality provided by the version of the browser you use.

Copying and pasting of catalog records with special diacritics, characters, or scripts into other applications depend on the ability of those applications to handle Unicode and bidirectional scripts.

Input Methods for Non-Roman Characters

Built into Mac OS X is support for the inputting on non-Roman characters. To enable these features, go to *System Preferences* and select "International":

The following screen displays. Select the "Input Menu" tab. Select input methods for languages you need. Make sure to check the box to "Show input menu in menu bar."

In order to use a language-specific input method, look for the "flag" icon in the menu bar for the application you are using:

More on Non-Roman Characters on Macintosh Computers

This information comes from the Unicode Web site:
http://www.unicode.org/help/display_problems.html

On Mac OS X, the *Safari Web* browser includes Unicode support as does *OmniWeb. OmniWeb*, however, does not currently provide support for all of Unicode (it can, however, take advantage of Unicode fonts for Windows if properly installed).

Earlier Versions

There are currently no Web browsers which provide direct Unicode drawing (font support) on the Mac OS 9.x or earlier. All the browsers use Apple Language Kits and WorldScript to varying degrees to support Unicode and international text.

Language Kits are installed using your Mac OS 9.x installation CD. Launch the Mac OS Install application. Proceed through the initial screens, selecting the appropriate boot disk. When you reach the "Install Software" screen, click on the "Customize" button. This opens up the Custom Installation and Removal dialog box.

Scroll down to "Language Kits." Click on the check box, and then select "Customized Installation" from the installation popup to the right. (It will say "None selected" at first.)

This brings up a dialog box with a list of all the available language kits. Select the ones you want, or use the menu at the top of the dialog box to select all of them. Proceed with the installation.

If you already have Mac OS 9.0 installed, you will be asked if you want to add or remove software after you select the installation disk. Click on the "Add/Remove" button. This will bring you to the Custom Installation and Removal dialog box.

The installation procedure is the same for Mac OS 8.6, except that you will be installing "Multilingual Internet Access" instead of Language Kits. For Mac OS 8.5.5 and earlier, it will be necessary to purchase the individual language kits.

Use the browser's **[Back]** button to resume searching.

>>Top of Page

Still Need Help?
Ask a Librarian

Reporting Catalog Errors?
Error Report Form

Library of Congress Online Catalog - catalog.loc.gov
Library of Congress Home Page
February 8, 2006

COMMUNICATION FORMAT & DISPLAY FORMATS OF MARC RECORD

COMMUNICATION FORMAT

```
01834cam  22003254a 4500001000900000005001700000900800410002690600045000679250042011295501940015401000170034802000350036502000350040004000180043504200140045305005200012100684540062008055050495008676500033013626500012013956500024014078560077014314132789162004041209570201314303071752004    ilua  c b  001 0 eng ▲ ▼a7▼bc bc▼corignew▼d1▼eecip▼f20▼gy-gencatlg▲0 ▼aacquire▼b1 shelf copy▼xpolicy default▲ ▼ajb10 2003-07-17▼ijb10 2003-07-17▼ejb20 2003-07-17 to CHI LIT▼alb00 2003-07-18 ▼dlb18 2003-08-22▼aaa07 2003-08-25▼a[s10 2004-03-08 1 copy rec'd., to CIP ver.▼f pv12 2004-04-08 CIP ver. to BCCD▲ ▼a 2003016135▲ ▼a1403448582 (hbk. : alk. pa per)▲  ▼a1403454329 (pbk. : alk. paper)▲  ▼aDLC▼cDLC▼dDLC▲ ▼apcc▼alcac▲00▼aQL73 7.C23▼bS586 2004▲00▼a599.756▼222▲1 ▼aSpilsbury, Richard,▼d1963-▲10▼aBengal tiger /▼cRichard Spilsbury.▲ ▼aChicago, Ill. :▼bHeinemann Library,▼cc2004.▲ ▼a48 p. :▼bcol. ill. ;▼c27 cm.▲ 0▼aAnimals under threat▲ ▼aDiscusses the plight of Ben gal tigers and why they are near extinction, as well as some of the ways humans can help.▲ ▼aIncludes bibliographical references (p. 46-47) and index.▲0 ▼aThe Bengal tiger -- Tiger country -- Tiger populations -- The body of a tiger -- A s upreme hunter -- Tiger ranges -- Courtship and communication -- Young tigers -- Conflict between tigers and people -- Poaching -- Dealing with poaching -- Tiger hunting in the past -- Destroying tiger habitats -- Fragmented tiger population s -- Saving tiger habitats -- Conservation organizations -- Tigers in captivity -- Tiger tourism and local people -- The future for Bengal tigers -- How can you help?▲ 0▼aTigers▼vJuvenile literature.▲ 1▼aTigers.▲ 1▼aEndangered species.▲41▼3 Table of contents▼uhttp://www.loc.gov/catdir/toc/ecip046/2003016135.html▲⏎
```

TAGGED DISPLAY

005 20040412095702.0

008 030717s2004 ilua c b 001 0 eng

906 __ |a 7 |b cbc |c orignew |d 1 |e ecip |f 20 |g y-gencatlg

925 0_ |a acquire |b 1 shelf copy |x policy default

955 __ |a jb10 2003-07-17 |i jb10 2003-07-17 |e jb20 2003-07-17 to CHI LIT |a lb00 2003-07-18 |d lb18 2003-08-22 |a aa07 2003-08-25 |a [s10 2004-03-08 1 copy rec'd., to CIP ver. |f pv12 2004-04-08 CIP ver. to BCCD

010 __ |a 2003016135
020 __ |a 1403448582 (hbk. : alk. paper)
020 __ |a 1403454329 (pbk. : alk. paper)
040 __ |a DLC |c DLC |d DLC
042 __ |a pcc |a lcac
050 00 |a QL737.C23 |b S586 2004
082 00 |a 599.756 |2 22
100 1_ |a Spilsbury, Richard, |d 1963-
245 10 |a Bengal tiger / |c Richard Spilsbury.
260 __ |a Chicago, Ill. : |b Heinemann Library, |c c2004.
300 __ |a 48 p. : |b col. ill. ; |c 27 cm.
440 _0 |a Animals under threat
520 __ |a Discusses the plight of Bengal tigers and why they are near extinction, as well as some of the ways humans can help.
504 __ |a Includes bibliographical references (p. 46-47) and index.
505 0_ |a The Bengal tiger —Tiger country —Tiger populations — The body of a tiger — A supreme hunter —Tiger ranges — Courtship and communication — Young tigers — Conflict between tigers and people — Poaching — Dealing with poaching —Tiger hunting in the past — Destroying tiger habitats — Fragmented tiger populations — Saving tiger habitats — Conservation organizations — Tigers in captivity —Tiger tourism and local people — The future for Bengal tigers — How can you help?
650 _0 |a Tigers |v Juvenile literature.
650 _1 |a Tigers.
650 _1 |a Endangered species.
856 41 |3 Table of contents |u http://www.loc.gov/catdir/toc/ecip046/2003016135.html

USING THE WEB ADDRESS GIVEN IN FIELD 856, USERS MAY ACCESS THIS CONTENT PAGE

TABLE OF CONTENTS

Bibliographic record and links to related information available from the Library of Congress catalog. *Note: Contents data are machine generated based on pre-publication information provided by the publisher. Contents may have variations from the printed book or be incomplete or contain other coding.*

Contents

Barcode in Library Management

Barcode Production

Automated circulation control systems use barcodes (a series of printed lines and spaces of varying widths which represent numbers, symbols, and/or letters) to track items through the circulation process. While some systems can accept either barcodes or optical character recognition (OCR) labels, barcodes are easier to print and scan. Barcoding is an expensive and labor-intensive activity. It is also the first critical project library staff undertake prior to automation. While not a glamorous undertaking, a well-planned barcoding project is an important step in helping to establish favorable staff and user attitudes toward the new system. Procedures concerning the recording and resolution of barcoding problems should be documented in advance of the barcoding.

Barcode Symbology

Many different barcode schemes are used in business and industry. The Universal Product Code (UPC), now ubiquitous in supermarkets as a means to control inventory and pricing, is perhaps the best known barcode symbology.

Only two barcode symbologies are commonly used in libraries; Codabar (or Code-A-Bar) and Code 39 (or Code 3 of 9). In library applications, Codabar generally consists of a string of 14 digits. The first digit represents a patron or item. That is, a first digit of '2' tells the circulation software that a patron number is being scanned; the number '3' signifies that an item is being scanned. The next four digits (digits 2 through 5) are the institutional identifier. The local system vendor either assigns this number or the library can make up its own institution code. For example, the library might use the last four digits of its telephone number or the last four digits in its extended nine-digit ZIP code. The next eight digits (digits 6 through 13) define the sequence ID number. Most smart barcode sequences begin with the number 1—i.e., 00000001. The final digit (digit 14) is a check digit used to verify that the barcode number has been scanned accurately. An eye-readable form of the item number is usually printed beneath the scannable number. To improve human readability, spaces are inserted between digits 1 and 2, 5 and 6, and 10 and 11.

Code 39 may contain fewer than 14 characters. For example in a ten digit number, the first digit indicates whether the code represents a patron or an item, the next 2 digits define the institutional identifier, and the last 7 digits identify the applicable code. While in theory Code 39 applications do not require a check digit, in practice many do add a check digit. Alpha characters can be used with Code 39 but they should be avoided if possible.

Both Codabar and Code 39 are self-clocking and permit bi-directional scanning. Library materials should not be barcoded before the library has chosen its local system.

SMART VS. DUMB BARCODES

Barcoding is the process of assigning a unique item number to each piece that can circulate and linking that item number to an item record, which in turn is linked to a bibliographic record. Library barcodes labels are classified as either 'smart' or 'dumb.' Dumb barcode labels are also referred to as 'generic' labels. Smart barcodes are always applied prior to bringing up circulation control, making it possible for library staff to concentrate on mastering the new system rather than the arduous task of making sure the right barcode gets put on the right item. Dumb barcodes can be applied prior to bringing up the system or at the point of check-out.

Smart barcodes have item numbers that are assigned by computer during the item field build on the basis of copy and volume holdings appearing in the bibliographic record. Because they are preassigned by machine to specific items in the database, their use avoids the tedious work of manually linking barcode numbers to item records. Smart barcodes come in a variety of sizes and styles and cost about four cents per label. Since proper shelf arrangement is critical to efficient smart barcode application, a preliminary shelfreading project should be considered prior to applying labels.

Smart barcodes entail extra costs in both database processing and label production and their use can reveal problems that will later demand attention. Smart barcodes have the added advantage of providing a quasi-inventory of the collection during their application. Whereas smart barcodes alert the library to database problems early on, dumb barcodes do not reveal these problems until the linking step occurs. From that point onward the clean up and correction process are similar. Dumb barcodes are less expensive to produce and can be applied at random throughout the collection. However, depending on the nature of the collection, they may be more costly when one factors in the time necessary to link the barcode numbers to item records. The great advantage of dumb barcodes is that they can be applied by unskilled workers prior to circulation or even at the point of circulation. Their disadvantage is that each barcode has to be manually linked to its item record. Even if the library has opted for smart barcoding, it still needs to acquire dumb barcodes for new titles and for those items for which a smart barcode label has not been produced. The latter can be caused by either the database vendor ignoring the library's actual holdings or the lack of holdings information in the catalog record. Libraries should not order more than a three-year supply of dumb barcode labels. Opinion varies as to whether smart barcoding is always the best approach to linking library materials to item records. As a rule, smart barcoding is recommended for collections having specific call numbers and only a single copy of most titles. Academic and special libraries will almost always benefit from smart barcoding. Public libraries, having multiple copies and non-specific call numbers (e.g. FIC), may encounter problems in applying smart barcodes, particularly if the bibliographic records do not contain adequate holdings data. Dumb labels are recommended for very small databases, e.g. under 10,000 records.

Barcode Location

The location of barcodes on library materials needs to be determined in advance. Given the expense of barcode labels, most libraries will only want to purchase a single label for each item. There are advantages and disadvantages to where the label is placed on the item. Affixing the label to the inside back cover endpaper offers good protection and, if book pockets or date due slips are used, increases check-out efficiency. Label suppliers recommend that labels be placed on the inside rather than outside cover or spine of books.

Placement of the label on the outside of the cover facilitates inventory and in-house scanning without having to open the book or in some cases even remove it from the shelf. As with other aspects of the automation process, consult with your local system vendor and other experienced users of the system before making barcoding decisions. Large libraries might want to review an Association of Research Libraries publication, Spec Kit 124 (May 1986) titled 'Barcoding of Collections in ARL Libraries.'

Pitfalls to Avoid

Opinion also differs on the wisdom of assigning dumb barcodes 'on the fly' as part of the cataloging operation before the local system is selected. This is accomplished by applying a dumb barcode to the item as it is being cataloged. The barcode number is either keyed into the holdings field of the catalog record or 'wanded' in with a barcode reader. Those recommending this practice argue that the library is getting a head start by reducing the number of barcodes that need to be applied later. LTI's experience has been that this practice always makes more work for library staff and limits the institution's flexibility. Whatever benefit results from having barcoded a certain portion of the collection in advance is more than offset by the new problems it creates. Since the library does not have online access to its database, there is no easy way to maintain barcode numbers assigned to records. In addition to the extra work of getting the barcode number into the record at the time of cataloging, staff will need to keep a log of replacement item numbers for labels removed or destroyed by patrons. When a record is reused, staff may need to rekey the barcode number(s) into the latest use. Database vendor programming costs will be higher because two different methods of building item fields are required. Moreover, the library runs the risk of adopting either a barcode symbology or check digit that will not be supported by the local system vendor.

Your library may find it expedient to order dumb barcode labels before the database vendor has completed the item field build and produced the smart barcode labels. If so, a comfortable margin should exist between the last possible machine-assigned item number and the first dumb barcode item number. As a guideline, academic libraries can estimate the number of item fields by multiplying the number of records remaining after deduping by 1.1 or 1.2. For example, if the library has 100,000 catalog records following deduping, one might project 110,000 to 120,000 item fields. Because of multiple copies, public libraries can have a higher ratio of item fields to records, in some cases as high as 1.5. Before ordering dumb barcodes, the library must confirm with the database vendor what the start sequence number should be for the dumb labels. Using the example above of 100,000 catalog records and an anticipated 110,000 to 120,000 item fields, the library might want to start the dumb barcode sequence at 300,000.

Thus, if the library is using a 14-digit item number and its institution code is 4921, and the first machine-assigned sequence number is 1, the first item number will be 3 4921 00000 001C, where the letter C at the end is a check digit whose value is a number between 0 and 9 calculated from the values of the 13 numbers preceding it. To eliminate any possible overlapping item numbers, the first item number assigned to the dumb barcodes might be 3 4921 00300 000C. The barcode producer must also be told how the check digit is to be calculated, e.g. MOD 10, MOD 43.

BARCODE LABEL "DRIVER" TAPE

Smart barcodes are printed using a photocomposition process from data written to a barcode label 'driver' file. Data used to format the labels comes from the item field and other fields in the library's catalog record. Because much of the information used in the label is derived from the item field, smart barcodes cannot be produced without first creating item fields.If the library has not yet selected its local system, the database vendor cannot format the item fields and, without item fields, smart barcodes cannot be printed. An exception exists for those database vendors that create generic item fields without regard to library holdings or the local system item field specifications. In addition to data taken from the item field (e.g. the item number, call number, branch/location code), smart barcodes must contain sufficient bibliographic information to match each label to the piece. On a standard 2" (wide) x ¾" (high) smart barcode label, two lines are available to print call number, holding library or location, and abbreviated author/title information. Other lines are reserved for the library's name, along with scannable and eye-readable versions of the item number. The only time the call number and related bibliographic information on the smart barcode label is useful is when the label is being applied to the item. Dumb barcodes are commonly printed on 2" x 5/8" stock and include the name of the library at the top, followed by scannable and eye-readable versions of the barcode number.

Prior to creating the barcode label driver tape, the database vendor must know if there are bibliographic formats (e.g. serials), types of materials (e.g. periodicals), or special collections (e.g. reference, rare books) for which barcode labels should not be printed. Barcode labels are usually arranged by holding library or collection and sorted by call number. Efficient smart barcoding depends on how closely the sorted barcode labels follow the shelving arrangement of the library materials.

MARC 21 Concise Formats: 2005 Edition

MARC: News and Announcement (May 15, 2006)

The 2005 edition of the *MARC 21 Concise Formats* is now available from the Library of Congress.

This new publication supersedes the 2004 edition of the "MARC 21 Concise Formats." It includes changes from the 2005 update (Update No. 6) and is current with all five full editions of the MARC 21 formats.

Major changes in this edition include:

- Addition of field 662 (Subject Added Entry-Hierarchical Place Name) in the bibliographic format

- Addition of field 766 (Secondary Table Information) in the classification format

PROCEDURE FOR INSTALLING THE SOFTWARE

System Requirements

1. Operating System: MS Windows 98 or above.
2. Software requirement: MS OFFICE 2000 or above
3. Processor: Pentium 3 or above (with SD RAM 128 MB or above).

Installation Guide

1. Uninstall any previously installed MARC 21 cataloguing program.
2. Close all other application in your PC.
3. Open the folder "Pack Marc21 D050906" in the CD ROM where 4 icons will appear—Support, Marc project, Setup, Setup.LSI.
4. Double click "Setup" icon. A message will show up. Wait till another screen titled "Marc21 Cataloguing Setup" opens.
5. Click "OK" button, if you want to continue.
6. Another form will open. A button (with SETUP icon) will appear on the upper-left corner of the screen. Click this button.
7. A form titled "Marc21 Cataloguing—Choose Program Group" will apear. Check if "Marc21 Cataloguing" is selected. Click "Continue" button.
8. A form titled "version Conflict" may appear—a few number of times. Click "Yes" whenever this form appears.
9. If another form titled "Marc21 Cataloguing Setup" appears with 3 buttons—"Abort", "Retry" and "Ignore" click "Ignore".
10. Finally a message will appear "Marc21 Cataloguing Setup was completed successfully".
11. Click OK.

Note: The above process may vary a little bit with different operating systems. The basic suggestions given above are only typical guidelines.